A LEAF
OF HONEY

and the Proverbs of the Rainforest

A LEAF
OF HONEY

and the
Proverbs of the Rainforest

JOSEPH SHEPPHERD

Bahá'í Publishing Trust
27 Rutland Gate
LONDON SW7 1PD

British Library Cataloguing in Publication Data

Sheppherd, Joseph
　A Leaf of Honey and the Proverbs of the Rainforest.
　1. Africa. West Africa. Tribes. Cultural processes
　I. Title
　305.8′966

ISBN 1-87098-902-3

Computer typeset by SB Datagraphics, Colchester, England
A member of the ICIAN Group

Set in 10½/11 point Baskerville

CONTENTS

This book is dedicated to the Ntumu people,
a tribe of profound wisdom and loving-kindness,
who taught me where to look
to find the world among the leaves

and

to Fanny, Samuel and Ruhieh
who helped beyond measure.

FOREWORD

by

Professor Sir Edmund Leach, F.B.A

When I first came into contact with social anthropologists around 1937, the senior members of the profession took it for granted that they were engaged in an objective classificatory science. Studying the many kinds of human culture in the rainforest was like studying the varieties of mammal in a zoo. The personal peculiarities of the anthropologist were not considered relevant. Things are much the same today. An ethnographic monograph is generally considered to be quite different from a chapter in the autobiography of the author.

At a recent gathering of professional anthropologists I asserted just the contrary. An ethnographic monograph is at least as fictional as a novel; the characters in the story are modelled on the author's self image. The author himself/herself should feature in the story. The older members of my audience were shocked; the younger ones agreed. I find Sheppherd's book specially interesting because of the solution he has provided to this dilemma.

But this is a unique book and its author is a unique man. The reader is likely to ask all sorts of questions which will not be answered in the text, so let me offer some clues. Joseph Sheppherd is an American citizen who resides permanently in England when he is not otherwise engaged in various projects in education, race relations and poverty relief in Africa and Latin America. He has a first degree from the University of California at Riverside and a Master of Philosophy degree from Cambridge, England. When he takes time off from doing other more morally rewarding things he will probably earn a Ph.D. in ethno-archaeology from Cambridge. He was born in 1949. He is a member of the Baha'i religious community. This last detail has been a major influence in his life. Peripherally, it is of considerable importance for an understanding of this book.

In an academic sense "A Leaf of Honey" is a linguistic study of proverbs recorded among the Ntumu tribal people of Cameroon during 1976 and 1977. At that time Sheppherd was notionally based on the Riverside Campus of the University of California, but he communicated with his director of studies, a "Dr Kilngott", only by letter. These letters constitute the even-numbered chapters of the book and provide the orthodox ethnographic content in the form of fieldnotes and drawings which have been produced here by the author. The book opens however with a narrative, an autobiographical account of how Sheppherd first learned of the Ntumu proverb upon which the title of the book is based: "Man is a Leaf of Honey".

The autobiographical account continues with every odd-numbered chapter. The "hard science" and autobiography are thus formally kept separate but their interdependence is clearly shown. It is this relationship between the two different kinds of text which provides the key to a true appreciation of the value of this work. The two types of text are interdependent but the fieldnotes become interesting only because of the autobiography, not the other way about. This is what makes Sheppherd's book a very important contribution from an academic anthropological point of view. That is a matter of methodology. But besides that the autobiographical bits are great fun.

14 February 1988
Edmund R. Leach

1

MAN IS A LEAF OF HONEY

There was that strange feeling that something was wrong for a few moments before I noticed the silence. Slowly it permeated my concentration until I had to look up from the fieldnotes in my lap. The village women had suddenly stopped hoeing for some reason and were all facing the far side of the clearing. I followed their eyes and tried to see what held their attention. At first there was nothing, only the sounds of the crackling fires in the planting area. In the distance, however, I became aware of a low but distinct rustling sound of something moving in the jungle. The women with their babies wrapped tight to their backs stood motionless, listening, ready to flee. The children among them were frozen still, their eyes fixed on their mothers, watching them, like statues in a churchyard. The noise grew and I recognized that terrifying sound of undergrowth being quietly pushed aside. I joined the collective alertness and fear that filled the clearing as the sound continued to approach. Slowly I laid down my clipboard and put my hand on the machete beside me. The villagers had taught me to always keep my machete nearby. Humans were strangers here and beyond the safety of the fires and the clearing, the rainforest was the home of many dangerous things. I waited with my back against the tree.

Suddenly the rustling ceased, and a single loud deliberate cough broke the silence. The women and children swayed and relaxed. It wasn't a gorilla. It was only Papa Atanga, coming back from the jungle. The women joked among themselves to relieve the tension and returned to their bent positions and the steady rhythmical thud . . . scrape . . . thud . . . scrape of hoeing. The children resumed the chore of carrying the weeds to the burning heaps.

1

A LEAF OF HONEY

The old tribesman had been gone about an hour. He emerged from the forest with his frayed work shirt now tied around his waist. Bits of leaves and dry grass clung to the sweat on his old skin. He held his machete in front of him as he made his way through the undergrowth. As he entered the clearing, I saw he carried a long pole on his shoulder with a beehive impaled on the end of it. Papa Atanga had brought back what he had set out to find. He carried his load to the tree under which I was sitting and laid it down in the shade. As he approached, I quickly stood up and moved out of his way. Most of the bees had apparently not yet vacated their hive and buzzed angrily about him. The old Ntumu gave me a bemused sidelong glance as I stood watching from a safe distance out in the noonday sun. The bees flew wildly about him and yet they didn't seem to sting him.

He left his prize in the shade, went back to the clearing's edge and soon returned with several broad green leaves, the kind I called "elephant ears" because of their shape and size. He squatted down and carefully laid out the leaves on the ground in front of him. He placed the hive in the centre of the leaves and slowly withdrew the pole. Honey oozed from the wound onto the leaves. The old man gently began to cut up the hive with his machete. The bees became even more agitated and covered his arms and back. I noticed that there were quite a few on my clipboard and tape recorder also but I suppressed the urge to rescue them. I had a healthy respect for bees. If fieldwork had taught me anything about Africa, it had taught me that even tiny things working together in large numbers could be deadly. The old man seemed unbothered by the bees swarming and crawling over his bare skin. He took each section of the hive and squeezed it in his hands. The clear golden liquid spread out in a pool on the leaves.

"My elder, why is it that the bees do not eat you?" I asked him in Ntumu.

" 'Sting', not 'eat' " he corrected.

I had been living among the Ntumu people for nearly six months as an anthropologist collecting data, and the tribesmen had by now become somewhat used to my lack of vocabulary and the inane questions I was likely to ask.

Without lifting his eyes from his work, he replied with a proverb:

"Homeless bees never sting."

A LEAF OF HONEY

The apparently simple truths of the Ntumu proverbs were the focus of my research and thus far I had collected quite a few by interviewing the elders of the village around the hearths and fires in the evenings. I believed that their proverbs and stories held the key to their deepest beliefs about life and how they saw the world around them. Papa Atanga was undoubtedly the oldest man in the village and presumably a wellspring of oral tradition, but he always refused to speak when my tape recorder was present. He usually ignored me when I spoke to him, so I felt fortunate now to hear him use a proverb in a conversation with me.

I was aware that the novelty of my presence in his village drew attention away from the authority he had earned by outliving everyone else. In the village council his voice opposed my efforts to record the oral tradition of his tribe. He often reminded the other elders that I was without a clan, a whiteman and above all too young for the wisdom of proverbs of the rainforest. In short I was unworthy of the knowledge. I realized that Papa Atanga's support and his knowledge of tribal proverbs were crucial to the success of my fieldwork. I had tried everything to win his confidence. However, he still mistrusted my motives in collecting someone else's oral tradition and often stated that the passage of time would reveal the real reason why I had come to the jungle.

This saying was similar to others I had already heard and, like all Ntumu proverbs, it was an oral palimpsest, a verbal statement which conveyed several messages, each at a different level of significance. This one was chosen to remind me of my place. He watched me to see if I understood the analogy of "homeless bees". The old man's eyes were dark and serious, his face was wrinkled with great age and rarely filled with the good-natured mirth of the other elders. His masterful use of proverbs was legendary in Ntumuland, and like the long curved Ntumu machetes, sharp on both edges, Papa Atanga could wield them and cut the air with the blade as well as the hook. In his eyes, I was a homeless little pest here in the rainforest of Cameroon, far from my own land and culture and, like these bees, mildly irritating to him; an uninvited visitor who was able to fly but not sting, an ineffectual stranger in the midst of his tribe and village.

When the all of the honey had been squeezed out of the hive the old man folded up the leaves into a cone-shaped package and sealed the top closed with a spine he had cut from a nearby vine. It didn't leak, a functional origami masterpiece. He stood up and brushed

3

the remaining bees and leaves off his back and put his shirt on. He put the residual wax from the hive and the package of honey into an old basket he slung over his shoulder and prepared to leave. Most of the bees had flown off, so I was able to collect my things from beside the tree.

He paused in his preparations and asked, "Do you want to hear an old proverb?"

In my ears, these were surprising words. Today was the first time he had ever spoken to me in other than complete contempt. I was more than a little bit wary of Papa Atanga. A few months back he had required that I ride the Ntem River at flood stage as part of a near fatal initiation test of merit. I had almost drowned. This was the same old man who opposed my repeated application to the council of elders and to attend their secret rituals. He was not the most winsome character I had ever met and living in the same village with him taught me to be cautious.

"I am the child who wants to learn," I said carefully, showing proper deference to my elders. He pointed to the package of honey and said: "*Mot ane oka woe*":

"Man is a leaf of honey."

The words rang with the antiquity of oral traditions nearly forgotten. For a moment he spoke in a mode of the language archaic to these times. I did not understand fully the syntax of this phrase and nothing of its possible meaning.

"How is man a leaf of honey?" I asked.

Papa Atanga started off down the path that led to the village of Meyo-Ntem and I followed, waiting for an answer. As we walked along he explained, "I will take this leaf of honey back to my village and give it to my first-wife to store. She will drain the honey from the leaf into a special bottle she keeps. When she is finished she will give the leaf to the children. Each will lick the leaf and find some honey to sweeten the tongue. When the last child has finished, he will throw the leaf out behind the hut where the goats sleep. They will have their turn. The other animals, the chickens, the flies, ants and so on will come and find their share of honey left on the leaf." I recognized the diminishing examples of "*ad infinitum*" in his story.

The old man paused and stared into my soul with his black eyes, and for the first time smiled at me. "Man is a leaf of honey. This is what you need to know about us." He repeated this several times to make sure I understood, and then continued: "Man is good and man is precious and, like the leaf of honey, his goodness is inexhaustible. When you think that there is none left, there is still some there to find. This you should not forget."

I couldn't think what I had done to change Papa Atanga's attitude towards me. The old man smiled with the pleasure of someone who has just given a gift to his grandson. This was his first act of kindness towards me. With a nod of his head and a gesture of hand, he silently indicated that he would say no more and that I should go back to the clearing and write his words down in my fieldnotes. Somehow I had finally become worthy of sharing some of the tribal wisdom that was locked in his mind. I watched Papa Atanga turn and make his way through the jungle until he was out of sight. I felt that this was the beginning of my research.

At last I had a definitive statement on the Ntumu view of human nature. This was the most important proverb I had collected. That night, back in the village, as I lay awake in my hammock, comparing it with all the sayings I had collected over the last few months, I saw the significance of this one proverb. It was the key to the pages of recorded proverbs I had and the key to the mind set of a people I truly wanted to understand. I recognized then that Papa Atanga's gift of insight was indeed great. He had begun to teach me and like in any good master-apprentice relationship, he knew what I needed to learn. In the darkness of my small wattle-and-daub mud hut, I realized that the old man had intentionally allowed me a glimpse of the mental world which held the proverbs of the rainforest.

2

CULTURAL PERCEPTION AND RELIGIOUS BELIEF

Several weeks before I left the University of California at Riverside to begin my anthropological research in Africa, I received a worrying message from Dr Kilngott asking me to stop by his office at three o'clock that day. It was a typical Dr Kilngott kind of note, hurriedly typewritten with words running off the right hand side of the page on a old manual machine with a typewriter ribbon worn through in places. The words in his notes always faded in and out. I looked at my watch and re-read the note. It was frustratingly brief and stated that he wanted to talk to me about my upcoming research in Africa. It left me wondering if my research proposal had been rejected at the last minute by the departmental staff. I looked for clues. Here and there, the occasional word was XXXXXXXX exed over where a more appropriate word was chosen. I held the sheet of paper up to the light and read what his first choice of words were. This didn't reveal much. I would just have to wait until three o'clock and see.

Dr Kilngott was my assigned research advisor and one of the more lovable eccentrics in the Anthropology Department. He was a good-natured and humorous man who I felt was sometimes struggling to be serious in a stuffy and unamused academic world. He was the kind of teacher who left his door open so that first-year students would feel free to wander in and ask questions. It worked. Even as a third-year undergraduate I had been there many times doing just that. Over the last year, he had become more than just my research advisor, he was a friend. He often left notes for me, but this time it was different. The tone was strange and formal. It worried me. If there was some problem with my Senior Honours

A LEAF OF HONEY

Research project, I didn't know what I would do at this late date. I was committed both mentally and financially. My wife and daughter had already left to spend some time with my in-laws in Colombia before we were to meet in Paris and travel on to Africa together.

If it was bad news I didn't know what I would do. I decided that I couldn't wait until three. When I reached Dr Kilngott's office, I found the door closed. I knocked and waited nervously. Nobody home. I checked my watch, there was a whole hour to wait. I loitered around in the hall hoping he might come along but finally I went to the Anthropology Department coffee room to kill the time. In the mornings the room was the social centre of the department but this late in the day it was deserted. Everyone was in class. I tried to read the notice board to keep from worrying. I soon discovered, however, that I had already seen most of the notices pinned up there. The only new item was an announcement for a departmental party and potluck:

"Potlatch, Friday 9pm, Dr Saltassi's place."

I chuckled to myself. This was a clever play on words decipherable only to fellow anthropologists. *Potlatch* was a Amerindian word which had been adopted by anthropologists as the term for a strange ritual-feast of conspicuous and excessive gift-giving and hospitality, a contest of one-upmanship by participants who tried to out-do the other contestants through generosity. Among the tribe from which this term originated the object of the *potlatch* was to emerge as the one who was able to give the most away. The ironic twist in the competition was that the winner was left with no material wealth, only a title of high esteem.

On another of the institutional grey walls of the coffee room was a large poster of a tired and bewildered old orang-outang. The caption read:

Just when I had
all the answers to the
problems in life
they went and changed
the questions.

7

Below this was an enterprising handwritten sign next to the coffee machine which promised:

COFFEE IS WHAT THEOREMS ARE MADE OF. 10 CENTS A CUP.

I invested a dime and took a seat with my cheap cup of promises, watched the clock and waited for the onrush of anthropological theorems. The coffee was terrible. Whoever brewed the pot seemed to have the philosophy that coffee was like medicine, it had to taste horrible to work. I tried to relax and not speculate about what Dr Kilngott would say. I focussed on my planned fieldwork. I wondered what Africa and life in a tribal village would be like. It would certainly be different from the places I knew in Latin America. I closed my eyes and tried to visualize myself in a village setting. It was difficult to assemble a coherent image because I had no direct knowledge of Africa. Everything I knew about it came from books and every mental image I conjured up came from the either short documentaries or the cinema. All I could imagine was a primitive circle of thatched huts in a misty jungle clearing at twilight. Surrounding the village lie the unknown, a dark and dangerous place choked with poisonous flora and vicious, lurking fauna. Around a fire in the centre of the village danced fierce warriors, their semi-naked bodies glistening with fresh paint. Their eyes and teeth flashed in the fire light. A series of drums beat towards a murderous climax while the tribesmen thrusted their sharp spears at unseen enemies in the death-dance. I opened my eyes and shook my head in self-disgust. It was disturbing how a void in one's own experience could be filled so easily with images straight out of Hollywood. Whatever I was to find in Africa would certainly not be like this.

Ten minutes later my cup was empty and I was still waiting. I got up and checked his office again. The door was open. Dr Kilngott was sitting there, pounding away on his old typewriter. I knocked on the door and he looked up.

"How are you?" he smiled. His room consisted of a cluttered desk surrounded by shelves crammed with reference books, Chinese ethnographic knick-knacks and stacks of old term-papers collected from students long since gone.

"Worried," I confessed.

"Come in and sit down and don't be," he replied motioning me to a chair. He sounded pleasant but looked serious, like he had something difficult to say.

"There was a staff meeting yesterday," began Dr Kilngott, "and seeing that the term is almost over and your fieldwork is approaching, some of the staff felt that we needed to have a little chat." He paused.

"A little chat?" I asked.

"A little chat," he repeated.

"As I recall, the last time anyone said they wanted to have 'a little chat' with me was when my father tried to tell me about where babies come from," I joked.

"This is not that kind of chat."

"Are you sure? There are a few things I would really like to ask about."

"It's about your research," he said seriously.

"My research?" I asked timidly. Dr Kilngott was my principal supporter in the department, but there were those who didn't approve of my being allowed to pursue graduate level fieldwork as an inexperienced undergraduate.

"And your . . . religion."

I didn't say anything.

"They wanted to know how your religion will affect your proposed linguistic and ethnographical fieldwork in Africa," he explained in an embarrassed tone. I could not see how my religion could be such an issue as to be raised in a staff meeting.

"What do you mean, and who are 'they'?" I asked.

"Well specifically, Dr Tanner and Dr Saltassi wondered if you had considered how your being a Baha'i will influence your interpretation of the data you will collect," replied Dr Kilngott. I realized that he was speaking to me in an official capacity. As he was my advisor, he had been instructed to ask these questions. I looked into his eyes and I could see that he was not enjoying this. He held a familiar-looking paper in his hand. "From your submitted research proposal here, I see you plan to 'investigate the beliefs and world-view' of a people totally different in history, environment and culture from your own. Some of my colleagues feel that considering that you seem to have strong views about religion, don't you think that this will colour your interpretations and perhaps even blinker you to ideas and concepts beyond your

9

cultural experience?" Dr Kilngott never spoke like this. I could see that he was paraphrasing someone else's misgivings, someone in the department less sympathetic to my religious beliefs than he was. This was the other side of his role as my advisor, he had the duty to prepare me for everything, from tribesmen to academics.

"No, Dr Kilngott, I don't see why my personal faith should handicap me. It may even help me," I said defensively. I was not longer in a joking mood.

"Unfortunately, there are some staff members who would contend that religion traditionally causes a narrowing of the mind in this field. Although I would disagree with this, you need to be prepared to respond to those who feel that religious affiliation restricts one's ability to perceive things which might disagree with dogma." He seemed uncomfortable in asking me these questions and whenever he was nervous he had an unconscious habit of holding the end of his nose in his fist while he talked, as if it were cold.

"Boy, if there is one thing I can't stand, it's intolerance," I said sarcastically. "Quite frankly, I find such a view of religion rather jaundiced. But I suppose it wouldn't be academically prudent to say that to them personally. But I must say that I feel more than a little indignant to know that people are even considering my religious affiliation as a negative factor in my research, even before it begins, or being viewed as some kind of religious fanatic."

"I am not defending them. I support your proposed research," said Dr Kilngott reassuringly. "What they see is this, no dedicated anthropological research has been done on this particular African tribe before. To be the first in documenting a people's language and culture is both a great honour and responsibility. There will be no previous ethnographic studies to which they can compare your findings. The staff will want to know if your Baha'i beliefs have affected your interpretations."

"Of course my personal beliefs will affect the way in which I interpret the data to some degree. I think everyone here in the department knows that all of one's experiences and belief-patterns will effect perception; but part of the Baha'i belief-pattern concerns the conscious expansion of one's personal understanding. Each Baha'i is charged with the responsibility to investigate reality and not live on dogma, religious or otherwise."

"What I think these members of staff are worried about is academic integrity," said Dr Kilngott.

"Please tell them that as I am aware of its possible influence, then I will try to remain objective and truthful so that I will be able to discover some of what is really there. Besides, what I report will be basically descriptive. If I go beyond that then I will qualify my interpretations. That way, what I write will be of some value to anthropology." At least he now had an answer to give them.

"Unfortunately," he began philosophically, "objectivity is not defined in the same way by everyone. Paradoxically, objectivity is in the eye of the beholder; everyone is essentially subjective about objectivity."

"You sound like a Woody Allen film," I interrupted. Dr Kilngott relaxed enough to let go of his nose and laughed.

"I don't feel the staff are concerned about your ability to describe and assess basic language structures or even ethnography, but because the goal of your proposed research is understanding something about another culture's world-view, they are concerned about personal religious-based interpretations. Basically, this is because world-view is almost pure interpretation. The reporting of another people's beliefs about their place in nature, the supernatural and their religion is not easy. It is not just descriptive. It requires explanation and it is in the explaining that interpretation leaks in. Dr Saltassi in particular is apprehensive that you will try to look into the depths of another culture's beliefs through the eyes of your own religion."

"Does he believe this will be a problem because I am a *Baha'i* anthropologist?" I challenged. "What about through the 'eyes' of *agnostic* anthropologists like himself. Dr Saltassi's agnosticism is almost religious in its intensity."

Dr Kilngott laughed at my spurt of indignation. "Just don't let him hear you say that. I'm sure that Dr Saltassi would maintain that being a Baha'i seems to dominate your life and that for him, being an agnostic doesn't."

"I don't know about that, but *agnostic* anthropologists potentially suffer from the same sort of short-comings as he feels I do. Just because agnostics don't have a religion doesn't mean they don't have beliefs and conceptional presuppositions. Dr Kilngott, I don't particularly want to spend my few remaining weeks in the department defending my religion instead of preparing for fieldwork. How can we solve this. Surely this is not the first time an anthropologist with a religion set out to do fieldwork. How did others cope with this problem?" I asked.

11

"Some academics have proposed that a way around this problem is to include an autobiographical statement of your beliefs and background in your thesis. This will allow its readers to know what the viewpoint and potential cultural biases of the author are."

"Personally, I don't see how this will enhance the work's impartiality and objectivity. There is nothing more subjective than self-appraisal, but if an autobiographical presentation is all that is needed to satisfy Dr Saltassi, then I will make sure I include one," I promised. "That seems easy enough."

Dr Kilngott paused in thought for a moment then compulsively seised the end of his nose again. This was not a good sign.

"The other issue they want to raise with you is the cultural impact you will have on the people you wish to study. I am sure you realize that you will be more than just an observer, you will be a participant-observer in a new society. While you are learning about their culture and beliefs, they will be learning about yours. Tribal peoples can sometimes be over-accommodating about what information they think will make you happy. If your aim is to understand something about their view of themselves, it is important to be careful not to end up reporting your own. What Dr Tanner and some of the other members of staff are concerned about is that if you reveal your beliefs or teach them your religion, then they may tell you what they feel you will want to hear." He paused for a moment, still clinging nervously to his nose. "Which brings me to the question they really want answered: do you plan to practise your religion in Africa?"

More inquisition by proxy.

"For me, religion is more of an ethical background than something you 'practice'. It is a frame of reference which is there as a moral standard for personal assessment and comparison. What I think Dr Tanner and Co. are worried about is that I will go to Africa as some kind of missionary. I do not plan to 'proselytize' among the natives, if that is what they mean by 'practice'. However, they need to understand that I will not suspend my faith for a year for anyone's sake. I will continue with my personal Baha'i responsibilities during my fieldwork."

"Perhaps if they knew what those were they would feel less apprehensive," he said.

"They are quite simple and personal. In private, I will continue to pray and read from the Baha'i Writings each day. If there are no other Baha'is in the area, my wife and I will celebrate the Feasts and Holy Days alone. If there are, we will celebrate these with them."

"What is a 'Feast'?"

"Well, basically, it is a social gathering for reading the Baha'i Writings together, discussing community service projects and having fun. It is sort of like a departmental "potlatch" party with prayers instead of booze. It happens every nineteen days," I explained. "I will also observe the nineteen-day Fast."

"You have a nineteen-day fasting period?" he asked with a twinkle in his eye. He incredulously looked me straight in the stomach and commented: "It's hard to believe." He let go of his nose to laugh.

"Luckily for me the fast is only during the daylight hours," I explained. As the time approached to leave the land of Big Macs, super tacos and finger lick'n good chicken, I had been a bit over-indulgent in stocking up. Although more charitable people would have described me as stout, my wife had begun to refer to me as her "beached-whale". I really wasn't bothered about my growing corpulence. It was temporary. I figured that African food would be more effective than Weight Watchers.

"I don't know a lot about your religion but aren't there some activities called 'Firesides' that I see advertised in the local Riverside newspaper?" Dr Kilngott paused and chuckled to himself and began to count on his fingers. "Given that there are 'Feasts', 'Fasts' and 'Firesides', do all of your activities begin with the letter 'F'?" he asked.

I had to laugh too. "No", I said.

"I don't think that the staff would be too concerned about these. I think that what they really want to know is whether you plan to carry out any kind of converting activities?" he asked.

"Dr Kilngott, please tell them that, at this point, I am more interested in learning about the African's beliefs and religion than teaching them mine," I stated. "There is, however, something that I think they should know. After I finish my undergraduate research and submit my thesis, I plan to stay on in Africa for a while, perhaps for a few years."

"This is news. What about your graduation and diploma? Will you come back for them?" he asked.

"No, I don't think so, but there is something you could do for me. Providing you find my work is good enough for me to graduate, could you please mail the diploma to me?" I asked.

"If that is what you want, I will inform the office when the time comes. Now that I have finished doing my academic duty to the staff, there are a few things I need to talk to you about. First of all, you understand of course that I expect periodical reports from you about the progress of your research. It would also be useful for me to see what you are doing. I assume you are taking a camera. African material culture is very colourful," he said.

"Of course. I plan to record as much of village life with my camera as possible. Developing the rolls of film, however, will have to wait until I finish my fieldwork and return to technological civilization and film processing. In the meantime, I will try to include some drawings of what I see in the reports I send. I will try to write every week," I answered.

"That will be interesting." He grinned and began to dig around in one of the piles of paper on his desk. He located my most recent term paper to his class on urban anthropology. "I hope your Senior Honours Research thesis will be more interesting than *Social Messages and the Proxemics of Affluent Retirement Garden Landscaping in Hemet California.*" He feigned a yawn as he handed it to me. It was graded A- on the cover.

"With this grade it couldn't have been too bad," I commented.

"It was well researched and written but the subject matter was rather boring," he replied. "Let's hope the African tribesmen of the rainforest are more exciting than your tribe of blue-rinse tinted geriatrics in Hemet."

3

THE LANGUAGE OF VEHICLES

I bought a series of fairly detailed maps in Yaounde to assist me in choosing the initial site of my linguistic and cultural investigations in southern Cameroon. I decided on the village of Meyo-Ntem for several reasons. It was a small settlement beside the major river of the region, the Ntem. Situated at the heart of a rainforest reported to be populated by the Ntumu tribe, it seemed to be ideally isolated geographically from other tribes surrounding it. The maps revealed that the village was just off a major road leading from the regional capital of Ebolowa, which suggested that it was not too remote from the amenities of civilization and ideal for my studies. The lines on these maps indicated that there were passable roads the entire 150 kilometres from the town of Ebolowa to Meyo-Ntem. These lines, as it turned out, were no more than some wishful-thinking cartographer's whim.

When it came time to make my first trip out to Meyo-Ntem, I took along a talented young Cameroonian who I met through an accquaintance. He not only spoke fluent English and French but was, conveniently, a native speaker of Bulu, a language closely related to Ntumu. His name was Robert and he proved to be a fine interpreter. However, he was young and had spent most of his time growing up in the relatively urban environment of the town of Ebolowa. Like me, this also proved to be his first trip into the rainforest of the Ntumu tribesmen.

There was no scheduled public transport and the only way Robert and I could get there was to go to the market square early in the morning and hire a vehicle. After negotiating with several drivers, we finally found one who didn't initially ask for an amount approaching the sale price of the vehicle. The driver we chose had an old grey four-wheeled-drive Land Rover, which was the property of some company which bought cocoa from the villagers in the area. He was short, good-natured, with a surprising number of scars on his face and his forearms, and obviously moonlighting. Speaking to us in French, he explained that he was not usually allowed to take passengers and was restricted to journeys which ferried empty sacks out into the bush and brought back full sacks of cocoa. However, he continued, because I was a rich American and stuck for a ride, he would make an exception and relieve me of my money.

We waited while he loaded the Land Rover. Once he had filled half the front seat and the entire back with bales of empty cocoa sacks and things to barter, we negotiated a price for what amounted to sitting room and airspace on top of the heap. Robert explained that moonlighting was not only a common practice in this part of Cameroon, but also a developing art and science. Not only did the successful moonlighting driver and entrepreneur have to employ artfully the company's restricted vehicle to his own benefit and not get fired, but, as we were later to find out, he was required to be somewhat of an engineering philosopher. He seemed to believe that one should be careful not to overload a Land Rover with too much non-paying cargo. The leaf springs were his gauge. Once the leaf springs over the rear axle were flat or inverted from the weight of the load, he would refuse to take any more baggage, only paying individuals.

Robert and I were the only ones in the Land Rover when we started out from the town square at Ebolowa, comfortably perched on the mound of sacks. But as soon as we rounded the first bend, past the police inspection post at the edge of town, the vehicle stopped and thirteen people, who had been hiding in the bushes and who had obviously booked in advance, climbed on. We were now sitting in a standing-only zone, eyeball to kneecap with a forest of brown legs.

The road on the map proved to be little more than a two lane foot-path, one for each wheel. After about an hour of patience, acquiescence and generally being a credit to my superior western liberal upbringing, most of the cultural veneer of smiling courtesy and passive forbearance blistered and peeled away. I elbowed and excused my way up nearer to the top of the heap and stood with my face in the wind, happy as a dog with his nose out of the car window.

The green landscape sped by on both sides of me and the brightest blue sky I had ever seen squeezed through among the parasol-like towering majestic trees.

"Hey! This is the life," I thought. "Now *this* is Africa." I wondered what my wife, Fanny, would think of this. She was waiting as agreed in Ebolowa until I made contact with the Ntumu tribesmen.

The equatorial sun was shining, the air was full of the earthy aromas of the jungle and, best of all, the cries and hoots of unseen animals wafted above the drone of the engine. This was the fulfillment of a dream of adventure that had been planted in me from the moment my grandmother took me to Disneyland and put me on the Jungle Ride when I was six. That same Walt Disney-like soundtrack was all around me again and I couldn't wait to see the heart of the Ntumu homeland.

However, the magic of novelty faded with each passing hour over what had to be the world's worst road. The bright sights and exotic sounds were slowly replaced by the reality and discomfort of dusty air and standing too long. The road became markedly worse with every mile. The occasional smooth stretches of ground finally surrendered to the perpetual pot holes and deep ruts. I began to suspect that I had chanced upon the hidden place to which trainee designers of automobile test tracks are secretly flown out for inspiration. I also found that there is a giddy stupor which arises from sustained suffering and fear for one's own well being. After about seven hours of dangerously fast driving, teeth-jarring bumps and breathing in my own weight of dust, some of the women passengers began to sing what my interpreter told me were church hymns.

"How very appropriate," I thought. "Funereal music."

Conversation through an interpreter was difficult on the crowded and jolting Land Rover. Once, however, after swerving to miss a herd of complacent goats sleeping in the middle of the road, I tried to strike up a nose to nose conversation with the man with whom I had been sharing my personal space for most of the morning.

"Ask him if the driver has ever had an accident," I told Robert, noting that the driver's scars were not there as a result of ornamental cicatrization. If I had been more observant of the exterior of the Land Rover before I got on, I would have known how self-evident the answer was. Do it yourself panel-beating and automobile body work is a full-time career in Africa. My interpreter spoke to him in Bulu and he shrugged his shoulders and answered with a proverb:

"Dying alone is bad."

"Tell the whiteman", he said, "there are many of us here, so not to worry". With this delightful news, I gave up the idea of making casual conversation and concentrated on worrying.

Finally, the fateful combination of bad driving, terrible road conditions and an erroneous loading philosophy convinced the strained leaf springs to snap. The vehicle rolled to a stop and the driver got out and surveyed the damage. As far as this trip was concerned, we were informed, the damage was terminal. Everyone climbed down from the Land Rover and stretched out to rest on the ground alongside the road. We had barely descended when another enterprising cocoa company moonlighter rounded the bend in a Toyota Land Cruiser just as overloaded as ours was. A dozen or so fellow Ntumu passengers jumped up and burst into a chorus of pleadings as the vehicle approached.

"Stop! Wait! Stop! Wait!" they chanted in English. I was puzzled and through Robert I asked the man we had spoken to before.

"Who are they speaking English to?"

"The machine speaks English," the man informed us.

"What machine?" I asked stupidly.

"That machine," he said pointing to the Toyota.

"Surely he means the driver speaks English," I said, and Robert asked again.

"Machines that roll speak English," the man reiterated.

By this time the Toyota had stopped and the stranded passengers were negotiating with the new driver. They were now speaking to him in what seemed to be Ntumu. Convinced that he must understand some English, I walked over to the driver's side and spoke to him in English:

"Good afternoon. Do you have space for us also?" The driver gave me a blank stare and Robert came up and translated what I had said. The driver's face instantly lit up and replied, "Of course!" He probably thought that I was the owner of the Land Rover. The driver carefully looked me up and down, as if weighing my financial resources. Little dollar ign reflected in his eyes. At the thought of passing a bedless night alongside this road, I closed my eyes and told Robert to negotiate any price.

We found an empty one-square-inch patch next to the man from our first conveyance. I jokingly told Robert, "Tell our friend here that this one cannot speak English like the broken down Land Rover. This one is a Toyota. It was made in Japan and therefore speaks Japanese."

The man became very serious and looked at me sternly as he spoke to Robert.

"Tell this whiteman", he said, "that all machines that roll speak English: cars, vans, trucks, everything. And if he expects them to respond to his wishes he had better learn to speak to them in the language they understand."

"This guy doesn't really believe this," I thought, "and is just trying to have me on." I decided the best culturally sensitive thing to do was not to argue.

The additional weight of the new load of passengers made starting difficult. The engine sputtered and stalled several times. After a few more tries, the assemblage of sardine-packed passengers, including the man, began to slowly chant, "Move! Go! Move! Go!" in English.

Suddenly, as if responding to the chant, the Toyota lurched to life and with every "go" it gained confidence and soon began to lumber heavily down the road. I tried to avoid eye contact with our friend, but finally he reached over and tapped me on the shoulder. I couldn't ignore him any longer. I turned and he stood there grinning triumphantly at me. He leaned over and said "See, just like I told you," to Robert and looked away smiling.

What was it that Dorothy said to Toto in the *Wizard of Oz?* "I have a feeling we're not in Kansas anymore." I knew how she felt.

4

THE NTUMU PEOPLE

Dear Dr Kilngott,

At last, I am able to begin sending the progress reports I promised. This letter was hand-carried to the nearest postal town of Ebolowa and then mailed by a friend of mine from there.

You know that I am interested in tribal technology and I will try to send you a few sketches of village artefacts with each report. I think that drawings will be better than dry and laborious descriptions. This time, I have enclosed a couple of drawings of a handmade sugarcane press I saw being used in one of the Ntumu villages I visited. It is a very simple but clever device. The sugarcane juice is squeezed out by placing a length of cane on a notched platform and pressing down on it with a stick which is levered through a hole in the back of the notch. The juice runs down a metal skirt and is collected in a bowl underneath. Fresh cane juice makes a fantastic drink and is often used as a sweetener in Ntumu dishes. However, if left to stand for a few days, the high sugar content in the juice soon begins to ferment and bubble as it becomes alcoholic. The villagers have long since discovered that a container of cane juice and little bit of patience will make a lot of rum.

Through these weekly reports I will try to reveal something of the social and spiritual significance of the culture of the Ntumu. I hope to do this by examining the structure and analyzing the content of one genre of their oral tradition: the proverb. I will describe the role of the proverb within Ntumu society, its use in the jurisprudence of the tribal council and its place in the spiritual understanding of its people. Before I begin, however, I feel that I should give you some ethnographic background.

The Ntumu are a West African Bantu tribe which inhabit the remote jungle of the Ntem River Basin of south-central Cameroon, northern Rio Muni in Equatorial Guinea and north-western

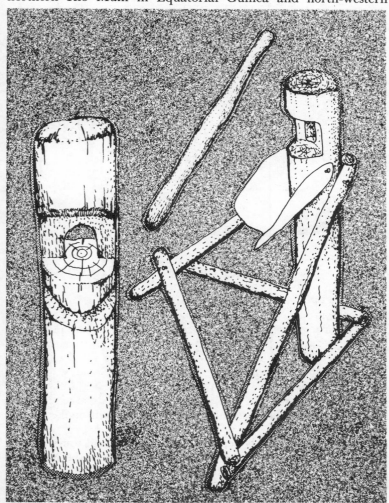

Gabon. The Ntumu are fundamentally a rural, agricultural-based people using "swidden" or slash and burn methods of ground preparation. They maintain both subsistence crops and small cocoa and coffee plantations as cash crops.

The Ntumu live in a rainforest and riverine ecology in a social environment little touched by modern technology. The region is sparsely populated and the village around which my linguistic and ethnographic description centres, Meyo-Ntem, falls within an area

calculated at having a density of approximately one inhabitant per square kilometre. Although mainly horticulturists, they are able hunters, trappers and fishermen. They are directly affected by their surroundings and are reliant upon the animals of the rainforest and the fish in the tributaries of the Ntem for most of their protein. This reliance is reflected in their oral traditions, especially their proverbs, their *minkana tsu tsu.* Literally: "teeny-weeny folklore".

These proverbs play an important part in Ntumu society. They not only serve as vehicles of transmission of wisdom and experience from one generation to another but are part of everyday life. Through these proverbs, ideas are expressed and exchanged, moral values prescribed and daily actions guided.

For the *nyamboro,* the elder males and tribal counsellors of the village, proverbs contain the traditional standards by which to live, advise and govern. The use of proverbs in speech is true oration and the rhetoric of jurisprudence. For the Ntumu young men, proverbs embody the goals of later life, the knowledge attained by virtue of age, the influential tongue of wisdom. For the anthropologist like me, proverbs are a distillation of complex beliefs and practices, boiled down to basic communicable images, the ideal place to begin my investigation of Ntumu world-view.

By the middle of june, a little less than a year from now, I will have collected the major body of Ntumu proverbs for my thesis. I plan to write a phonemic description of the language and several short articles concerning tribal technology before tackling the thesis on Ntumu world-view. I am learning to speak Ntumu and I have begun to collect some of the folklore. I plan, for the most part, to collect the majority of proverbs from recorded interviews. I have come across a couple of small handwritten collections of proverbs and stories by Baptist and Catholic missionaries living in the region. These sources are written using Bulu sound symbols, and I suspect that they are more Bulu than Ntumu. I intend to use these to verify proverbs collected from my interview recordings. They will undoubtedly help to expand the body of oral tradition I collect for myself.

I have placed individual proverbs on separate cards and as relevant information is obtained it will be added to these cards. The following headings appear on each card:

ET : English Translation
Nt : Ntumu Proverb
Ex : Explanation
C : Content
P : Personae
S : Style
Co : Collected from (coded)
FN : Footnotes

To illustrate the codification, indexing and handling of the proverbs so far collected, the following is a sample of my card entry system:

(001) ET : "I wanted to build a fence around you thinking that you were peanuts, while all the time you were *obo obo zen*."

Nt : "*Me yi wo lon akak onyo wa mebum na one owono, nde wo one obo obo zen.*"

Ex : *owono* (*Arachis hypogaea*) and *obo obo zen* (another quadrifoliate) are similar in appearance as young sprouts. The peanut or groundnut is one of the basic staples and the other is "an absolutely useless plant".

C : Don't be fooled by appearances.

P : 1st person, Generic human, Specific plants.

S : Declarative, Affirmative, Analogous

Co : E.A.M.C. of M.C.

SEE : Compare : (386)

FN : Swidden agriculture. Cross-reference with (017) Fence types : *afup, afan* and *nnam. Obo obo zen* literally means : "it lies down alongside the path."

I have started to record proverbs from anyone who will consent to give them to me. All of the proverbs obtained from direct recording thus far are from males over the age of 50. Most females and younger males state that they do not know any proverbs. They often say that only the old men of the village know the "wise sayings". However, usually only the older males consent to be interviewed. I feel the ones who decline do so because they do not, as yet, trust or understand my motives for collecting their proverbs.

Once a proverb is recorded from an interview, it is transcribed onto the cards. For the purposes of my reports to you and ultimately my analysis, the Ntumu transcriptions for individual proverbs will not be included. Only individual terms will be occasionally presented for clarification of meaning. The Ntumu terms which will appear will be presented without their tonemic diacritical markings.

To assure a higher degree of accuracy, both the recorded interviews and the transcriptions will be used in the translation process. My translator assistant will listen to individual proverbs from the recordings and translate literally, term for term, while I follow along with my transcription, taking notes and asking for amplified meanings to specific words. After this literal translating process is complete, we will discuss what the proverb means and the circumstances under which it might be used. Up until now, my assistant has been able to translate all of the proverbs. Only occasionally is he unable to explain their underlying message.

Aside from that, everything is progressing. However, the food is quite different here and as bad as it was, I am even beginning to miss the coffee in the Anthropology Department.

Sincerely yours, Joseph

5

THE CROSSING OF PATHS

The Toyota went as far as the village of Ma'an. *Ma'an* means: "the crossing of paths" and the namers of this place knew what they were talking about. It had a double row of mat roofed wattle-and-daub huts along the path at one end of the village and a cluster of zinc-roofed huts around the market at the other. From the air it must have looked like tin foil litter in the jungle. For another reason Ma'an was aptly named. It was the first place where my path crossed that of the Ntumu.

It was late in the afternoon when we finally arrived and although Robert and I were exhausted, we began to look for somewhere to spend the night before it got dark. Sunset in equatorial Africa was a phenomenon that I was not quite prepared for. Unlike the long and lingering dreamy summer evenings in the California desert where the twilight between sunset and dark can last two hours, nightfall here in the rainforest was as subtle and lingering as turning off a light switch. We had just begun asking about lodgings when suddenly, click, it was night.

In the dark, everyone we asked either declined to speak to us at all or softly refused us a place to sleep. I was sure that if Robert were alone he would have no trouble. I sensed a combination of fear, annoyance and embarrassment at being asked to house a whiteman. I asked Robert to try it alone and he soon came back with the news that under the circumstances only the village chief could help us. We started knocking on hut doors trying to locate the chief but everybody we asked didn't seem to know in the most unconvincing manner. We finally went to the marketplace and sat

down to wait, not for anything in particular, just wait. There was
nothing else to do.

I sat under a starless sky against a tree in the dark. The night was
so complete that the only things that could be seen were the tiny
pin-pricks of flickering yellow lantern light leaking out of the mud
walls of the huts across the way. It was interesting to watch but soon
the fatigue of the journey caught up with me. My mind nodded in
and out of drowsiness and thought. I saw the irony of my
circumstance and remembered the time during the first few years
after becoming a Baha'i. The early Sixties seemed long ago and
filled with impractical idealism. It was a time of great racial unrest
in America. The struggle for and against Civil Rights was the lead
story of every newscast. I remembered that intense but hollow kind
of concern that only distance and racial ignorance can spawn and
my armchair involvement in the distant racial confrontations in
the American South. Some years later, in 1968, after having passed
through Alabama in a racially mixed musical group called
Ubiquitas, I realized how naive I had been. In the tense aftermath
of the beatings, lynchings and riots, I had at last seen that I should
have more actively supported the process toward racial equality.
The empathy I felt while watching the marches and the sit-ins on
the six o'clock news was not enough. As a Baha'i, I should have been
in places like Selma and Birmingham, instead of wasting time
trying to become an opinionated legend in my own lunchtime, by
engaging in discussions about the social issues of the day with my
equally idealistic friends over school meals at Victor Valley High
School.

Since then my perception and self-awareness had changed. Five
years in the poverty and violence of Central and South America
had made me a little more streetwise about life and forced me to
realize what I had really been during that time: just another idle
fool sitting in the safety of my room watching a colour television
with a black-and-white mind. Just another hypocrite with my eyes
misted by the tears of social injustice, living in a comfortable white
house on a complacent white street in an exclusively white
neighbourhood. The irony of it all was amusing. "And where am I
now?" I thought. "I am on the other side of the tracks, the singular
anomaly in a place where no one will rent me a roof to sleep under
because I am different." It is impossible to know what fear,
prejudice and avoidance is without ever having been their victim.

A LEAF OF HONEY

After awhile the sporadic reflections gave way and I drifted off to sleep. In what seemed like a few seconds, I was roused by a light shining in my eyes and people talking at me. Robert was telling me to wake up. The local chief had returned to the village. An elderly but not ancient man with a kerosene lamp stood before me squinting in the glare of the flame. This was the chief of Ma'an. I stood up quickly and with a few terse words he directed us to follow him. We shouldered our belongings and tried to keep up with his circle of light as he wove his way through the stalls to another part of the market. He stopped in front of a small zinc-roofed hut that from the fermented cocoa smells must have served as storage depot. The chief invited us to enter and wait while he went off to look for some beds and a couple of chairs. We thought about something to eat but we were too tired even to open a tin of sardines.

We summized that the chief of Ma'an was the village businessman and bought cocoa from the surrounding plantations and sold it to the Greek buyers in Ebolowa, for a profit, of course. It was his slack season and I imagined he looked upon us as an opportunity to make money. He soon arrived with what must have been someone's entire household of furniture. I could imagine his wives and children sitting on the bare floor of an empty room cursing the likes of us. This could not be good for intercultural understanding. He sat down on one of the chairs and I could see that the time had come to find out what all of this was going to cost me.

When I had first hired Robert in Ebolowa to interpret for me, I explained that the initial contact with the Ntumu people was very important and that there was a specific form I wanted the translation to conform to, one that minimised paraphrasing. I taught him first to *metaphrase* or translate literally into English what was being said to me so that I could begin to understand the images with which the Ntumu spoke and begin to isolate specific words in the process of learning the language. Then he was to translate the meaning of the statement into English equivalents. When translating what I said into Ntumu, he was to be as literal as possible. We had practised this method before we had set out, but this was the first time he had been required to do it in a formal setting. He had already managed to teach me some of the more rudimentary greetings and polite sayings.

"*Mbolo!*" I said, greeting the chief in Ntumu.

"*Mbolo,*" he replied with a nod of the head.

A LEAF OF HONEY

So as not to deplete my entire repertoire of Ntumu sayings, I asked Robert to introduce himself and explain that he would translate for me.

"I am a traveller", I began, taking the chair opposite the chief, "and I come from a far place to this place."

"You are a son of what land?" the chief inquired.

"I am a son of the land of America," I answered.

"For what purpose have you come to this place?" he asked.

"I have come to see the Ntumu, I have come to hear you speak and to learn to speak with your tongue. I have come to listen to the telling of your stories and to learn your wisdom," I said. The chief thought about this for a moment.

"How long will you remain in this place?" he asked.

"I will stay in the land of the Ntumu for one year," I announced.

The chief made a clicking sound deep in his throat and Robert explained that this simply meant "I have heard you" and that I should continue the dialogue. The room continued to fill with the elders of the village but only the chief and I were seated. Every time something weighty or profound was said by the chief, the assemblage of old men would emit this same attending glottal click.

Both Robert and I were very tired and I suspected that this kind of exchange could last a long time. I realized that I had no idea what the etiquette of formal speech might entail, so I decided to risk being rude and get to the point.

"I give you thanks for this house and the beds and chairs and the kerosene lamp," I said, listing everything. "I am an unexpected stranger in the night. How do I repay your sacrifices?"

The chief thought for a moment. *"Deux mille francs,"* he said in French. Robert didn't even translate it. Two thousand francs. A long silence filled the room and the elders watched their chief in the dark glow of the smoky lamp. This was about a month's wages for a labourer during the cocoa season in this part of Cameroon. I was not in the best bargaining position having just been awakened from under a mango tree alongside the road, but nevertheless I did not want to establish an expensive precedent just because we were exhausted.

"Two thousand francs is money", I began tiredly, "it is a great pile of money."

"It is what the sons of Greece pay to sleep one night in a hotel in Yaounde, the capital." The chief definitely knew the law of supply and demand.

"I am not a son of Greece and this is not a hotel in the capital," I replied.

The chief gave a knowing glance toward his gallery of elders and said that he was:

"Shooting gorillas because of a lack of boars."

There was aloud and sustained chorus of clicking approval in the room, and I could see that the chief was well-pleased with his own wit. He turned half around in his seat to his tribesmen and laughed.

Robert leaned near and translated that the chief was obviously declaring that he was overpricing me because the Greeks were out of season. They weren't around at this time of year. I had to do something, and fast, or I would be obliged to pay.

"*Ane minkana!*" I announced loudly in Ntumu, this was another of the phrases I had learned to say. "It is a proverb." I hoped it was. The clicking subsided and the room grew quiet. I waited until the chief turned back and faced me before I addressed him.

"When a wayfarer comes", I continued with Robert's help, with the exaggerated gestures of a mime, "to a new land to build a hut for his wife and child, he looks for a place where the water is not muddy or bitter, for what man would build a hut beside water he could not drink?" I hoped the accompanying gestures helped communication and I paused to see if the chief was following my spontaneous analogy. "Muddy water is easy to know and does not need to be tasted. But how can a man know if clear water is sweet without tasting it?" I pointed at the chief and spoke to the elders employing the same indirect speech gesture the chief had used on me. "I have found a place with much clear water, this I can see." I motioned around the room. "Now the time has come to taste the water. If it is sweet my family will follow the path I have taken to this place." Robert had translated almost simultaneously, and I hoped the chief had understood what I was driving at. I sat back and awaited his answer.

Now the chief's gaze was different and after a moment he softly said:

"One never throws away the walking-stick before meeting
the earliest wayfarer on the path in the morning."

He added, "You have come this far and cleared the path of dew and met me. The rest of your path is dry." The chief stood up and the elders made a pathway to the door. "I am the father of the people of this village and the people who live in it are my children. One does not ask a son to pay to stay in the house of his father." With that he went out of the door.

I was left totally bewildered by the rapid change of attitude and was quite convinced that I had offended the chief with my hastily contrived allegory. The chief was gone but the elders still remained, whispering to one another. I asked Robert what was happening and he said he didn't know. After a few minutes of uncomfortable silence the chief returned with a chicken with its feet tied. He held it up for me to inspect and then offered it to me. Robert told me everything was fine and took charge of the conversation. He stood up and told the chief:

"One never eats a spoilt chicken when he has a friend."

Robert lowered his head and received the bird with an impressive and respectful gesture. He took the gift in his right hand while holding his right wrist with his left hand, a gesture I quickly learned. The gift of a chicken, he later explained, was a sign of honour and respect, and the custom of not only the Ntumu but also the Bulu, the tribe to which Robert belonged. Robert handed me the chicken and I copied the gesture of respect. The chief was satisfied and bid us both good night.

After he and the elders left, Robert and I discussed the exchange with the chief. I was no longer sleepy. Robert could not explain the meaning of the proverb about the walking-stick the chief had used, but he felt that it was somehow linked with the story I had told. He was convinced, however, that the chief had indirectly stated that I would never pay to live in his house.

It wasn't until months later, after I had learned to speak a little Ntumu, that I was able to ask one of the elders who was present that night what the chief had meant. By chance, the images of the allegory I had chosen and the literal translation of words themselves had unintentionally referred to an ancient saying.

"During the night," the elder explained, "the mist comes and clings to the jungle, and the plants along the paths through the jungle become heavy with dew. In the morning, the first person to use the path will take a branch or his walking-stick and shake the dew off the plants ahead of him as he walks so that his clothes do not become soaked. He takes this precaution only until he meets someone coming from the opposite direction. After passing, there is no longer any danger of getting wet because the other wayfarer has already shaken the plants dry." He added that this proverb also referred to the initial caution and care one must have when entering a new situation.

6

STYLE, PERSONAE AND CONTENT

Dear Dr Kilngott,

I have found that many of the proverbs incorporate examples of Ntumu food and cooked dishes, something you are interested in from your fieldwork days in China. I will try to send some of the tribal recipes as I promised. Food, planting and cultivating tools, personal belongings and firewood are carried by the women in homemade baskets which are worn on their backs. A strip of cloth is laced through the weave to form shoulder straps. I have enclosed a quick drawing of one. Root crops, plantains and some grains are pounded in wooden mortars with long pestles. I have drawn a couple of these pounding mortars and pestles used in the village of Meyo-Ntem for you. The mortars are carved from the trunks of a tree with soft light yellow wood and the pestles are cut from a reddish hardwood.

ANALYTICAL HEADINGS:

I have decided on some of the specific headings within the methodology we discussed before I left. I will employ these to make sense of the folklore I am accumulating. From next week I will be enclosing some of the proverbs assembled so far. These have been analyzed by the three different means we agreed upon and are classed and grouped accordingly:

1 The literary style in which the proverb is expressed, its manner of presentation.

33

2 The personae: who or what figure in the text of the proverb.

3 The content: the ideal the proverb communicates, its underlying message.

All the Ntumu proverbs that are translatable will be presented. However, only a representative few will be cited as examples and included in the text. Those proverbs which do not appear in the main text will be included at the end and referred to for the purpose of comparison. Tables at the end will also list the proverb numbers which correspond to types of style, personae and content.

STYLE:

As you predicted, the literary composition of Ntumu proverbs varies quite a bit. Several different manners of expression are employed to help convey, through the means of analogous elements and situations, the underlying meanings. Many of these styles overlap in particular examples and can be classified under more than one stylistic category. For the purposes of presenting the diversity of style which the Ntumu proverbs manifest, the following somewhat synthetic categories have been isolated:

1 DECLARATIVE
2 INTERROGATIVE
3 AFFIRMATIVE
4 NEGATIVE
5 ANALOGOUS
6 IMPLICATIVE
7 DIDACTIC
8 METAPHORIC
9 SYNECDOCHIC

Before I continue I would like to say that although the proverbs I collect will be examined with an interest in stylistics, this analysis will be rudimentary. I do not have the level of training in stylistics to hypothesize anything profound. I hope to be more pragmatic than theoretical in my research and I do not propose to postulate some basic underlying stylistic principle that connects each of the maxims I record. Similarly, I will not deal with the issue of the truthfulness of the proverbs or how informed the people from whom I extracted them were. I feel that considering the time constraints involved, it is sufficient to describe the manner and situation in which they are given and try to explain them as they were explained to me. I expect that there will be proverbs, regardless of their having been translated, which will be so self-explanatory as to be trans-cultural, while others will necessitate the presentation of background material to make them understandable.

I know that there is another stylistic factor to consider which I have not included above: satire or irony. I will present the proverbs I collect in a non-satirical, non-ironic fashion because this is the manner in which they were used. From what I have seen, the Ntumu do not employ sarcasm. They use more direct and sincere means of expression, even when putting down someone who is being haughty or arrogant.

Personally, I suspect that the juxtaposition of proverbs when linked together in a rhetorical exchange may reveal that these categories are sometimes more syntactic than stylistic. Time will tell. For the time being, I will send you only a few proverbs as examples of each of these styles. As I have said, these stylistic categories are synthetic and imposed by this anthropological and literary analysis and are not necessarily those which the Ntumu might readily isolate themselves. Some, however, are acknowledged as being distinct types of proverbs by those elders of the village who are willing to speak about this. The identification of these types reflect their sense of style. They clearly recognize analogous, implicative, didactic and synecdochic formats in their oral traditions. I hope that the more in-depth analysis of individual proverbs later on in my investigations into personae and content will reveal more about their own stylistic taxonomies.

Whenever I present an explanation of the meanings of these proverbs I hope that you will not think that I have endeavoured to "solve" them, because they are likely to be far more mysterious than I will ever be able to unravel and whatever simple explanation of them I give can never suffice. All that I can hope for when I give an explanation is to be as accurate and truthful as possible. Even the most succinct proverb will never be totally self-explanatory.

Sincerely yours, Joseph

7

A VISUAL ENVIRONMENT WITHOUT HORIZON

Robert had a bedroll and took one of the raffia pole beds to sleep on. I had brought a hammock along with me which I had had since I left South America. Robert wrapped himself up in a sheet-like cloth and covered his head to escape the insects. This was mosquito country. Mosquitoes, I soon discovered, produce a special constant humming sound which can defeat the normal ability of the human ear to detect the direction of the source of the sound. They are the insect kingdom's master ventriloquists. They can have you searching for them in one direction and, zap, get you in the back of the neck from another. On the inside of the hammock I attached a mosquito net that I had made for myself soon after my wife and I got off the plane in Douala. I strung the whole thing up to the rafters and got in. The trick was to lie at a slight diagonal so that your back was level with your heels. The mosquito net was a lifesaver. Just as long as you didn't sleep up against the net where the mosquitoes could get a shot at you, you were promised a fair night's rest.

The children of the village moved into the room after the elders had left and were very interested to see someone "sleep in the air" as they called it. They chattered among themselves while we talked, Robert through his sheet and me through my net. After a while, we shooed the children out of the room, turned the lamp down low and settled into sleep. I didn't realize how dead tired I was.

The next morning I awoke with the fleeting dream-like memory of a group of little black and brown faces framed in the doorway. I recalled peering over the side of the hammock in the middle of the night and squinting at this blurred scene for a while, trying to

36

decide if it were real or not, and finally deciding I was too tired to care and drifting back to sleep. What had woken me now was the sound of Robert trying to evict a noisily protesting family of goats which had joined us during the night.

Robert and I started out early in the morning with a frying pan, the hammock, odd personal belongings and a chicken tied by its feet to the outside of our backpacks like things attached as afterthoughts. We looked like a pair of desperate hobos trudging out of a scene from *The Grapes of Wrath*. I felt ragged and blurry around the eyes but Robert looked bright and energetic. He had even brushed his teeth. He had with him a special root which he chewed the end of until it was reduced to fibres. He then brushed his teeth with the frayed end of it. He called it a "toothbrush root".

It may have been early to us but it was obviously late for everyone else. The market and village were absent of the people who already had gone to their fields. The whydah birds were loudly bickering and fighting among themselves for building rights in the short coconut trees that lined the road. Some of the trees were stripped bare of every last leaf to weave their nests. You wouldn't expect anything so small to make so much noise.

The distance from Ma'an to Meyo-Ntem was seven kilometres on my map, but the trek intimated that the cartographer was wrong yet again. We first followed the muddy and tyre-rutted road out of the village through the jungle to the west until we reached a strangely out of place little red-brick house with a Cameroonian flag, a swing barrier and placard which read: *Control de Douane,* Customs Checkpoint. According to the map, there was a good fifty kilometres of uninhabitable virgin jungle between here and the Equatorial Guinean border, land that my grandfather would have simply called "boondocks". Certainly it was a very long way to come to declare your duty-free. A smartly-dressed official in a freshly starched and ironed brown uniform and foreign-legion type hat came out of the hut with a clipboard to inspect us. It turned out that he was the only customs officer for the entire District of Ma'an. I suspected he had committed some heinous felony somewhere else and had been sent here as punishment for his crime. He asked us in French where we were coming from and where we were headed. Robert told him what he already knew. There was nowhere else to come from and nowhere else to go. I asked him if he got many people through his checkpoint. He sighed that we were the first he had seen for two weeks and that in the two years of manning this post by himself he had never stopped anyone for a customs violation. Yep, it was just him (and all the crocodiles in the Ntem river basin) that deterred people from smuggling. He lifted his little barrier and we passed through. About a hundred paces on, we turned left down a path that branched off through the bush to the south to what we hoped would be Meyo-Ntem. There were no road signs, just a calculated guess.

The jungle above the path had three distinct layers of vegetation. At the bottom, in the root zone, the red laterite soil was covered with waist-high grasses. Small trees and vines grew out of this and formed a constant canopy of foliage over our heads. At the top, enormous *dum* trees towered over the jungle. The crowns of these giants were mostly veiled from view by the smaller species of trees and the morning mist, but the trunks and root complex of the *dum* dwarfed everything else on the floor of the jungle. The *dum* rose more than thirty meters and the roots began three or more meters up on the trunk as a fin-like protrusion that curved and wove its way out from the tree into the ground. I could see why the road and path skirted around the *dum* trees that stood in the way. Cutting one down at ground level would be nearly impossible. The labyrinth of protective snarls of roots alone would defeat any tribesman long before his axe reached the main trunk. Among the roots there wasn't enough room to swing an axe.

I wondered what effect this plant-choked environment would have on the Ntumu tribesmen. The landscape was obscured by the wall of matted foliage and the path through it was a shadow-rich winding tunnel of overhanging leaves and beaten-down grass under foot. A thin mist still hung in the trees and by noon the scene was accentuated at random by luminous narrow shafts of vertical light that ended in sunflecks on the ground. It was an environment which lacked one phenomenon that is fundamental to human orientation — the concept of a horizon. The eyes had nothing to focus on at a distance. No surface was more than thirty meters away. Visual perspectives and vanishing points were limited or non-existent. The sky and clouds could not be seen except as small bits of white peeking through the garment of green foliage. The spectrum of light was narrower here and green was the standard to which everything was compared.

It was a world where there was no vantage point onto which one could climb and see the lay of the land. Any sense of the topography of the terrain had to be pieced together from small short-range observations of the incline of the path and stored in three dimensions in the mind. One could not anticipate the imminent danger of something approaching and rely on distance as a safety factor here. It was visually impossible to perceive anything approaching. In the jungle there was no distance, only enveloping nearness.

The sphere of perception around a dweller of the California desert, like myself, includes about ninety percent of things I would term as static scenery. These are things like the sky, distant mountains and background, things that I didn't have to worry about because they were predictably static. They always kept their distance and I never had to keep an eye on them. In the rainforest nothing is scenery, nothing is static. It is a jack-in-the-box world, where things suddenly jump out at you from nowhere. I could see how dangerous it was not to be awake and attentive in an environment where everything was foreground and potentially interactive with you. Seemingly innocuous things in your peripheral vision become as important to your well-being as objects you are focusing on. For the native dweller of the jungle, I imagined that it is a relatively closed and microcosmic world which would encourage close range and accurate perception of the condition of the immediate surroundings, a constant state of heightened awareness.

Any Ntumu world-view would be conditioned upon this and be the basis upon which any mental image of a wider reality would be built. Surely Ntumu world-view transcended this blinding verdancy. How different it must be when compared to my own. I held in my mind assumptions about the shape, size and configuration of the world I live in. These were based upon images I had built up from memories, maps, globes and pictures taken from satellites. I had never seen the white cloud-enshrouded blue-green orb of the planet from space for myself, yet this was one of the images I used as the foundation for all sorts of assumptions about the universe and my location in the world. I knew about the unseen range of mountains that lay beyond the hills that skirted the desert of my homeland because I had seen maps of the region and I could recognize features in the landscape that corresponded to the features illustrated on the map.

I had a set of identities and affinities with groups I had never met but were nonetheless part of my social make-up. I wondered if they did. Although I could readily see myself as a son, a brother, a husband, and a father to one group of people I knew, i.e. my family, I was also affiliated with other individuals outside my family and shared a more abstract relationship beyond kinship with a lot of people I had never met. There were different layers to my social make-up. If my allegiances included a dedication to my family, a camaraderie with my friends, a mild sense of patriotism as an American, the religious sodality of being a Baha'i, and an even more abstract feeling of brotherhood and solidarity with the rest of mankind, it would not be unreasonable to assume that the Ntumu were just as socially complex. These were levels of social unity which were not solely dependent upon technological advancement. However, for me personally, within each of these layers or circles of complex social interrelationships, the concept of my own position was based upon some geographically related image. For the most part, these images were the result of the way I had been exposed to the world. My self-image within the social, cultural, political and religious structures I recognized was a complex blend of many factors, but one of these was surely the way in which I had been exposed to the physical world around me.

The Ntumu must certainly have a different basis for their complicated and layered world-view and therefore live in a different psychological universe than I did. By reason of the different nature of their environment, they would be able to perceive things in the world that I couldn't. One of the principal reasons I was here was to acquire the linguistic skills to enable me to find this different mental world and thereby perhaps understand my own a little better. This wasn't the first time. The years I spent in Colombia among the Latins and the Guajiro Indians had taught me:

"El que adquire una nueva lengua, adquire otra alma."

He who acquires a new language, acquires another soul.

It was going to be a learning experience for Robert as well. His home village was near the town of Ebolowa and this was the first time he had been in virgin jungle as dense as this. Robert was aware of most of what the jungle contained, but many of the animals here he had never seen for himself. We were like two little school children on our first outing to the zoo. The grass was alive with a rainbow of oblivious butterflies and crawling insects, and the intermediate trees directly overhead were full of wary and flitting squirrels and jabbering monkeys while the *dum* played host to the clicks and cries of a myriad of unseen birds high above. Every turn in the path gave us a glimpse of the wealth of life hidden around us as new species of little animals scurried out of our way.

A kind of music surrounded us. The jungle could sound soft and sweet in the gentle twitter and tweet of a solo performance of a distant bird for a time and then, without warning, erupt into a riotous cacophony of screeches and hoots. In the ever-changing melody of the morning we ate up the distance along the path, the aluminium frames of our heavy backpacks squeaking in time to the slosh of our boots through the puddles on the path. We saw no one on the path and our trouserlegs were soon soaked from brushing against the wet undergrowth. We had not yet learned the practical wisdom of the proverb of the night before.

About halfway to Meyo-Ntem we came across an area beside the path which had been recently trampled. Branches on the smaller trees had been broken and stripped of foliage. Strips of bark and bits of fruit had been strewn about. It was obviously the work of some large animal and I sensed the danger in the extent of such destruction. I suggested we keep moving but just as soon as we passed the area we heard a snapping noise. We stopped and looked back and saw a small tree shaking violently and its fruit falling into the grass around it. Moving in the grass near the tree, we could see the black head and back of a large foraging animal. I repeated in a low voice my suggestion of getting the hell out of there, but Robert didn't seem to hear me. He stood mesmerized by the activity in the bushes. I could not see enough of the animal to tell how big it was, but from the way it shook that tree, its size could be speculated upon later from the safety of the next village. Presently the shaking ceased and the animal stood up and peered over tops of the high grass at us.

"Oh oh!" I whispered to myself, "A gorilla!"

It's funny how the same stimulus can elicit completely different responses from two individuals. Robert seemed enveloped in a bubble of calm curiosity, while I, on the other hand, was scared spitless.

In that slow motion of heightened awareness that often accompanies times of danger, I flashed on my only previous encounter with a live gorilla. I vividly remembered going to the San Diego Zoo as a child in the autumn. There was an enormous male gorilla in a barred cage that paced angrily up and down on his knuckles. A large crowd of sightseers with cameras were gathered around the cage, shouting and jeering at him to perform. The gorilla grew tired of the unrelenting harassment, and approached the front of the cage, squatted down and lazily scratched his backside. The crowd pointed and laughed at the comical scene. They leaned forward against the rail and raised their cameras to capture the performance. The crafty old ape then suddenly stood up with a freshly deposited handful of his own faeces and slung it through the bars. His aim was impeccable. He splattered a wide swath of people, many of them with their mouths open in astonishment.

Unfortunately, there were no bars around *our* gorilla. He just stood there, head and shoulders above the grass, making menacing grunting noises. As if sleep-walking, Robert began to move toward it.

"I've never seen one before," he said absently. I couldn't see the rest of the gorilla, but I was sure he wasn't standing on any box to make himself look taller. He was at least as big as Robert.

"Robert!" I cried in disbelief, "Where the hell are you going?" I reached out and grabbed him firmly by his backpack and pulled him back.

"I want to see it," he said in a faraway voice. I started tiptoeing away backward as slowly and unalarmingly as possible down the path with Robert in tow. This careful and deliberate retreat only lasted a few seconds. The ape charged. The backward shuffle turned and became a terrified dead run.

Convinced that the ape was in hot pursuit, I didn't pause to look back until we covered about a kilometre. The relief of not finding the gorilla on our heels was total. The adrenalin suddenly ran dry and panting exhaustion consumed me. Robert was just as breathless, and more than a little bit indignant that I had panicked at the sight of such a harmless animal and literally dragged him away from a chance of "catching a gorilla". Between gasps, I tried to explain what I felt were the dangers of fraternizing with gorillas, especially ones his own size. Nothing I could say could convince him of the danger we had just escaped. Robert accused me of being silly and became sullen.

We continued down the path in silence toward Meyo-Ntem and about a half an hour later we came upon a lone opened-sided hut with six men sitting around a smouldering fire. Robert greeted them and they offered us wooden stools to sit on. Five of the men looked as if they had been out hunting because they had spears and a shotgun. The sixth was strange. He sat with a towel over his head, which he held closed like a veil in front so just his eyes were visible. Robert chatted for a few minutes and then mentioned that we had just seen a gorilla. Upon hearing this there was an excited exchange of information and the five hunters suddenly jumped up with their weapons and ran off down the path from which we had just come.

Robert looked surprised and asked the remaining man what all the excitement was about. A series of muffled and distorted words came from behind the towel. Robert's eyes widened as he listened in silence to the laboured speech of the man. The sounds he made were almost inhuman. For the first time I could see fear in Robert's eyes. The man removed the towel and exposed the horror of a gaping hole where his face should have been. Most of his cheeks and all of his nose, upper lip and front teeth were gone. His pink tongue lolled around in the hideous nasal cavity and drooling skeletal orifice. It wasn't a recent wound and the skin had healed as much as it ever would. The man didn't wear the towel to hide his nightmarish image. It was there to keep the flies and bloodsuckers out.

Robert sat stunned. The fresh image of his foolish approach to the animal still flickered in his eyes. Robert slowly stood up and we left the man sitting in the hut without a word. As we walked on towards the next village he explained what the man had said. A year ago, the man with the towel had been attacked on the way home, near this spot, by a huge gorilla. The gorilla had held him by the hair on each side of his head and had bitten him full in the face, ripping out the hole we saw.

In the distance, we heard two sharp blasts resound through the trees and undergrowth followed after a long time by a single shot. Robert and I didn't stop and kept moving down the path. A while later the group of hunters overtook us. They were hurrying toward the village. The man with the towel was not with them. They had loaded the dead gorilla in a wheelbarrow from somewhere and wheeled it along. As it passed me, I could see the fatal wounds across the chest. The head bore a larger wound to the face fired at close range in apparent vengeance. The gorilla overflowed the wheelbarrow as they rolled along ahead of us, its limp arms hanging over the sides and dragging on the ground.

8

NEGATIVE ASSERTIONS, AFFIRMATIVE QUESTIONS

Dear Dr Kilngott,

Sending this preliminary analysis to you piecemeal as you suggested is proving more difficult than I anticipated. I have just discovered that the last report I sent you never reached my friend in Ebolowa for him to mail. The person to whom I gave the envelope to deliver to Ebolowa went somewhere else. About two weeks later, I saw the man in the market-place at Ma'an and he still had the envelope with him. It was rather mutilated. From the curve of the envelope you can tell he must have had it in his back pocket. I have now found someone else, who I hope will be more reliable in delivering the letters to my friend. Every letter I send has to run the gauntlet of being hand-carried about 120 kilometres before it faces the real enemy. The Cameroonian postal system is beyond description. One look at the sorting office in Ebolowa and I was convinced to make multiple carbon copies of my work just in case a dozen or so of my reports fail to reach you. It must be difficult for you to read my thesis in this serialized and tattered form. Although I plan to write my reports weekly, I will sometimes have to wait for someone to travel the distance to Ebolowa. Please excuse any delay.

I have been looking at some of the playthings the children of the village make. In particular, the young boys. They produce some of the most amazing toy cars and trucks. The drawings which I will be enclosing over the next few weeks do not do them justice. The production of these toys seems to follow several progressive steps in their development and there is a clear correlation between the technological complexity of the toys and the age of their makers.

This is interesting because Ntumu children don't appear to share their toys. Instead, they share the technology of how to make them. Each boy discovers how things work for himself as he makes his own toy car or truck. The process is one of sequential learning. The child learns about basic technology in a very sound and effective way. As he makes his first simple "truck", he is learning the fundamentals he will need to build upon when he upgrades his toy in the future. Unlike the steel and plastic in the toys of the more technological world, the raffia which the Ntumu use does not last forever. When the toy wears out the Ntumu child must make a new one. When he does, he makes one better and more technologically advanced than the old one.

The first sketch shows the push-stick "truck" which very young boys make. Boys of about five or six will find a long bent stick and push it along in front of them. As they do this, the point will bounce and jump. Children a little older modify this with the addition of an axle and a pair of large green fruit as wheels. The second drawing shows how a smaller fruit in the middle is used to connect the axle to the push-stick. Sardine tins are also fitted with green fruit wheels or rubber disks cut from the soles of sandals as the last drawing portrays. These sardine-tin cars are the only toys which I have observed being pulled. Everything else is pushed.

DECLARATIVE STYLE:

I have, for the purposes of my analysis, termed those Ntumu proverbs which are statements rather than questions as declarative. In the body of folklore collected so far, declarative proverbs greatly outnumber interrogative proverbs. Representative of this assertive style are the following two examples:

(002) "The wife of a fool never divorces, the wife of a lazy one does."

Here, by non-analogous means, the literal message is conveyed. And again in the declarative style:

(003) "Many pigs, take care of each."

Through analogous means, the message here is: "One must pay attention to even the smallest things because each individual part of one's life is important". The analogy here is that usually in a litter there are many piglets, nevertheless care must be taken with each to ensure that all will survive, even the runts.

INTERROGATIVE STYLE:

Many proverbs are phrased in an interrogative or questioning mode. These are formed in several different ways: some use prefixual interrogative markers on the pronouns, others incorporate tag interrogative words at the ends of otherwise affirmations. They reflect a sense of the Socratic method among the Ntumu.

(004) "If you say something is true, is it as if it becomes true?"

The message here is obvious: saying something does not make it a reality. This is the Ntumu way of teaching one to avoid rationalization and self-deception. In the following example, a situation is created in which animals figure. From this an element is drawn and made reference to as analogous to that which hides the truth from sight.

> (005) "If the panther kills an animal, it hides it in the grass; if you eat the grass, where then will you hide?"

The message is one of "if you are not careful your secrets will slip out."

AFFIRMATIVE STYLE:

Simply, this category groups those proverbs which are grammatically positive as opposed to negative.

> (006) "The weak chimpanzees and the strong chimpanzees together."

Another animal analogy. It takes all kinds to make up the world, or there is a place for everyone.

(007) "If *osen* brings news from the branches that *mvein* is sick, who will doubt him?"

Osen and *mvein* are two different tree-dwelling squirrels which live in close proximity to each other in the forest. In this proverb, they are symbolic of close relatives in humans. If someone tells something about one of his own family, in Ntumu society it is taken as truth because as it is said: who else would know better? The lesson here is that one's opinion is valid in proportion to one's experience or familiarity to the subject in question.

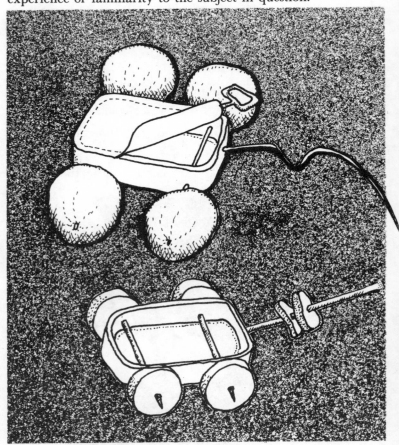

A LEAF OF HONEY

NEGATIVE STYLE:

In many proverbs, examples or situations are presented which are shown to be counter or opposed to that which is proper or prescribed. These negative types can be either analogous or literal. "One never . . ." and "One doesn't . . ." are common formats for such proverbs:

(008) "One doesn't throw a stone where he hides a piece of zinc."

The zinc referred to here is the corrugated zinc roofing sheets which some of the more wealthy plantation owners use to roof their houses. Since the exploitation of bauxite in Cameroon, these corrugated sheets are nowadays made of aluminium. However, the word "zinc" is still retained for this new material. A stone striking such a sheet of metal would make a lot of noise. The message here is: Don't give your secret away, steer clear of situations and conversations which will lead to the discovery of private matters.

(009) "A child will not stop eating raw caterpillars until he has vomited."

This is the Ntumu version of the universal lesson of Western children sticking their fingers in the fire. The *nkon* caterpillars are much relished when specially prepared and well-cooked. Before you begin looking through the footnotes for the recipe for "cooked caterpillars", forget it. I have tasted them. One bite and my mouth thought it had died and gone to hell. There are some things in the world which need to be missed and left to slip into merciful oblivion, those things which we regard as ethnographically unrecorded. This is one such thing. I have no doubt that this intentional omission on my part with regard to "cooked caterpillars" will save the life of some future anthropologist trying to reconstruct Ntumu culinary practices.

Sincerely yours, Joseph

A REMNANT OF TRIBAL SOVEREIGNTY

The hunters wheeled their grim trophy through the forest and Robert and I followed the blood-stained trail. They were jubilant and laughed and took turns pushing the wheelbarrow. Soon we entered a long clearing with about thirty-five red mud huts lining the path on either side. One of the hunters informed us that this was the village of Meyo-Ntem. I took another look. After nearly six months of planning and academic preparation and about 10,000 miles of journey, I had finally arrived. It was much smaller than I had imagined, and I thought about the prospect of spending a year in a place this isolated and small. First of all, the village appeared abandoned. There was no sign of either people or animals.

In the centre of the settlement was a distinctive square structure without walls. It was built nearer the path and out of line with the neat rows of huts. It contained the only evidence of recent occupation. A slim wisp of pale blue smoke rose from an open hearth and lingered as it was caught in the thatched roof.

The open area between the two rows of huts was a patchwork of ground that had obviously been cleared systematically but at different times. The grass grew at different lengths in front of each hut, each forming a large rectangle. I noticed that there was a little square green bottle buried in the ground at the intersection of each rectangle. I tapped one of the bottles with the toe of my shoe. It was firmly set in the ground upside down, with the square base flush to ground level. I guessed that they were tribal bench marks or survey markers of some kind. I was told later that they had been buried by the council of elders to mark out the boundary of each hut owner's responsibility to keep the common area clean and the grass cut.

A LEAF OF HONEY

We went to the wall-less hut and sat down on some stools in the shade of the roof. The hunters left the wheelbarrow outside in the sun. The flies soon found the blood. Presently, a few people came out of their huts and greeted the hunters. They appeared to know them. The children gathered excitedly around to stare at the dead gorilla. They whispered amongst themselves as if not to awaken the beast. I noticed that all the villagers were either very elderly women or children between about three and ten years old. It was obvious that the working-age members of the community were absent, but I was surprised at the lack of mothers and infants. No "housewives" here. The mother's carried their infants to work. The hunter who was toting the shotgun told the story of the killing to the small crowd with gestures which vividly re-enacted the event. It was then that I understood about the third shot to the face. One old woman brought a gourd of cool water and we all drank.

Having learned the key role the local chief would play in finding us accommodation, we asked the hunters to find out where he was. The hunters asked the villagers and we were told that the chief of Meyo-Ntem lived in the large hut at the far end of the clearing, but that he was away. I was beginning to suspect that tribal chiefs were like policemen: never around when you needed one. Someone explained that this was only part of the village of Meyo-Ntem and that the larger half of the settlement was on the Ntem river two kilometres further to the south. The hunters suggested that that was probably where the chief was. We thanked them for guiding us and said that we would rest here. They said they had to press on and that they wanted to make it back to their village across the river before the meat began to spoil. The hunters continued down the path wheeling the gorilla along, promising that if they saw the chief, they would tell him that we were here.

After the hunters had left, the crowd of villagers remained. They seemed moderately interested in me, but I could see, that as a white man, I was no rival to a dead gorilla. The children cautiously approached me and began carefully to touch my face and hair. Robert told them my name was Joseph and a delightful chorus of voices began to shout "*Yoser, Yoser, Yoser.*" Up to this point I had not yet spoken. Back in Ebolowa, before Robert and I set out, I asked him to teach me some silly phrases which I felt might help break the ice. They were simple enough to be understood clearly yet totally ludicrous.

51

A LEAF OF HONEY

"*M-bo-lo*," I said carefully, so that the children would understand. The eyes of the children lit up with glee.

"*Mbolo!*" they cried in unison. I leaned forward.

"*Iwa zu ma dji?*" I whispered with feigned concern. "Are you going to eat me?" The children's faces dropped in horror and they bolted out of the hut in every direction. An instant later they were slapping themselves on the legs and rolling about on the ground in great fits of laughter. The older villagers were also laughing at the absurdity of the question. This was the last thing that they had expected a whiteman to say.

Children are usually the best initial teachers of an unwritten language in a village setting. They are the ones who have the time and interest to play language building word-games. Learning the language had to be the first priority, and the success of my present research depended on it. Employing Robert as my translator I saw as a necessary first step, primarily to facilitate my introduction to the people I wanted to learn about. However, without a personal knowledge of their language, the meaning of their oral tradition could never be grasped. How could I ask questions which were meaningful to them without using their own concepts and images of life? If I ever wanted to understand more than just the patently obvious and be able to find the best equivalents in my language for the nuances in Ntumu beliefs, I had better learn to see with their eyes.

As a conscientious anthropological fieldworker, I wanted to eliminate carelessness and inaccuracy from the product of my work. I could not rely on Robert forever. Sooner or later he would have to return to Ebolowa and continue his schooling and, more importantly, he was Bulu and not Ntumu. His translations would be full of personal interpretations and unintentional cultural bias. People always edit when they translate. Educating my tongue was the key to opening my eyes to the separate world within their culture. I knew that some of the concepts which lay hidden in the minds of these people may not even exist in my own native English, and that the only means I had of discovering their subtleties was through learning Ntumu.

For the rest of the day, Robert and I wandered around the village and the children followed us wherever we went. I felt like mother duck leading her line of trailing brood. Every so often I would stop and the children would gather around me. I would touch something and ask: "*Enye ane dje?*": "What is this?" I got my clipboard out and my old 1949 edition of *The Principles of the International Phonetic Association* and began to note down the words I was learning using the International Phonetic Alphabet. I pointed at things and asked the names of rocks, goats, huts, trees; everything I could see. The children never grew tired of teaching me.

By the end of the day, I had acquired a long list of words phonetically transcribed as sound-symbols. I sat down and began to collate my data. Robert looked over my shoulder and shook his head. It must have looked like Martian to him. He pointed at a group of symbols.

"What is that?" he asked.

"An initial syllabic retroflex nasal assimilated to a voiced plosive velar, an ascending tonemic half-open back vowel and a terminal alveolar-dental nasal," I said. I pronounced the word for him: "*ngon*".

"Pumpkin seeds!" said Robert. "All that just to say 'pumpkin seeds'. Why do you have to write it like that, why so complicated?"

"If I want to learn to speak Ntumu without an accent and be able to hear the subtle tone differences which change the meanings of words, then I will have do this. At least in the beginning," I explained.

I read through the words I had collected. In the end, I was relieved to find no duplications. My project advisor at the University of California had warned me about apparent duplications and told me a story about an anthropology fieldworker who went to Australia.

The student had begun his collection of the Aboriginal names for things from an old Aborigine. He did this without a translator. The student sat on the ground near the man and pointed at a tree and the Aborigine said, "*Ungumba*" or something like that. I forget the real word. The student wrote down "*ungumba* means: 'tree', possibly a specific tree species". He then pointed to a bush. The Aborigine said "*Ungumba*". The student thought to himself, *ungumba* must be more generic than just "tree" or "bush" and he set out to find the category of things which *ungumba* described. He made his first working hypothesis: *ungumba* meant "foliage". Now it was time to test his hypothesis. He pointed at several kinds of trees. In each case the answer was "*Ungumba*". So far so good. He then pointed at several types of bushes, "*Ungumba*" again. He permitted himself a smug self-satisfying smile. Now all he had to do was find which plants were not *ungumba*. He pointed to the grass, again the answer: "*Ungumba*". The student frowned. "Possibly vegetation", he wrote as an amendment. He pointed to every plant he could find. Everytime the same response: "*Ungumba*". He stopped and thought: "Maybe this is the only word he knows." He dismissed the idea. "Maybe it means 'green' or 'verdant'," he thought. He was wearing a green cotton shirt, and pointed to it. "*Ungumba*". He then pointed to his brown pants. "*Ungumba*". "Definitely not green," he wrote. Thinking about his cotton clothing, it occurred to him that perhaps it had a wider meaning, a meaning which combined concepts which were separate in his own language. Maybe it meant something like "growing" or "has once been alive". It was possible that it was not a noun or an adjective at all, but a verb. The student pondered for a long while trying to think of a test which would prove or disprove this. All this time the Aborigine patiently waited for the next question. At last he had a plan. The student carefully pointed to a stone. Yep, you guessed it: "*Ungumba*". He picked up the stone and silently pointed at it. "*Ungumba*". He threw the stone straight up and quickly pointed to it in the sky. "*Ungumba*," said the old man watching it fly. The stone came down and fell dangerously close to the man. It was at this point that the Aborigine jumped up and said many things, none of which were *ungumba*. The student sat on the ground watching the Aborigine stalk away shaking his fist in the air and grumbling to himself. It was more than a week before the student found out that *ungumba* meant "finger".

In the afternoon the chief of Meyo-Ntem returned. He had been working in his plantation of cocoa trees and knew nothing about us. I am sure he was startled to see strangers, one of them white, occupying his village. He was a head shorter and thirty years older than me with just a few strands of grey among his short-cropped hair. Robert entered into a long conversation with him, explaining who I was and what I intended to do. His name was Ekotto Fang and he appeared to be a serious but likeable man. After asking several questions about the length of my proposed stay, he said that we were welcome to stay the night in the *aba* and that he would call a meeting of the elders the next evening to determine the long-term arrangements for our stay.

The *aba* was the name of the open hut in the centre of the village. Robert and I had seen many of these on the last leg of our ride in the Toyota. It seemed the *aba* was a special type of Ntumu structure because Robert commented that the villages in adjacent Bululand lacked these.

As the evening drew near, the chief brought a kerosene lamp for us to use that night. One of the children came with an armful of kindling and stoked the smouldering fire into flame. The rest of the huts were roofed with raffia mats and the walls were made of a type of construction called wattle and daub. There appeared to be basically two kinds of huts: large rectangular single-room structures and smaller multi-room huts. The larger huts Robert recognized as *nda mininga*: "women's houses". These had two door openings, one looking out onto the centre of the village and the other opening onto the forest at the back. These were single rooms in which the wives cooked and slept along with the children. The smaller huts were multi-roomed dwelling places for men known as *nda fam*.

The women's houses were cluttered with raffia beds and cooking fires. There were no chimneys or openings in the roof which caused the rafters and roofing mats to be encrusted with the black soot from years of smoky fires. The dark air was full of the smells of smoke and fish. Trays of woven raffia hung over the fires filled with dry fish being smoked and cured. Each of the curled fish had its tail forced through one of its gills and out the mouth, like little doughnuts.

As night descended it became chilly and I sat nearer the hearth in the *aba*. The chief came and sat on one of the raffia beds to talk with us. He laughed and told Robert that I was "bathing in the fire", trying to get warm. I asked if the chief would tell me about the *aba*. Robert translated as the chief told the story.

The *aba* was a kind of *nda fam* like some of the other huts in the village. It seemed to be a remnant of a time when the chief was the tribal sovereign. Near the center of every present-day Ntumu village is situated a similar structure. They are all called *aba*. They are usually open-air huts constructed of upright wooden poles holding aloft a gabled raffia-thatched roof lashed in place with rattan-like vines. The *aba* is distinguished from the other structures in the village by its central location and its usual lack of walls or doors. Although the *aba* huts differ in design from village to village, some having low walls and others a perimeter fence, they all allow a person sitting inside easy visual access of the entire village and road. The shape of the *aba* is usually square or rectangular and the size varies according to the population of the village.

A LEAF OF HONEY

The *aba* is not only the predominate structure in the village but also an important social unifying institution. It is the site of most male social activities in the village. It is the centre of male handicraft and recreation, the communal dining hall, the gathering place of visiting and resident males, the focal-point of messengers and newsmongers, the seat of tribal consultation and justice.

The existence of this structure and the institution of the *aba* is traditional. For the Ntumu it is eternal in the past, no one can recall a time when there has not been an *aba*. Even those things which outlive the recollections of the oldest in the village, the oral traditions, speak of the *aba*.

The *aba* has nonetheless changed over the years. The older elements of the Ntumu society tell the stories told to them by their forefathers of a time when the *aba* was far more important than now. Before the advent of the whitemen, the Christians and the cocoa trees, and before the roads were built to transport them, the Ntumu villages were linked together by footpaths. Each village was built so that the dwelling and the cooking structures lined either side of the path. In the midmost heart of the village lay the *aba* with the path running through it.

The chief and village men would sit in the *aba* and pass the hours after coming from their farms occupied in handicraft and discussion. As the only path through the village led directly through the *aba*, the men of the village could easily scrutinize the visitors and wayfarers who were obliged to pass through it. Familiar individuals, upon arriving in the village, would enter the *aba* and greet the men there before going to the individual huts of their friends or relations in the village. This practice for the most part prevails today.

Strangers, however, were treated far differently than they are today. The chief then had more power. Folktales tell how strangers who had to cross the village *en route* to their destination would have to present themselves before the chief and elders in the *aba*. They would be invited to remain awhile and answer the questions put to them by the elders. These questions would concern the genealogies, villages of residence and destination of the strangers. These things were asked to determine if they were related to any tribe or clan presently at war with members of the village. Strangers unlucky enough to be declared enemies because of their individual reputations or relations were sometimes subsequently enslaved or put to death by their interrogators.

Likewise, because of the situation of the *aba* on the footpath, the chief was provided the opportunity of reviewing the passing females. Wives accompanying their husbands on their journeys ran the risk of becoming a new wife of the chief of any hostile village. If the chief found such a traveller attractive, he would direct her to go and place her belongings in the cooking house of his other wives. The prudent ex-husband would then continue, as directed, alone on his journey without voicing any complaint. Those men who refused to relinquish their wives upon command or who challenged the rights of the chief soon found themselves either enslaved or dead.

Each elder male of the village, by virtue of his age, won the right to construct a low bed in the *aba,* thereby showing to all his earned rank and position in the authoritative hierarchy of the village. In the *aba,* this bed was his alone, a place marking his presence or absence at meetings of the council to the chief, a physical reminder of his social niche in the community.

The *aba* served as the communal dining hall for the men of the village. Male children, upwards of seven years old, were required to cease eating with their mothers and sisters in the cooking hut and join their fathers and male relations in the *aba* for meals. At meal times the chief would ring a bell summoning the women of the village to bring the food they had prepared, and the assorted bowls were brought and placed at the feet of the entire assemblage of men gathered in the *aba.* After the chief, one by one, from the oldest to the youngest, food would be taken from the receptacles irrespective of which wife had cooked what. In this manner, old and young, married and unmarried ate from the bowl of communal effort.

Inside the *aba* were left the implements of craft and recreation. Under the beds and low stools and wedged in the rafters were stored carved and woven objects each at different stages of completion. The long-handled machetes, knives and rattan used in their hewing and weaving could also be found there. Often sheaves of smoking tobacco were stashed among the leaves of raffia thatch. Conveniently placed in the corner were the split halves of thick bamboo which had been cut to the length of seven segments and lashed together forming the fourteen cavities necessary for playing *songo.* Suspended from a peg hung a bag of the seventy oilpalm nuts used as counters in the game.

A LEAF OF HONEY

In the evenings, the ashes which perpetually smouldered in the *aba* would be stoked into flame and fed with the wood shavings of the day's carving. On colder evenings, individual fires would be built between the beds of the elders. It was the children's responsibility to keep these fires burning. This was the time of day that the older children would remain in the *aba* after the younger ones went off to sleep and listen to the tales and songs of the elders. In the morning, the older children would share the tales with the smaller children while they played.

Since this time, the authority and power of the chiefs have waned and have partly been replaced by the distant and abstract powers of government and law. The diminishing influence the chief has over the affairs of the people in the community has caused the institution of the *aba* likewise to lose some of the functional aspects it once had.

During the cocoa season, trucks and jeeps roar and grind through the village unaware of the gaze of the chief and the elders who sit in the *aba* watching and waiting for the wayfarers to stop and pay their respects to the lost authority of the village through which they pass. Of course, the new and wider path no longer passes through the *aba*. The *aba* is now built as close to the centre of the road as possible.

On a bench beside the *aba* now lay enticements to stop: cut lengths of sugarcane and hands of bananas and a receptacle of cool water, free to the wayfarer who is no longer obliged to stop.

The fire in the *aba* which has been burning since before the coming of *keke* missionaries, the *flesi* French, and the motor vehicles, still smoulders during the day and burns bright during the night. Men still gather around the fire to do their carving and weaving but now most men eat in their own huts. Some even eat with their wives in the cooking huts. There is no longer any set time for meals and the chief's bell is gone from the *aba*. Occasionally a woman will bring a plate of something to the *aba* for whoever is there.

The unspoken prohibition against resident women sitting in the *aba* has prevailed over the years. The *aba* has remained the pivot of male activities. It has, however, lost much of its significance as a symbol of the chief's power and authority. Many Ntumu villages now have more than one *aba*, it no longer being the sole possession of the chief. It has become but a remnant of the sovereignty he once enjoyed.

10

THE USE OF ANALOGY

Dear Dr Kilngott,

This week's drawings show the next step in the development of wheeled toys. As the fruit wheels wear out or rot, they are replaced by a pair of more durable raffia-wood wheels. These are made by bending strips of raffia around stout raffia spokes. Sometimes the fruit wheels are replaced by a single hardwood disk mounted in a wooden fork and handle.

ANALOGOUS STYLE:

The vast majority of Ntumu proverbs are analogous rather than direct in their manner of conveying a concept or relationship. Typical of this style is the employment of the literary device of substituting non-human elements from nature for human attributes and relationships to illustrate or prescribe correct attitudes and actions. This type of proverb is usually fablistic: animals and plants, from the environment of the Ntumu region, are cast into roles and situations which resemble or symbolically parallel real-life Ntumu roles and situations.

In some proverbs in this style, the animals and plants act in roles natural to their own reality:

(010) "Hummingbird went up to the branches with leaves and all the birds started dying."

(011) "Squirrel came down from the branches with leaves and the animals started dying."

In these equivalent Ntumu proverbs, both hummingbird and squirrel are cast as carriers of a certain poisonous leaf. Symbolically, they are the introducers of foreign and poisonous elements into an environment in which they have no beneficial place or use. Size is also an analogous element here, for both these characters are relatively small members of the forest. The Ntumu believe that small and extraneous things can lead to the demise of things larger and stronger.

In some of these proverbs, both human and animals figure in naturalistic roles. The following three examples also concern themselves with death:

(012) "No one knows which fly goes into the grave with the dead body."

A LEAF OF HONEY

Especially in the swelter of the dry season, flies are often a part of a funeral, buzzing about in irreverent clouds. It is said that there is always one that gets buried with the body but that it is impossible to tell which it will be while they are flying around the corpse during the funeral preparations. This proverb draws an analogy between flies and deeds. It is explained as follows: No one knows which of one's deeds in life will follow him, whether good or bad. No one knows which will find its way to the end of life and into the grave. In life, if one tries to make each deed good, it won't matter.

(013) "Tortoise tells the birds that they should eat only a little of *enyo* because of death."

Enyo is a jungle fruit not eaten by the Ntumu and seen as poisonous. Here, the message is more than just "do not over-indulge in things". Showing moderation in life may well show you what is detrimental, and therefore what is to be avoided in the future.

(014) "*Medza* asked *amang mbong*: How is it that you accompany me in my dying? You died a long time ago and I have just died. How is it that we are going into the same grave?"

This is a conversation between two different kinds of cooked dishes. One dish is made of a type of greens and the other of cassava. Whereas the greens are fresh, the cassavas were picked, fermented, pounded, rolled in leaves and cooked days before; nevertheless they are served at the same time. The grave here is the mouth of the consumer of the meal. The proverb, in a rather humorous way, illustrates that whereas events may occur at the same time, they do not necessarily take the same time to come to fruition.

This dish, by the way, is not bad, although Colonel Sanders may never put it on the menu. The Guajiro Indians I lived with in Colombia make something similar to it.

Sincerely yours, Joseph

11

SPEAR HUNTERS AND DOG BELLS

In the early afternoon, as we sat in the shade of the *aba*, a hunter armed with several long spears and a machete came into the village. He was accompanied by two skinny black dogs of indeterminate breed. The shirt and trousers he wore were old and torn in places, especially at the knees. He had wrapped his ankles with pieces of sackcloth and laced them around like first world war army leggings. His stout shoes were scuffed and muddy. He had a bag hung over one shoulder and the weapons he bore were tied together and carried on the other. He greeted us and came into the *aba* and sat down. He was hot and tired from walking and his two dogs followed closely at his heels. With a command they lay down at his feet. He explained that he was returning from an unsuccessful hunting trip to the uninhabited jungle to the west.

Around the neck of each dog was tied a curved bell stuffed with leaves. The bells were made of wrought iron but differed in size. The hunter explained that they were hunting bells and made by a tribal ironmonger across the river in the neighbouring Equatorial Guinean province of Rio Muni. He untied the bells and handed them to me to look at. I turned them over in my hands. Both bells were crescent-shaped with the pointed ends curved around to form tying loops. A long slit formed the opening along the convex side. I asked if I could remove the leaves and hear the bells. The hunter agreed. The clacker inside was a free rolling handmade metal ball. I rang the bell loudly and the man shook his head as he showed me how they worked. The hunter took one of the bells and slowly moved it back and forth for me. The ball rolled from side to side along the slit opening and produced a clunkity-clunk sound. He told me to do the same with mine. The sound mine made was similar but with a different tonal quality. Each bell had its own tone so that the hunter could recognize his dogs during the hunt. The bells, he said, were his eyes in the jungle.

The hunter told us that in the jungle the animals could run faster than man; that was why he had dogs to chase them. The dogs, however, often ran so fast that the hunter was left behind. The hunter put bells on his dogs so that he could locate them and "see" what was happening at a distance. The hunter could tell the speed of each of his dogs by the sound of its bell. He demonstrated by shaking the bell: when his dog was moving slowly, the bell would make a certain sound with the sway of the dog's walk; but as the dog increased its speed and changed its gait to a trot or a run, the sound the bell produced changed. This enabled him to visualize the scene of pursuit. Based on these sounds the hunter would shout instructions to his dogs until the game was cornered or captured. When the hunter reached the dogs and quarry he would kill the animal with his spear.

The hunter finished his explanation and said that he must continue on his way. Robert and I thanked him. He put the bells in his shoulder bag, picked up his weapons and headed off down the path, preceded by his dogs. Some months later I heard the only proverb about dog bells I collected:

"It isn't because one dog went to the forest
with a bell that you say that the ones
that stayed in the village can't hunt."

This simply means that the demonstration of ability by one person doesn't mean that others cannot do just as well.

Shortly after the hunter left, Robert and I were sitting in the *aba* when some of the young men of the village came by and invited us to see a plantation of new cocoa trees they were planting. I thought it was a good idea. Cocoa was the only cash crop this part of Cameroon had and, aside from this, Ntumu agriculture was the mainstay of the tribe's subsistence economy. Seeing how the men of the village co-operated would be useful to my understanding of their society. One man had a wheelbarrow full of saplings. Each little tree was about a foot high. It had been grown from seed in a plastic bag which the government provided. The villagers had punched small holes in the bags to allow the planting soil to drain.

64

A LEAF OF HONEY

The man with the wheelbarrow led the way. The path was narrow and the rest of us followed in single file. Robert followed the wheelbarrow and by the time I got in line I found myself second from the last. As we walked along there were many questions I wanted to ask Robert to translate but he was too far ahead. I decided to wait until we stopped instead of shouting to him or trying to pass the tribesmen in front of me. The man behind me was about the same age as myself but he was tall and had muscles. He had the kind of build that weight-lifters would achieve after a lifetime of pumping iron and taking steroids. Sometimes life is so unfair. After twenty-seven years I was chubby and soft in the middle and the man behind could have been an Olympic boxer. Without Robert I couldn't even find out his name. All I could do was look back and smile at him as we walked along. I walked slower than the rest and soon there was a distance between me and the group of villagers ahead. All of a sudden, I felt a tremendous slap on the side of my head. I turned around and the man behind me just looked at me and smiled as if nothing had happened.

In a deep voice that matched his physique, he uttered a one-word explanation: *"osun"*. I didn't understand. I frowned and kept on walking. I hadn't a clue what *osun* meant or what I had done to deserve such a slap. In my cultural ignorance, it could have been anything. I looked up along the narrow path. Robert was ahead of me, too far away to ask his advice or have him translate. I wondered if I wasn't moving fast enough or I had stepped on something I shouldn't have. I was in the middle of this thought when . . . Wham! He hit me again. I stopped this time and looked him squarely in the eye. He didn't say anything this time and looked down on me and gave me that same wide innocent grin. He motioned me to continue. The side of my head really smarted and I was becoming angry. If this was some kind of mischievous prank or game the Ntumu played on each other while they were walking in the jungle, I didn't find it amusing. Perhaps he was trying to provoke me. He was the last person in the line and no one could have seen him slap me. He could deny it. We walked along in silence for a few minutes. SLAP! He did it again! This time it was much harder and I stumbled off the path. The same man reached out and grabbed me so I wouldn't fall. I turned on him and shouted in a very loud and angry voice. There would be no mistaking my tone. Shaking my finger under his nose, I kept repeating the one

65

word I knew in his language that I felt was appropriate.

"*Amu dje! Amu dje! Amu dje!*" I screamed. "WHY! WHY! WHY!"

The man just stood there staring wide-eyed and blinking at me as if I was having a deranged fit.

Robert came back to see what the trouble was. I told him that the man had slapped me three times and I demanded to know just what the hell he thought he was doing. Robert asked the man what had happened. The man reached forward, toward my head and picked something out of my hair. He held a small dead insect in his huge hand for me to see and simply said: "*osun*" again. Robert turned to me and translated: "tsetse fly." I stared at the insect in disbelief and felt rather foolish. All of the indignation, anger and aggression I had boiling in me drained away and was replaced by apologetic embarrassment. Instead of trying to harm me, the man behind me in the line had kept me from being bitten by a carrier of the sleeping sickness.

Robert explained that it was always the duty of the person walking behind to watch and protect the back of the person in front. It was one of the basic responsibilities of life. Any child knows that. Robert said he was surprised that I had not learned that yet. My friend would have been even more surprised if I told him that it was the social norm *not* to watch and *not* to protect and, above all, *not* get involved in the dangers of others in the jungles of places like New York.

12

IMPLICATIVE ELEMENTS

Dear Dr Kilngott,

The crown of wheeled-toy development is the truck. By the age of ten the village boys seem to have mastered all the emulative skills of the art of model-building. It is common to see them pushing recognizable makes and models of pick-ups and trucks along in the village. The sophistication is remarkable considering the tools and material these children have to work with. Using only a machete, raffia wood and bits of scrounged rubber, they are able to

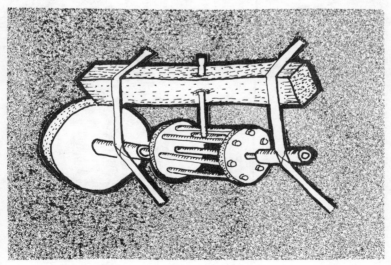

incorporate functional details of real vehicles into their toys. The enclosed drawings illustrate some of these features. These include a rigid chassis, steerable wheels, independent suspension, doors with working hinges, and a sound-producing clicking drum on the back axle. The sophistication in these toys reveals sharp minds and an early understanding of basic technology.

IMPLICATIVE STYLE:

Ntumu proverbs sometimes set down analogous statements which imply a relationship between two propositions such that the

second can be logically deduced from the first. These proverbs contain situations or events which are presented in such a manner as to show that they are conditions which are the effects of certain causes. Often these *a priori* relationships are more significant as conveyors of latent meanings than they are in establishing actual relationships between the isolated elements or situations. Following are three implicative examples, all utilizing the conditional *ngu* form, i.e. the "if" implication.

(014) "If you look at the chicken's pecking, you will not eat the gizzard."

Gizzards are highly prized among the Ntumu as being the best and tastiest part of the chicken. At any meal, the *nyamboro* or eldest male of the family has the unquestionable right to this organ. It is one the privileges of his age and a sign of his position. If a meal in which a chicken is served lacks a gizzard for a particular reason, the

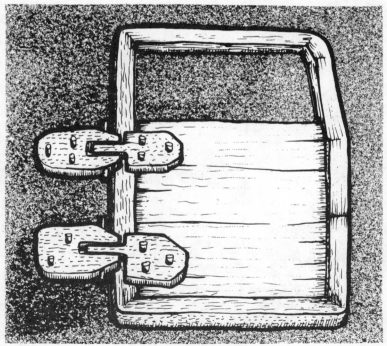

nyamboro may very well refuse it and send back to the women's hut with the command to bring him a chicken with a gizzard. The image used here is that if you watch what the chicken consumes, you won't want to eat the organ through which such things have passed. The analogy here is that details are not as important as the whole.

(015) "If you don't know a whiteman, look at an albino."

The whitening of the skin is something that the Ntumu sees as debilitating. It happens to the Ntumu only if the person is defective, either from birth as in the case of an *evulu* albino or from certain pigment-altering kinds of *zam* leprosy. In either case this victim is seen as less able than those who are healthy and black. Aside from being called *mfum* or "white", whitemen are also pejoratively called "lepers" or by the word *ntangan* which means "he who has not suffered". This cutting proverb suggests the same defectiveness and weakness in whitemen as they see in albinos. It also implies that if you do not understand something unfamiliar to you, then find something familiar that you do understand and compare them.

A LEAF OF HONEY

The proverb is also used in the same sense as the expression: "If the cap fits, wear it".

(016) "If you put your basin of water on your knee, God will help you in putting it on your head."

Clean drinking water is a problem in southern Cameroon and most Ntumu villages lack wells or running water. They are usually situated near small tributaries and water must be carried to the village for cooking. This is most often the task of the women and children. To carry this water, large aluminium pans or basins are used. As in most places in Africa, the Ntumu traditionally carry their loads balanced on their heads. Water is heavy and often groups of women will go to the stream together to help each other. Placing the heavy pans on top of the head without spilling them is the hardest part. When in groups, a couple of women will hold a pan aloft while the carrier gets underneath it. Getting a full pan atop the head in one go can be a near impossible task to do if she is alone. It has to be done in stages. The pan is first picked up and rested on the knee, it is then lifted the rest of the way to the top of the head. This appears to be a proverb born since the advent of the Christians to Ntumuland. It merely employs a familiar setting to express the old proverb:

"God helps those who help themselves."

Men also carry water, but less frequently and, from what I have seen, only under duress from their wives. Women are the workers here. I am sure a time-and-motion study would reveal that women do about eighty percent of the actual physical labour and bring home the majority of the cultivated and gathered food.

Sincerely yours, Joseph

13

SEE HOW LONG THE HOLE REMAINS

A few days after our arrival in Meyo-Ntem a summons was sent to the southern half of the village for all the elder males to come. Towards evening the old men began to arrive in small groups of two and three. They sat in the *aba* and talked and laughed among themselves while Robert and I wandered around the village practising my feeble Ntumu. Unlike earlier in the day, the village was now full of life. Children of all ages were everywhere running around and playing clapping games. We finally sat on the ground just outside the *aba* and waited for the council meeting to begin. The *aba* was filled with a dozen or so elderly men. Robert said they ranged from about forty-five to ninety years old. I was surprised. Africans certainly did not show their age as quickly as the senior citizens of my own race. Robert pointed out the eldest man present. He was called Papa Atanga and had a balding head ringed with a hoary crown, much like my grandfather.

In the languor of waiting, I thought about my grandfather. He was a rustic western American farmer who spent his life growing apricots, citrus fruit and being cantankerous. I loved him dearly, but he was set in his ways, and his beliefs and mine seemed to be separated by more than just two generations. Discussions on religious topics invariably led to his contention that the Baha'i Faith was all right except that it encouraged its members to be too self-sacrificing and that Baha'is didn't look after their own sufficiently. What really irritated him was the idea of going off to foreign lands and trying to "help" other people. When I told him I was planning to leave California again and go to Africa he became quite annoyed.

A LEAF OF HONEY

"What is this missionary thing with you?" he demanded. "You just came back from South America. Weren't all those years down there enough for your religion? Think about your family for a change. Do you think your wife and daughter want to go and live in some God-forsaken place like Africa?"

"Granddad, first of all, I'm not a missionary and secondly Africa is not God-forsaken, just man-forsaken. Living among a tribal people will help me to be a little more understanding and responsive in trying to help other people," I tried to explain.

"Help yourself first and let the devil take the hindmost," he replied, repeating one of his favorite sayings. Granddad had his own selection of potted proverbs.

"I know you well enough to know that you don't believe that," I said. My grandfather was usually very generous and used to give to several charities and church missionary societies, but the years had taught him that trying to help others in this manner somehow never made a dent in the poverty, misery or ignorance in the world. It was just a waste of time and money. Things never change. I am afraid he saw anthropology in this light, as just another futile waste. He firmly believed that people, over there, should stop being lazy and help themselves.

"Granddad, please try to understand. I just want to be effective," I tried to continue. "I am ignorant of poverty. I really know nothing about the people in the world who need help the most. I must go see their needs for myself."

"Let me explain about how poverty is," my grandfather interrupted, "It was there before you, and it will be there long after you have gone. You take yourself too seriously, son. If you think you, or your religion, will have any real long-term effect on those people, then try this: stick your finger in a pail of water and pull it out. See how long the hole remains. Sure, you can go over there for awhile and make them dependent on you, but the minute you leave, things will revert to what they were before. Progress only comes from working hard. You know what they say: God helps those who help themselves."

"They also say: God helps those who help others," I retorted. This kind of tit-for-tat argument never led anywhere. My grandfather was speaking from a deep conviction based on a lifetime of struggling to make a success out of farming. He had worked hard over a fifty year span which began by ploughing fields behind a mule and ended in mechanization and retirement.

A LEAF OF HONEY

Subsequently, he had learned to loathe laziness. Unfortunately he attributed Negro poverty to idleness and sloth. In my heart, I felt it had more to do with social injustice than with such stereotypical characteristics. We also disagreed on the subject of injustice. I felt people had basic spiritual and moral responsibilities as human beings. It was impossible for me to compare my own condition with that of my fellow man and blame God for injustice in the world. Injustice was something which man had created. This belief was even more intense after I become a Baha'i. If I wasn't part of the solution then I was still part of the problem. I saw the importance of engaging in activities which would promote an ever-advancing civilization which looked after all the segments of society. Moving to Africa, I felt, was one such activity. I hoped that this year of fieldwork would prepare me for later service, and show me which were the beneficial avenues towards social development.

I must have been lost in thought for some time, because I realized that the last of the elders had arrived and the chief was ready to begin to speak. As I sat on the ground and watched the circle of faces around the fire, I knew what dignity was. Although I could not understand more of their conversation than what Robert translated, their demeanour and gestures revealed a cultural standard of dignity beyond the mere acquisition of years. Here were members of a jungle society, which my culture would mistakenly term as primate or uncivilized, demonstrating a level of character development far above my own. Lamentably, in America, pride of culture often means pride of technological achievement. The Ntumu might lack the technology of exploring outer space but they certainly possessed the social mechanics which allowed the exploration of the inner space of character potential. The elders were engaged in respectful debate, each man spoke uninterrupted when it was his turn and listened intently when it was not. There was none of the impatience, interruptions and apparent competitiveness so common during shared discussions I had attended in America. In fact, some of the committees I had served on could have learned a thing or two about the consultative process from watching these men. Although I could see that oratory and verbal persuasion were the backbone of their kind of consultation, nevertheless they were serious truthseekers trying to find viable answers to their problems. And at the moment, I was their problem.

A LEAF OF HONEY

They seemed to employ a method of communication which relied heavily on traditional standards. For the Ntumu, proverbs contained these standards. Proverb after proverb, each a pearl of traditional verity, was masterfully strung to the next, as each man spoke, to reveal the sequential line of thought of the speaker. The subject matter was treated in an indirect and analogous manner. Sharp specifics gave way to smooth generalities and the individual points were seen as eddies and ripples in a collective pool of ideas. Each speaker's point was made by the sequence of the traditional proverbial guidelines. This type of rhetoric required not only a complete knowledge of both the interaction of individuals and the overall socio-economic condition of the population but also a vast knowledge of the oral tradition of the people.

I was overwhelmed by what I saw. My religion taught that mankind should behave in a manner worthy of its station. These men certainly did. As the time approached for my turn to speak to them, I hoped I would be able to say what needed to be said in a manner seen as significant and dignified to them. If I expected to be allowed to stay in their village, I would first have to gain their respect and be worthy of their trust.

Robert told me it was my turn and I stood up to speak.

"*Mbolo!*" I began.

"*Mbolo!*" they returned.

"I have come from Ma'an to this place. I came from Ebolowa before that and Yaounde before that. I am a son of the land of America. I have come from a far place especially to meet with you," I said.

"For what purpose have you come?" asked the chief.

"I have come to learn your language and learn your *minkana,* your folklore," I said. A few clickings could be heard.

"Why do you want to learn our *minkana?*" asked the chief.

"The *minkana* of the Ntumu is full of wisdom and it is wise to seek wisdom. I can see that I lack this wisdom, I want to learn to become wise," I said more sincerely than my words could express.

"How long will you stay?" asked the chief.

"I want to spend a year in Meyo-Ntem," I replied. There was a round of guttural clicks from the elders. The old man Robert had pointed out remained noticeably silent. Age carried clout and influence because with a wave of his hand the crowd went quiet.

"What do you bring us? What will you take from us?" asked Papa Atanga.

75

A LEAF OF HONEY

I held up my hands in the fire light so that they could see my palms. "My hands are empty. I have brought nothing in my hands, because I do not intend to take anything away in them. My hands are empty now, and when I leave, my hands will still be empty. I have not come to take your wealth," I said.

"You are too young learn *minkana*," said Papa Atanga dismissively.

"You are right, I am a child, but a child becomes a man," I said. "I want to become a man and I have come here to become one."

"We have seen other whitemen before. You are not new to us. They come and say that our ways are not good," said Papa Atanga to the other elders.

"I am a stranger here from far away and a guest in your land. My elders are also wise, like you, but they are not here. While I am here, *you* are my elders. I have come to learn from *you*. I have not come to teach you that the leopard has spots." This analogy was as near to the message of: "Don't try to teach your grandmother to suck eggs" as I could think of on the spur of the moment.

I sat down and the chief then spoke to the elders on my behalf. Robert advised this course of action and explained that there was a relevant proverb for this:

"One never tries his own case."

The chief presented my case and told them of my wish to build a hut for my wife and child. When he had finished, Papa Atanga rose and with a firm voice, spoke against my request to stay and live among them. He made his points almost entirely in proverbs, one strung after another, with dramatic and meaningful pauses between them. Robert leaned near and whispered the translation in my ear as Papa Atanga began:

"The leopard is in the animal enclosure." (A great misfortune has occurred, there is a danger amongst us.) "It is as the spot on the leopard's face." (It is a self-evident sign.) "The river is crooked because it goes alone." (The whiteman has come alone, how can we trust him? He may say what he wants and do what he likes, because none of his peers or elders are here to make sure he is straight with us.) "Are we to carry water in a cocoyam leaf?" (This is a precarious situation and we must give it all of our attention.) "We should get out now that the water in the hole has climbed only up to the knees."

(We should foresee the misfortune he will bring and avoid it while we have a chance.)

Papa Atanga finished and then sat down. There was a moment's silence as the chief collected his thoughts. At last the chief stood up and responded in my defence:

"The leopard never misses a rendezvous." (An honest man will keep his promises. We do not yet know if he is crooked or straight.) "When you fetch water you look at your empty basket and you think about matters in the village." (Perhaps he will bring us good fortune.) "Make your bridge when the river is dry so that when the flood comes, you can walk on it." (Now is the time to be friendly, we may need a friend later.) "The river is always dry except during the flood." (Times of adversity are always followed by times of prosperity.)

The chief then sat down. It was like a pair of sagacious old lawyers summing up a case. It was now Papa Atanga's turn:

"The noise the river makes increases on the rocks." (The voice of truth is heard during the test.) "Girls are renowned by the number of lovers, a man is known by the number of his feats." (A man's worth is known by his achievements.) "The river goes, the stones remain. One knows that the hearth stone is the brother of the fire-place only if it is covered with ashes. Who would fall in the river because of mere shouts?"

Robert's translation began to lag and said that the last few proverbs were asking for some proof of my being a true brother and that a brother should not be frightened by tests. Papa Atanga sat down with a self-satisfied smirk. It was the chief's turn again:

"Does the panther become a cat because it crossed the river?" (Will testing him change what he is?) "Spearing the panther often makes the spearer unskilled." (Will testing him make us any wiser?) "All water descends to the sea." (Good character belongs to those who already have it.) "The leopard makes a catch and goes to eat it in its den." (Every man should choose a village where he is at home.)

A LEAF OF HONEY

As the chief sat down Papa Atanga stood up to reply. He spoke directly to the chief:

"The leopard catches the chief's goats also." (The adversity he may bring will spare no one, not even you.) "But the small kid cost the life of a powerful leopard." (Our response will be more terrible than this.)

Things were heating up and the chief was coming under personal attack for defending my application. But it was now the chief's turn:

"Lizard stirred up the water and made it murky by itself." (You are trying to cloud the issue.) "You are striving to save a falling drop from under a large basin of water." (You are overlooking that which is of value for the thing which has no value.) "The weight of water sometimes crushes the basin." (Do not overstretch my patience.)

However, Papa Atanga would not be intimidated. He pointed towards the river and said:

"The weight of the water breaks the dam." (Sustained efforts will arrive at the desired results.) "There is no waterfall for nothing."

With this, Papa Atanga sat down for the last time. He had declared that he had rested his case.

"There is no waterfall for nothing?" asked the chief. There was no response and he paused before he spoke again. All of the elders remained silent and waited for the chief to think.

"There is no waterfall for nothing," repeated the chief with an attitude of reluctant resignation. At that he stood up and the rest of the elders stood. The meeting had ended.

Robert translated this exchange as it happened and explained most of the proverbs and their relevance to my situation. This last proverb, however, proved enigmatic. It seemed to be pivotal to my application and had somehow drawn the meeting to a close. It must have been very important. Robert explained it was especially difficult to translate it into English because of its double negative. It had a variety of possible meanings, but he felt it meant something like "everything has its purpose". We were informed that the elders would meet again at some later date to decide if I could live in the village for the full year. For the time being, Robert and I could stay in a room in the hut of one of the young men of the village, Sylvain. Sylvain turned out to be my Olympian head-slapper. The accommodation was fine but something else was bothering me. I asked Robert if the chief had said that the elders would decide if I could "live" or "stay" in the village for a year. Robert said that the chief had distinctly used the word "live". I didn't like the nuances which the word could carry in this context.

14

DIDACTIC MORALITY

Dear Dr Kilngott,

A few days ago I met a hunter with a couple of dogs. The dogs wore very unusual bells around their necks. I asked to see them and had a chance to sketch them. I have enclosed the drawings I made. The hunter also showed me a very old and rusty ceremonial spearhead he called *ekwele* which I also drew for you. This *ekwele* was quite different from the steel points he used on the business end of the spears he carried to hunt with. He told me that several tribes on the Ntem river used to exchange these ornamental wrought iron spearheads as money in commerce. *Bikwele,* the plural form of *ekwele* is the name of the modern day currency of neighboring Equatorial Guinea.

As you predicted, most Ntumu proverbs are prescriptive in nature. Some are real lodestars of guidance and morality. Most prescribe a model for specific actions and attitudes. They often contain analogous situations or relationships which offer solutions to particular moral problems. As mnemonic devices the proverbs are easily retainable and in the older ones the cadence and rhythm is as identifiable as iambic pentameter. The Ntumu use them in many formal settings to analyze real-life situations by recalling analogous or parallel situations in the proverbs. They are indispensable in the judgment-making process of the council of elders and are also employed in informal problem-solving. Proverbs pervade most of Ntumu society and are often referred to as undisputable traditional guidelines. These prescriptive proverbs utilize situations and relationships both symbolic and literal and

80

often deal with abstract generalities and concepts which serve as delineations of morality.

DIDACTIC STYLE:

For the purposes of my study, this type of proverb will be called didactic. This is a stylistic category which my hosts would call *sosu'u*. These proverbs are intended to instruct, often excessively. They contain a moral message to which aesthetic considerations are subordinated. They deal with scruples. A good example of this didactic style regards comportment:

(017) "Rightness is not that you are in your father's place."

Proper personal bearing or demeanour should not change or diminish with the setting. It should be an immutable part of one's character. "Rightness" is the same word *sosu'u* in Ntumu and translates as "proper comportment".

Along the same lines business ethics and conscience are defined:

(018) "Sell, sell and be glad."

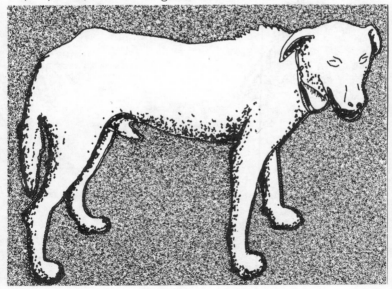

This is the Ntumu equivalent of the English tautological proverb employed to justify profit: "Business is business".

The concept of honesty is the subject of the following two proverbs:

(019) "My friend, tell the truth, death is bad."

Awu ane abe can read either: "death is bad" or "dying is bad". In this case, the syntax of Ntumu does not allow the subtle distinction between the moment or act of dying, and the state of being dead. This kind of proverb smacks of other truisms, platitudes, and obvious truths used by the missionaries in their occasional visits to the village. Another example:

(020) "Engutu Akulu says: Tell the real facts."

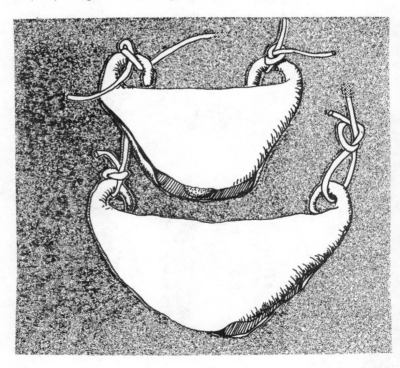

A LEAF OF HONEY

Engutu Akulu was a famous Ntumu wise man of the *yekomto'o* clan, and this was what he always said to people. Even in Ntumu, this proverb has that "Confucius say . . . " ring to it.

The prominent concept of forgiveness within the tribal social setting is stated:

(021) "The matter of today doesn't spoil that of tomorrow."

Although clear and simple in its message, this proverb is more: it is one of the Ntumu's most important social philosophies in a capsular form. Resentment, at least manifest resentment, is an emotion which is not long enduring among the Ntumu. Violent disputes are rarely physical, but however verbal and intensely vehement they are, they usually end in apparently complete resolution in a matter of moments, leaving the two parties interacting with a levity and ease that belies the preceding conflict. It is a very admirable and emulous social characteristic, at least as seen through these Western eyes. We sometimes seem to forget our own proverb of: "Forgive and forget", which seems to have been modified to the saying attributed to Robert Kennedy: "Forgive your enemies but don't forget their names".

The didactic notion of cleanliness is put forward in the following:

(022) "Beauty is not in the hair, beauty is in the cleanliness of the skin."

Beauty is defined as cleanliness among the tribesmen just as "Cleanliness is next to godliness" is expressed in America.

For me, staying clean in the jungle without running water is a real achievement. I think Pigpen, that great Schultzian philosopher, said it better:

"Cleanliness is next to impossible".

I must admit that I sometimes dream of showers and bath tubs.

Another genre of Ntumu folklore, the riddle, is also used for a didactic end. In this, one type of incest is defined:

Question: "What is the pear that can never be picked?"
Answer: "Your sister."

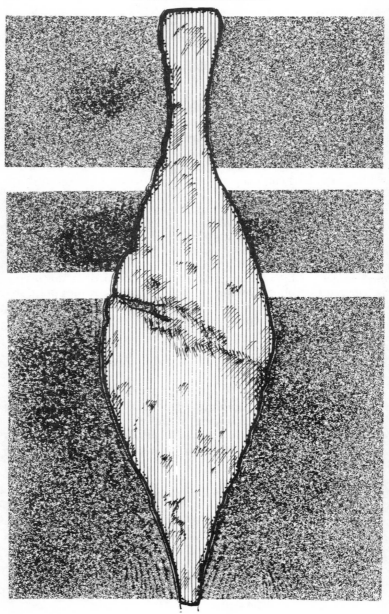

A LEAF OF HONEY

The Ntumu have clear prohibitions against incest, which I suspect date from before their contact with Christianity and its didactic missionaries. The term "pear" refers to several types of sweet fruit which are greatly enjoyed. When two Ntumu-speaking strangers meet, they spend a long time asking about each other's tribe, moiety, clan and family. An important function of this kinship and genealogical questioning is to allow people to determine how closely they are related, thus avoiding liaisons which could be defined by the tribe as being incestuous.

Sincerely yours, Joseph

15

THERE IS NO WATERFALL
FOR NOTHING

The next morning, the chief asked if I would like to see the other half of the village near the river, and I agreed. The chief and all of the men of the village accompanied Robert and me on the short trek to the south through hectare after hectare of cocoa trees. At last we arrived. This part of the village was indeed larger than where we spent the night. It had almost forty huts and a much bigger *aba*. I asked why Meyo-Ntem was divided into two halves and separated by nearly three kilometres of plantations. The two places, I was told, were settled by different clans, the northern part was *eba* and the southern was *esamengon*. The path led through the centre of the village like before, but this time the settlement ended at the Ntem river. The river was swollen and obviously at flood stage. I judged it to be about 300 meters across. We walked to the edge of the fast-moving water and out onto a small rickety old jetty or pier. On either side of it were clusters of dugout canoes, tied fast to the vegetation along the bank.

We had attracted a fair number of villagers who wanted to greet us. The chief said he would like to show me the *olam kwas,* the fish trap downstream, but first he asked if I would like to see something in the river up around the bend. The way it was worded, I guessed it was more a request rather than an option. As I learned later there is a very appropriate proverb for this:

"Choice is not like a recommendation."

Robert was told he was to stay with the others along the riverside and that I was to go with some of the village men, alone.

A LEAF OF HONEY

I was shown three large dugout canoes made of hardwood on the up-river side of the pier. They were each about the length of a Cadillac El Dorado and must have each weighed half a ton or more. Papa Atanga handed me a truncated stick with no blade for a paddle. There were seven of us, and I did some quick mental arithmetic, remembering that seven doesn't go into three evenly. It didn't. The six men each had their own wide-bladed oars and entered the two other dugouts and indicated that I should get into the third alone. I had done some canoeing in Colombia but what I knew about white water would be of little help here. Manoeuvering one of these massive boats by myself in placid water would have been quite a chore, let alone in this kind of current. The river was murky brown and laden with bits of flood debris. In places the water swirled around snarls of fallen trees and branches. I had no idea what I was supposed to do, but this had áll the trappings of initiation or the test of merit my research adviser had warned me about.

The men pushed off and paddled upstream a distance and motioned for me to follow. I struggled to keep the boat moving upstream and not be swept out of control downstream. The two other canoes always stayed just out of reach. I avoided the swift-moving current in mid stream and manoeuvred the heavy dugout along the relative shallows of the banks. I had to paddle furiously with the useless stick they had given me; it was too short to use as a punt pole and hopeless as an oar. With great effort, I inched forward, only stopping for a few strokes in the calmer areas by holding on to an occasional overhanging branch. After three hours of unrelenting work, I had travelled less than two hundred meters. I still couldn't see around the bend.

Despite the immediate danger of the circumstances, my mind was miles away, burning as much energy as my arms were. I thought of what a ludicrous sight I must be, kneeling in an oversized canoe in the middle of Africa muttering prayers between breaths, flailing the water on either side of me with a silly little stick in an effort to save myself from drowning. Was this happening to me because I had somehow missed a chapter on how to anticipate an initiation rite? Maybe a couple of vital pages stuck together. In any case I was not prepared for this. The whole purpose of coming to Africa was the establishment of enduring bonds of friendship in a different culture. I hoped I lived long enough to establish some. If this was somehow a test of my sincerity, I would prefer a written multiple choice examination, please.

The other oarsmen finally allowed me to catch up with them and one of the men jumped into my dugout. I felt a mixture of relief and dread as I recognized him as Sylvain, the man who had slapped me upside the head. With one adroit turn of his paddle we swung about and in less than a minute we were back at the pier where we started. I was shattered. Robert and some others had to help me out of the canoe. My hands were covered with burst blisters and my knees were badly bruised. It seemed that every muscle in my back was screaming for mercy. I knew for sure that it was an initiation test, but I didn't know if I had passed it. They let me lie on the ground for a long time until my body stopped retaliating for abusing it. As the pain slowly subsided and I was able to catch my breath, a thought went through my head: "Someday, these will be the good old days". I then remember shaking my head and saying to myself: "God help me, if these are the days I will someday refer to as: 'the good old days'." They helped me into the shade of the *aba* and I rested for several hours.

In the afternoon, the chief and the elders came to get us. Robert and I were taken downstream from the village and shown the promised fish trap. After a short hike there was, sure enough, a fish trap. But behind it was the *waterfall;* the great big, enormous, swollen, frothing at the mouth, enraged and incredibly unsubtle *waterfall.* The fish trap was substantial in size but a match-stick construction in comparison to the awesome spectacle of tons of water hurtling out into the void and crashing down onto the rocks below. After watching this for a moment, Robert turned to me, with that expression one sees in cartoons as the light-bulb switches on overhead, and said that now he understood the meaning of the proverb of the night before.

"There is no waterfall for nothing," he said. "It is so simple, everything has its uses in life, even a waterfall." Some things are better to know sooner than later. This was unfortunately an analogous proverb being used in a literal sense. Papa Atanga had been simply facetious. The waterfall was what awaited me if I had failed to go upstream. Looking down at it from the river bank, I felt that death over a waterfall was rather a severe consequence for failing an unrequested initiation test. It was inordinately cruel and final. It was like finding your puppy dead, run over in the middle of the road, and someone saying, "That'll teach him not to run after cars". No matter what I felt at the moment, the fact of the matter was I had survived and passed the test. I was very happy to be alive. I sarcastically commented to Robert that if this was a long-standing initiation practice, adherents of the "survival of the fittest" theory at my university might suggest that the Ntumu must well be on their way towards isolating the human chromosome responsible for canoeing prowess. I laughed at my own wit. Robert joined in and laughed concurringly for a moment and then, straight-faced, asked what chromosomes were.

When we arrived back at the village, the chief informed me that the elders had met and that I could "live" in the village as long as I liked.

16

METAPHORIC COMPARISONS

Dear Dr Kilngott,

An initiation test, and I passed it! Just what every anthropologist dreams of. I feel honoured. It was a test of endurance on the Ntem river which consisted of paddling a dugout canoe upstream for about three hours alone. I have enclosed some drawings of the dugouts which the Ntumu build and the lashing technique they use to construct their fish traps. When I have a chance, I hope to produce a complete drawing of one of these fish traps. I expect that having passed my test will be helpful to my research. I hope that it will open the door to the Ntumu's confidence in me.

The use of words to imply a resemblance is common in Ntumu proverbs as with all proverbs. The Ntumu people do not seem to divide this expressive practice and make the subtle distinction between simile and metaphor. The Ntumu language is just not constructed that way, and for this reason I have described this style as simply metaphoric.

METAPHORIC STYLE:

Metaphors are effective in isolating specific attributes or characteristics in mankind by comparing it to other things in nature. I have already told you about one such metaphoric proverb:

(023) "Man is a leaf of honey."

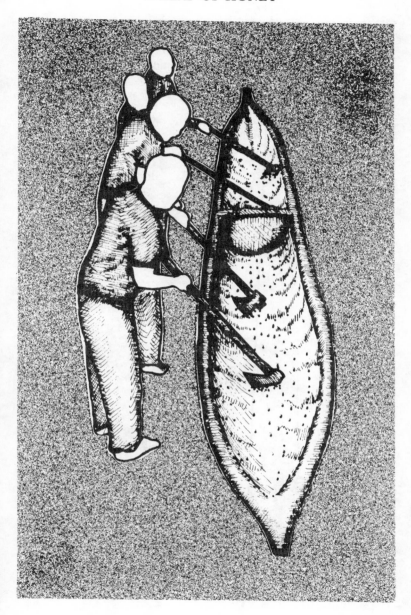

Others in this style include:

> (024) "Someone's brother is blood of the tongue, when you cut it,
> you spit some, you swallow some."

Here, the concept of "blood is thicker than water" is mixed with
a sense of "with the good, comes the bad". To the Ntumu, no matter
what happens between two brothers, the bond of kinship is stronger
than any conflict or condition. Survival in the jungle demands

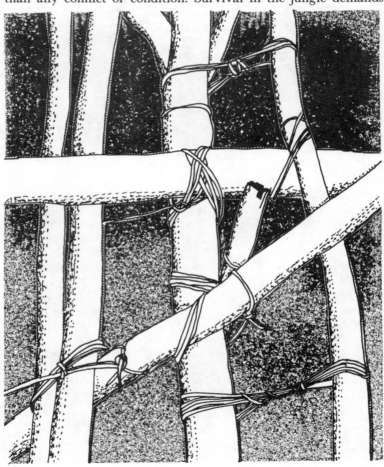

cooperation. Anger is short lived and arguments do not seem to become enduring resentments. Vendetta and feud would be difficult concepts to translate into Ntumu.

Another proverb metaphorically talks about what is called in California as "twenty-twenty hindsight":

(025) "The future is blind, the past is sighted."

Many European proverbs convey this idea as do several of oriental origin: "From the past you may foresee the future".

This particular Ntumu proverb is certainly applicable to something that happened to me a couple of days ago. As an anthropologist, no matter how careful I am not to offend my hosts' cultural sense of propriety, there are things which can only be discovered by accident. I have tried hard to be observant, but I haven't been able to anticipate every adverse reaction. Some of these reactions are very interesting.

A few days ago, I was sitting in front of my hut reviewing the material I brought with me on kinship systems. I had an old square-sided green bottle next to me that I had found in the jungle. I keep finding them; they seem to be everywhere. Anyway, the village was busy. Absent-mindedly, I lifted the bottle to my lips and blew across the opening. The bottle made that resonating low-pitched note like a foghorn. I looked up and the entire village had stopped dead in its tracks and everyone was staring at me in wide-eyed silence. They looked afraid. I calmly put down the bottle and began to hum to myself a little tune, making believe nothing had happened. As soon as I put the bottle down, the villagers went back to what they were doing. Every so often they would give me a sidelong glance to see if I was going to do the same thing again with the bottle. Later that day I called one of the children aside and asked him what had happened. He was about ten years old and looked at me as if I were one brick short of a full load. He shook his head and chided me, saying, "Don't you know, if you blow across a bottle like that, it will cause all the crops to die." Have you ever heard of this kind of sound-taboo before?

Sincerely yours, Joseph

17

GESTURES AND THE KINESICS OF COUNTING

I spent the next few days getting to know my new hosts, especially Sylvain and his wife. I joined in with as many tribal activities as I could. When they would go off to their plantations before dawn, I would go with them. Market-day came and Robert and I went with Sylvain to Ma'an to buy some food. Sylvain had shot some monkeys to trade. He toted them like shoulder bags. He had opened a hole in their necks and laced their long tails through to make handles to carry them by. The market stalls were full of people. There was a great variety of fruits, tubers and cooked items which looked like cassava paste wrapped in leaves and tied with banana twine. The meat department was amazing. There were four different kinds of monkey, whole goats, half goats and quarter goats; wild birds and chickens; eggs with rubbery shells of unknown origin; dozens of different kinds of dried and fresh fish. Many of the traders came from outside of Ntumuland, with things like tins of sardines, condensed milk and hand soap. These traders apparently did not speak Ntumu. I was interested to see that a lot of the transactions were carried out without speaking, only with gestures. Asking price and offered price were the most important issues here, and much of the haggling was done using a system of counting which everyone seemed to understand.

Gestures of the hands are dangerous things and always open to a wide variety of interpretations. In travelling around the world, I had learned that anything having to do with extended fingers could very well offend and as I didn't speak very much of the Ntumu language yet, I was keen to learn their counting system as soon as possible.

A LEAF OF HONEY

You can never predict what a common everyday gesture might mean in a new culture. You can be sure that particular fingers or combination of fingers will make someone unhappy and offended wherever you go. The problem is to find out which fingers mean what. In California, it was unhealthy to wave a particular finger about in a crowd of strangers, whereas the same finger in Guatemala was perfectly acceptable to point with. Similarly, the first two fingers held up with the palm facing the wrong way could get you into a lot trouble in Britain, but not in America, where it only meant "peace". Germans begin counting with their thumb, but this certainly would not be interpreted as the number "one" among Iranians who see the "thumbs up" gesture as quite rude.

I watched the traders as they showed on their fingers the asking price of their wares. With the help of Robert and Sylvain, I was able to work out the kinesics of their counting system.

The Ntumu use both hands and all the fingers in counting and displaying number amounts. The Ntumu system, like the standard American system, begins with the extension of the right index finger to display the amount "one". The amount "two" is similarly shown by both the right index and middle fingers. The Ntumu mode of expressing the amount "three" departs from the American way. The right index finger is doubled inward to the palm and held in place by the right thumb. This leaves the middle, ring and little fingers extended. This configuration is incorporated in a common Ntumu gesture which is used to express verity and is used in swearing an oath. In the course of an oratory, it is common to see the speaker place his right thumbnail supported by the right index finger, behind one of his upper front teeth while uttering the word *bubula*. The nail is then clicked outward and the arm is raised skyward with the other three fingers extended. The *bubula* gesture is a Christian logogram. The word literally means "the Three", and the accompanying gesture symbolizes the triune God of the Trinity of Christianity. This gesture is quite effective when executed in a dramatic pause to punctuate the termination of a statement with an emphatic kinesic exclamation point asserting the absolute verity thereof. Individuals can sometimes candidly be observed to solemnly bring to a close a moment of private and silent introspection or thought with this gesture. I had seen this configuration for swearing an oath before in Colombia. It was the one I had to use during the civil wedding with my wife when we took our vows before the local magistrate.

The amounts "four" and "five" are displayed by the full extension of all the fingers of the right hand, the former having the thumb closed across the palm and the latter with the thumb tip joining the tips of the other four fingers.

Amounts greater than can be displayed on one hand are shown with the use of both hands in configurations which are symmetrical for even amounts. The amount "six" is displayed on both hands, fingers down and palms outward, with the middle, ring and little fingers of both hands extended. This configuration is simply a double display of the amount "three". Literally, "three with three". This Ntumu configuration differs from the American one for displaying the amount of "six" both physically and conceptually. Although both systems display a total of six fingers, the American one projects a concept of "five and one more" and contrasts with the Ntumu "three and three".

The amount "seven" is displayed by one hand showing the amount "three" and the other the amount "four". The configuration "eight", like that of "six", is symmetrical "four and four".

The amount "nine" is interesting. It can be displayed in two different ways. The first and more common is a composition of the configurations for the amounts "five" and "four". The other option is "ten" with the left thumb withdrawn. Each of these configurations projects a different number conceptualization of the total amount. The first displays the idea of "five and four" as would the American configuration for the same amount. The second projects the concept of "ten less one".

The amount "ten" is displayed by joining the tips of all the fingers and thumbs of both hands together, with or without joining the base of the palms.

This configuration of "ten" is easily repeatable allowing the facile display of amounts greater than ten. For amounts between ten and twenty, the configuration for "ten" is displayed and followed by the corresponding configuration on either one or both hands. For amounts greater than twenty, repeated tapping of all the finger tips together displays the number of "tens" in the total amount. For example, the amount "thirty-five" is conveyed by tapping the finger tips together three times and then displaying the configuration for the amount "five" on the right hand. Basically, what is conveyed is "ten and ten and ten and five". This is pretty clear evidence that the Ntumu have a base 10 mathematical system.

A LEAF OF HONEY

For greater amounts such as hundreds or thousands, the above scheme is not employed. The Ntumu do not spend hours banging the tips of their fingers together trying to accumulate enough "tens" to make up "thousands" or "millions". Either kinesics are not employed or a different kind of simplified scheme is used. Often for these greater amounts, the configuration for the amount of the decimal unit is used. That is, if the amount to be conveyed is "1700", the index finger of the right hand is extended, displayed and acknowledged, and then retracted and the configuration for "seven" is displayed. The observer of such a sequence would know from the content of the accompanying conversation what the primary unit was and that the kinesic sequence did not refer to "17", "170", or "17,000". This is significant in the light of the Cameroonian currency system. The franc CFA is a high denomination currency. The smallest paper money begins at a unit of 500. Ntumu children learning how to count money would be dealing in practical units of hundreds rather than ones.

At either end of this counting and amount displaying system are the kinesic expressions of "none" and "all". The idea of "none" (literally, "no nothing") is conveyed by slapping the palms together once and, as the hands separate, turning the palms until they come to rest in the palms up position some distance apart. This gesture does not convey the notion of "zero", just the absence of something. "All" is conveyed by passing the right hand, palm inward, across the face and blowing across the extended fingers from index to little.

When we got back to Meyo-Ntem that evening, Robert, Sylvain and I got into a conversation about gestures and what they meant to different cultures I had met. I told them about the diminutive Kuna Indians who live off the northern coast of Panama on 300 or so tiny islands called San Blas. I gestured that these Indians were almost as short as the pygmies who lived near the Ntumu. Sylvain looked puzzled when I tried to describe the San Blas Islands as being so small that the roofs of the huts cover almost all of the island and hang out over the sea. He knew what a sea was, but had never seen one. It was hard for Sylvain to understand about living on the sea. Many of the children of the village gathered around to listen to the story. Story-telling is an important form of entertainment in the village and a good story-teller will act out some of the scenes and gather a large crowd. I decided to leave off telling them about the Kuna people, and told them instead about the Guajiros of

Colombia. I asked the children to sit in a circle and I would act out what happened as best I could. Robert translated:

"One day I wanted to go visit a friend called Marcos Ramirez. I had never been to his village before, but I had been told that it wasn't too far to walk from Riohacha. I set out early in the morning and walked along the road for about the distance from Ma'an to Meyo-Ntem. The Guajiros live in a flat desert land that has many "porcupine plants", tall bushes and thorny trees like porcupines called 'cactus'." I turned to the children and asked, "Can you say that?"

"*Katu, katu, katu!*" cried the children together.

"Between each bush and cactus there was a path, and it was very easy to get lost. I left the road near where I thought his village was. I had been walking for some time when I met an old Guajiro Indian." I stopped the story for a moment and explained that *guajiro* meant "people like us", and then I continued: "The old man wore very few clothes. He had no shirt and a brightly coloured cloth wrapped tightly around his hips and up between his legs. He was completely naked except for this and his shoes. His shoes were handmade from looped string and had a little pompom on each toe. I asked him where the village was and he pushed out his lips and said: '*watus*' and pointed his finger back the way I had come. *Watus* meant 'far'." I paused and raised my eyebrows at the children.

"*Watu, watu, watu,*" said the children enthusiastically on cue. I went back to the story.

"The old man went off and I turned back the way I had come. I walked around for a few hours and could not find the village. I finally met another Guajiro, a young man this time, with a herd of goats. Again, I asked him directions to the village. He lifted his chin a bit and stuck out his lips just like the old man. '*Watus*', he said and pointed his finger off to my right. I turned to the right, in the direction he pointed, and started to walk again. I thanked him and left him in the middle of his goats. He watched me go and shook his head.

"Just before dark I reached a village. It wasn't the one I was looking for. It was getting dark so I asked if I could stay the night. The chief agreed. In the morning, I asked an old lady how to get to the Marcos' village. She pointed to where the sun came up and stuck out her lips. I started to walk toward the east and she called after me.

'Where are you going?' she asked.

A LEAF OF HONEY

'I am going east, the way you pointed,' I answered.

'No, the village is *that* way,' she said. This time she didn't point. She turned me around and faced me in the opposite direction and stuck her lips out again.

"I went off the way her lips pointed and in a little while I found the village where Marcos lived. I told him about what had happened and he laughed.

'When a person sticks his lips out', he explained, 'he is pointing out the direction.'

'Now I see. I was following his finger. But what does the finger mean?' I asked.

'The angle of the finger is the way we describe distance,' he demonstrated. 'If I hold my finger straight up that means far away, and if I hold it out straight, that means near,' concluded my friend Marcos."

The children laughed and clapped and asked for another story, but I said "That is enough for tonight. I want to go to bed now." I stuck out my lips in the direction of my hut. The children laughed and shouted again. For the next few days all the children went around the village with pointing lips and shouting, "*Watu, watu, watu!*"

18

BREVITY AND THE SYNECDOCHE

Dear Dr Kilngott,

Although brevity is the subject of this progress report, the drawings I have enclosed this week have nothing to do with it. They show an armlet and a couple of hair ornaments, things the Ntumu women use to accentuate their beauty. The hair comb is attractively carved from red hardwood and decorated with a cut-line design. The hairpin is less well-made and has the letters: "PS" cut into it. Presumably this is not a souvenir from Palm Springs — more likely, the owner's initials. The armlet is worn above the elbow and consists of five curved ribs of smooth raffia wood with a loop on each end. The maker has used a locking-pin to hold the ten loops together. The armlet is tight fitting and the locking-pin must be pulled before the armlet will slip past the elbow. Leaving beauty behind and returning to brevity, let me get on with this letter.

As in many of the other cultures you reviewed in your lectures, the Ntumu are a totally oral society; they have an unwritten language and because of this the wealth of their knowledge is storehoused in their oral tradition. Their history, genealogies, law, tribal technology and sayings — all of their accumulated wisdom — are passed on from mouth to ear, generation after generation. The volume of this load of information can be staggering and the Ntumu have learned the beauty of brevity. If the meaning of something is to be memorable, it must be short. However, some of the elements of their oral tradition are too long-winded for practical everyday use, so they have found that the best way to communicate the wisdom of these is to take the pithy centre of a story — shorten it and make a mnemonic saying out of it. In a sense, a proverb is substituted for an entire story.

SYNECDOCHIC STYLE:

Proverbs are an appropriate medium for this because they can then be used in the rhetoric of jurisprudence. These then serve to bring to mind portions of oral-traditions familiar to everyone without resorting to retelling the entire story — sort of like just telling the punchline to a well-known joke. Everyone laughs, not because the punchline is funny but because it is mnemonic of something that is. Sayings which have this same function I have termed synecdochic proverbs: key words spoken to trigger the memory of a long story. Here are a few examples:

(026) "Going out with children, coming back in pieces."

This proverb advises not to expect children to act like adults, or that a child should not be sent to do an adult's job. This is the Ntumu way of saying, "Children are certain cares but uncertain comforts." This proverb encapsulates the following story:

"One day a man took some children with him into the forest to help him with his work and to keep an eye on them. They had gone quite a distance from the village when the man became very ill and could not continue. He lay down on the ground for a while in the hope of regaining his strength but he grew worse and was unable to get up. He asked the children to help him back to the village where he could be treated by the local doctor. With the children's assistance he

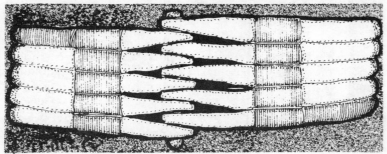

started off for home. Soon, however, the man lost consciousness and no longer could help them in his own conveyance. The children tried to move him in this state but found that they did not number enough to carry his weight. For a while they stood around him, perplexed as to what to do to comply with the man's wishes to be taken back to the village. Finally they had the answer. They took the man's machete and cut him into pieces small enough for each child to carry. With each child carrying his share and a few trips back and forth, the man was finally transported back to his village."

Another proverb I have collected apparently stems from this story:

(027) "He who travels with children is buried in five graves."

The following proverb is the synecdoche of another:

(028) "A lot are coming behind."

This is short for:

(029) "If you die for one, you don't know that a lot are coming behind."

or:

(030) "The stranger ate something because he didn't know something better was coming after."

The implication here is similar to the European proverb: "As good comes behind as goes before". These three proverbs advise the Ntumu not to knock himself out or kill himself trying to attain something, when, if he just waits, another will come to him later, without trying. This seems to be a combination of the concepts in "Everything comes to him who waits" and "There are many fish in the sea". Another synecdochic proverbs reads:

(031) "Parrot killed chicks."

This mnemonic proverb is taken from an Ntumu fable about a parrot who kills five of a hen's chicks. In revenge, the mother hen pecked out one of the parrot's eyes. Subsequently, the parrot never spoke about his lost eye, although it was something that could not be hidden, because it was the result of his having killed the chicks. It was the symbol of his crime.

The basic message of this proverb is to remind people to avoid subjects which will arouse feelings of sadness or guilt. Like all of us, the Ntumu do not like to talk about their sorrows or misdeeds. In other cultures this concept appears in proverbs such as: "Loss embraces shame" and "When sorrow is asleep, wake it not."

Sincerely yours, Joseph

19

THE ISLAND OF RIDVAN

I had to begin thinking about finding somewhere more permanent to live so that my family could join me. Fanny and Anisa were still staying in Ebolowa with the Elakas and I wanted to bring them to Meyo-Ntem. The trouble was that each hut in the village was built for someone and there weren't many empty huts to be had. The only solution was to build a hut. I wanted it to be made almost entirely of locally found materials like the Ntumu huts. I wanted to build it with my own hands and present it as a surprise to my wife.

One day Sylvain, Robert and I went up river to explore. I secretly wanted to find out what was "around the bend" that Papa Atanga and the chief had sent me upstream to see. We paddled upstream for quite a ways. The scenery was beautiful, but I didn't see anything special. The banks of the river were very similar on both sides with their overhanging branches of mangrove, raffia and bamboo. The river twisted and turned and I didn't know which bend the chief had been referring to, so we kept on going. I knew that there were crocodiles, but I didn't see any. Sylvain said that there were only little ones in this branch of the Ntem. The really big ones were south of here.

After a while we turned around and drifted downstream towards home. We had passed several small islands in the river on the way up but we were too occupied with paddling and didn't have time to stop and look at them. The largest of these consisted of an outcrop of rocks about a quarter of the size of a soccer field. It had an elevated flat area at the upstream end with a clump of mangrove at the other. The bases of trees were ensnarled in a Gordian knot of intertwining aerial roots. On one side of the island there was a small jetty of rocks with a patch of calm water behind it. We swung around and approached the island from that side. It was like a little harbour. There was even a place to disembark without getting our feet wet.

As Robert and Sylvain tied up the dugout and talked, I sat on the rocky end of the island and looked around. The place was fraught with possibilities. The ground was flat here and the mangrove roots nearby had snared a good supply of driftwood for a fire. There was plenty of raffia and bamboo upstream that could be cut and floated downstream to the island to make a hut. On the left were many vines for lashing. The clay at the roots of these vines would be ideal for daubing the walls of a hut. The jetty sat in shallow enough water that it could be extended to make a stepping stone causeway to the village side of the river. The right hand bank had a small beach of white sand. Best of all, it was only two and a half kilometres from the village. I could see it all: an "A"-frame hut made from the local materials. It was the perfect present for my wife.

Just as they had finished tying up the boat I was ready to go and see the chief about living on the island. My mind was made up. I told Robert about my idea and he told Sylvain. Robert was surprised at my choice of building sites but Sylvain smiled knowingly and remained silent on the subject.

That evening I asked to see the chief. Since my escape from the waterfall he had been rather pleasant. Papa Atanga, on the other hand, remained disappointed at my survival. I tried to avoid him. Luckily he wasn't there when I asked the chief if I could buy the island.

"No one owns the island so it cannot be sold," he explained logically. I suspect that this was the kind of response the American Indians first gave to the Dutch when they asked to buy Manhattan Island.

"Could I build a hut and live on the island?" I asked. He thought for a while and said I could use the island.

"If you want, live there," he said. I was convinced that the chief thought that all whitemen had been standing out in the sun without a hat for too long.

"What do you call the island?" I asked.

"We call the island, 'island'," he looked at me and laughed at the stupidity of my question.

"No, I mean, does the island have a name?" I asked.

A LEAF OF HONEY

"The island has no name," he said. "Why should a place have a name if no one lives there?"

"When I live there, may I give it a name?" I asked.

"If you want, give it a name. What will you call it?" he asked.

"*Ridvan*," I said.

"*Wezban?*" asked the chief.

"*Ridz-van,*" I pronounced. The chief tried again. The initial sound "r" and the consonant cluster "dzv" were alien to his tongue. I had to laugh. What he said was closer to "wristband" than *ridvan*. He kept trying to say it like I did.

"*Wristband? Wristband?* What a difficult language you have. What does it mean?" asked the chief.

"It's not actually my language," I said. "It is a word I know in Arabic." I told him that *ridvan* meant "paradise", and that the jungle was a garden paradise to a person like me from the Mojave Desert of California. It was the chief's turn to laugh.

"Paradise? It seems that not many of you whitemen go to heaven then, if this is what you call 'paradise'. Your 'wristband' island is not only small, but empty." The chief and I laughed a long time at his joke.

After a moment I was able to continue. I tried to explain about the two island gardens of this name associated with my religion. It was not surprising that the chief had never heard of places like Baghdad and Akka, but when I explained that I had seen the latter when I was in Israel, he became very excited.

"Have you been to the *Terre Sainte?*" he asked using the French term for "the Holy Land". The chief was serious now. It was obvious that he was no longer interested in contrasting the desert and jungle environments.

"Yes, I was in the Holy Land a few months ago, on the way to Cameroon," I explained. The chief addressed some of the other tribesmen present and they consulted among themselves. Presently he started to ask more specific questions.

"Have you seen Bethlehem?" he asked.

"Well, no," I said. But before I could explain that I had only a few days in Israel he continued.

"Nazareth?" he asked with disappointment in his old eyes.

"No." I felt I was letting him down.

"Judea?" he asked hopefully.

"I think so," I said, trying to remember exactly where Judea was.

"Jerusalem?" he asked with his voice full of hope.

107

A LEAF OF HONEY

"Ah yes," I said with relief. "I have been to Jerusalem."

The chief stood up and called his wife and sent some of the children to call the others. In a few minutes I was surrounded by people asking questions about the holy places of the Bible. They had never met anyone who had actually been to the Holy Land. Not even the priest who visited the village once or twice a year had been to the Holy Land. I spent the rest of the evening telling an enraptured audience about places they knew from the biblical stories.

At the time, it seemed like an ideal place to build a hut. However, living on the island of "Wristband" was more romantic than practical. The hut wasn't going to be anything fancy, more "Robinson Crusoe" than "Swiss Family Robinson". Resources, time and manpower limited my design. After a few days' preparation and transferring our equipment to the island, Robert and I began the process of building a hut. There are no prefab kits in the jungle. Sylvain helped to cut down and strip the long raffia poles. He would throw them into the river upstream and I would retrieve them as they floated past the island. I tied a small stone to the end of some light cord I had brought with me, threw the weighted line across the raffia "logs" and pulled them into shore. The system worked rather well. I missed a few, but not many.

At night we would sleep on the island. We made a tent out of a plastic ground cloth for Robert and I strung up my hammock between two trees with a little plastic roof to keep it dry. Sylvain went home at night, back to his hut. It rained every day. Not all day, but most of the day. We lived like weekend campers, not minding the temporary inconveniences, cooking the fish we caught over an open fire. The hut was progressing and life was wonderful. That was until the rain stopped.

After about a week, the weather changed and with it came the flies. One of the most appalling aspects of the mixture of a little naivety and lots of good intentions is that it leads to a lack of foresight. The river was infested with large black flies. It was a kind of fly that swarmed down the river in the morning and then swarmed back up in the afternoon every day it didn't rain. Although they didn't sting, they were so bothersome that they could drive you insane. The trouble was they were irresistibly attracted to body sweat — my body sweat. They didn't seem to notice Robert or Sylvain. I joked with my more fortunate companions about the prejudicial treatment from the flies. I was beginning to develop a theory about this selective attraction based on diet, body chemistry and blood type when Sylvain put his finger on a simpler explanation: fresh meat. In the presence of so awesome and succinct an answer, I laughed and immediately adopted the "Fresh Meat Theory". Sylvain had a great sense of humour. From then on, whenever the flies were due to arrive, Sylvain would stop what he was doing and shout, *"Fresh meat!"*. Sure enough, they would come every time.

Looking back on those times, I think it was the salt in the sweat. Robert and Sylvain didn't sweat much. The flies loved me. They would cover every inch of my body and just lick or whatever flies do. The other insect visitors would disappear when they came. Air traffic control had clear guidelines on this matter: sweatsuckers during the day, bloodsuckers at night. The only way to escape them on such a small island was to run around in ever increasing circles, luring them away from the mosquito net, and then make a dash for it. It was like a scene from an animated cartoon. Me running around, flapping my arms like an deranged chicken, being pursued by a cloud of black flies. Once I got enough of a head start on them, I would throw the net over me and just stand under it for awhile. Respite. It was the only way to escape the flies and regain a bit of composure and sanity.

Sylvain assured me that they were only seasonal. He couldn't say, however, how long the season lasted. We got most of our work done early in the morning, at noon and in the late afternoon, between swarms. Sylvain taught us how to tell time in the jungle. There was a special kind of hornbilled bird called *mzakunuk* that would cry out the hour, four times a day. He said it would cluck or click at six in the morning, twelve noon, four o'clock and at sundown at six. I took Sylvain's word for this, but to me, the bird would just cry: *kooooo-nuk, kooooo-nuk, kooooo-nuk* every so often. Every time we heard it, we knew that a unit of time had past. The rain also came like clockwork. Around midday the heavens would open and it would pour. The Ntumu have a saying that whenever it rains and the sun is shining, that "a baby elephant is coming". What this means, I do not know.

In the year I spent among the Ntumu and the entire seven years I spent in Africa, I never once saw a live elephant. The path that went through Meyo-Ntem led to elephant territory to the south and I saw many illegal hunting parties bring back diminutive tusks of baby elephant. I always felt very sad at the size of the tusks and what each one of them meant to the encroaching extinction of the west African pachyderm.

Occasionally, I was asked to share a pot of elephant stew in some of the villages I passed through. It was gristly and covered in chili sauce in an effort to mask the taste of rancidness. The women would tell me about how difficult it was to butcher an elephant. Nowadays, an elephant is never killed for its meat but the villagers take advantage of the large source of free protein. Once the hunter removes the ivory, the carcass is excavated where it lies by the men and women of the nearby villages. It takes days. They start at the top and cut away slabs of meat until they have enough to carry back to the village before dark. The carnivores feed on the remaining carcass at night. The next day, the villagers return and resume their work. They butcher it until they reach mud level. Anything sunk into the mud is lost but by then several days have passed and the meat isn't fit to eat anyway.

20

PERSONAE AND PERSON

Dear Dr Kilngott,

There is a wide variety of personae in the Ntumu proverbs collected so far. By personae I mean the "who" or "what" which figure in the proverbs. These include both human and non-human characters. Many Ntumu proverbs contain elements from nature that act as characters. These non-human elements are often symbolic and their interaction in the settings created in the proverbs are analogous of humans and human interrelationships.

Perhaps not directly relevant to this, but graphically interesting, is the drawing I have enclosed. It is of a smoking pipe the chief showed me. It is cast in brass or bronze by the lost wax method and has two parts: a pipe stem with a finger ring and a bowl shaped like a man in a cap. The chief said his father smoked it. He thought that it dated from the time when this part of Cameroon was a German colony. What, do you ask, has this to do with personae? It is a pipe with a personae.

PERSONAE GROUPINGS:

I have grouped the personae thus far discovered in the following four categories:

1 HUMAN
2 ANIMAL
3 PLANT
4 SUPERNATURAL

As with the literary styles, I have selected only a few to represent each of these.

HUMAN PERSONAE:

Human personae in Ntumu proverbs are varied, although not as varied as the animal and plant personae. Reference to humans is

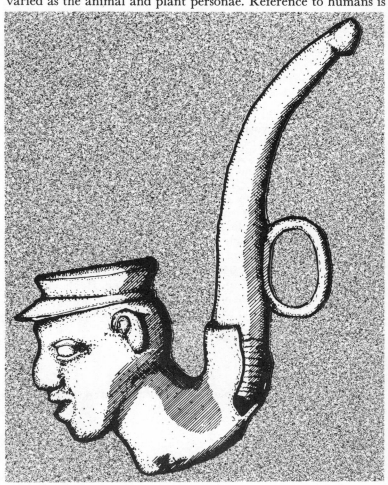

112

made in several different ways. Aside from the common
pronominal references, both definite and indefinite, the most often
occurring human characters are presented in proverbs in terms
which mark distinctions in age, sex, kinship relation, rank or social
status, and profession or skill. The use of such terms in the text or
manifest presentation of the proverb helps to convey a sometimes
abstract and complex underlying message. As enigmatic as some of
these proverbs is the mask I chanced upon the other day. I have
drawn it for you. I don't know what it is called or where it came
from or anything else about it. I sketched it because it is the first
mask I have seen so far in Ntumuland.

PERSON:

I have not chosen to use the English grammatical three-by-two
paradigm of the three possible persons, multiplied by their singular

and plural qualities, to categorize Ntumu proverbs, because the "we", "you plural" and "they" are all but absent. Most Ntumu proverbs are spoken in the third person; characters and events are spoken about. A few do, however, appear in the first person. You will remember this proverb from my first letter to you. Here the "I" of the proverb addresses a "weed" and laments at being deceived:

(031) "I wanted to build a fence around you thinking that you were peanuts, while (all the while) you were *obo obo zen.*"

Here the common proverb "all that glitters is not gold" is expressed by using a commodity just as important to the Ntumu subsistence economy as bullion is to national economies. Restated with more culturally relevant imagery, this proverb could read: "All that quadrifoliates is not peanuts". *Obo obo zen* literally means: "it lays down alongside the path". This "weed" is described as being an absolutely useless plant, even though it looks like *arachis hypogaea* as a sprout.

The Ntumu build and use several types of fences. These fences function either as boundary lines or barriers or both. What did Robert Frost say about good fences making good neighbours? A common boundary line marker is a tree which is skilfully felled into position rather than felled and then moved into position. Other fence types include those which are designed to keep people and livestock separate and short fences in the jungle to lead animals into snares and traps.

Peanuts, or "groundnuts" as they are called in anglophone Africa, are one of the Ntumu staple cultigens and are planted on swidden prepared farms. At harvest they are pulled up and left to dry, often suspended in the fields on "Y" shaped branches set in the ground. When dried and the pods separated from the rest of the plant, the peanut fruit is stored in trays that hang above the fire or in large baskets near the cooking area.

The following interrogative proverb is spoken in a chiding second person:

(032) "Do you have another part of the river in the village?"

Restated: "Do you have another hope or opportunity of gain somewhere else?" Caustically, this conveys the message of "don't shirk the work". Portions of the lengths of streams are owned by

114

individuals and this ownership entails the right to fish that portion of the stream. The streams are "cut" or dammed for short periods of time, usually during the dry seasons, and the exposed portions downstream are fished of almost all piscine and crustaceous life. Ownership of such a stream portion also includes the right to bury cassava in the stream-bed mud to ferment.

In the third person, the following proverb describes how the mother and unborn child are linked:

(033) "The herb the mother eats is the same (one) the child eats."

Many of the taboos which restrict or prohibit the consumption of certain foods are applied towards pregnant or virgin females. The above proverb is a warning concerning this. If such a female eats one of the tabooed foods it is said that the child will be born deformed or mentally deficient. When defects do occur, breakage of such food taboos is blamed.

Sincerely yours, Joseph

21

THE MOON IN A CLOUDLESS NIGHT

The children of the village had a guessing game similar to a game called "I spy" I have seen played by English school children. "I spy" is played like this: one child will say, "I spy with my little eye, something beginning with the letter . . ." The other children will then look around for objects that begin with that letter. Whereas this English game requires some degree of literacy, the Ntumu game only demands attention to detail. To play the game, one Ntumu child will ask, "How many eyes does an elephant have?" This is the cue to begin. The other children will look about them and answer, "Two!" The child who initiated the game will then ask, "What does the elephant see?" The other children will guess and guess until the object is discovered. It is then the turn of the one who finds the object to ask, "How many eyes does an elephant have?" This was an ideal game for me because it was simple and generated many one word answers. I exploited this to increase my Ntumu vocabulary.

We went to the village every two or three days and the children would follow us back to the edge of the river opposite the island. We often played the "elephant eye" game on these short trips as we walked along through the cocoa plantations and jungle. Sometimes the objects would be animals and birds but most of the time the answers would be specific names of tree types and flowering plants. I think I learned more of the Ntumu language from the children than the adults.

The children wanted to see the island, so we piled them all into the dugout Sylvain had lent us and took them over to see the hut. By now the frame was almost finished. The hut stood on stilts two

116

metres high and the floor was made of smooth raffia poles lashed tightly together. The sides sloped upwards from the ground and met in a high gable roof. The hut was divided into three sections. The large dry area underneath the floor was for storing firewood and building materials. Above that, there was room for an ample living space and cooking area. Above the main room, there was enough storage space under the rafters for our food and personal belongings. The children climbed all over the hut inspecting the construction until they were ready to be taken back to the river bank.

The news of a whiteman building a hut on "wristband" island spread and we started to have regular visits. The customs officer who usually wore a crisp brown uniform showed up one morning at dawn in his pyjamas, bathrobe and slippers. He had a toothbrush root in his mouth and a machine gun over his shoulder. He called to us from the river bank and we sent the dugout over to pick him up. He had brought us three chicken eggs. We stoked up the camp fire, put the coffeepot on and opened a couple of tins of sardines in mustard sauce. I cooked the best sardine omelette I had ever made and we all ate a hot breakfast sitting in the morning mist. He never mentioned the machine gun and neither did we. Machine guns speak for themselves.

Robert and I worked on the hut almost every day. We were beginning get tired of it and needed a change. At the end of one particular week, Sylvain invited us to have dinner with him and to spend the night at his house. His wife Jacqueline cooked a chicken and several other delicious dishes. The moment I met Jacqueline I knew my wife Fanny would love her. She was shy and witty with a radiant smile that lit up their home. We ate in Sylvain's man-house. It wasn't the wattle-and-daub construction of most other huts in the village. It had window frames and walls made of thin split-log planks. The roof was made of the usual raffia matting but Sylvain said he planned to put up a zinc roof when he had the money. He had built it all himself and was very proud of his hut.

When Jacqueline brought the chicken stew, Sylvain fished around in the pot ceremoniously until he found the gizzard and put it on my plate. I understood the honour he was showing me and I thanked him. We ate and talked about the coming cocoa season. Jacqueline sat on a stool by the door and brought the dishes of food in from the woman's hut next door. She always ate a little of each dish to show us that she was not afraid to eat her own cooking and that the food was not poisoned. She never took a plate for herself. She said women usually ate in the cooking hut with the children. Germaine Greer would have had a coronary. It was a wonderful meal, and Robert and I thanked our hosts. We knew that having guests over for a meal like this had cost Jacqueline and her husband a lot of time and resources.

When we finished our meal Sylvain and Jacqueline asked us to come outside with them. The night was warm and the entire population of the village was outdoors. Jacqueline said that tonight the village danced. Sylvain explained that the combination of a full moon, a cloudless sky and a Saturday night would inevitably result in a night-long village dance and music festival. The quality of this spontaneous music would have put Clara Ward and her Gospel Singers to shame. All the village instruments were brought out into the common area around the *aba*: the tall conga drums, the shorter drums, the marimbas with their hardwood plates and gourd resonators, the beaded rattles, several stringed *mbet*, and above all, the one brass whistle. The one who wore and wielded the whistle was the chorus leader of the church choir, a position of manifest honour and skill. This whistle seemed to be a vital part of both the Saturday night music and the small Christian Sunday services in the village church-hut every weekend.

The chorus leader started the music with a loud trill and the drums began a complicated and rousing beat. With a whistle, he then introduced and cued each new instrumental section as it joined in. The rattles were next. These were large gourds in a loose fitting mesh of beaded strands and the men who played them tossed them from hand to hand to the beat of the music. Occasionally they would throw them high in the air and catch them on the next beat. Trrill. The marimba players started up and produced both the melody and the harmony lines. Trrrill. The mbet players plucked out the bass notes. The whistler marked the crescendos. In the height of a frenzied rhythmic beat he would accentuate the tempo with a series of staccato bursts on the brass whistle. The women sang songs of praise of *Zamba,* the Ntumu word for God. I compared the joy of what I saw with my experience of attending white churches in America. I watched the villagers and knew what the difference was. Both had reverence, but among the Ntumu religion was fun. I could hear the origins of the music the African slaves had brought with them in their heads and hearts to America.

118

A LEAF OF HONEY

I loved Gospel music back in California but this was something
beyond anything I had ever heard. Any record company would
have signed up the entire village in a second. The music involved
the contribution of every individual in the tribe. The children and
the women danced and swayed to the music, sometimes their feet
hardly moving on the ground. The rest of their bodies, however,
moved in perfectly synchronized rhythm to all the beats of the
music. The head moved to the beat of one drum, the shoulders rose
and fell with the rattle of the gourds and the hips kept pace with yet
another drum. The women folk danced in a great circle and took
turns in the centre singing solos and improvising steps and
movements. Outside the circle the men played their instruments
and worked up a respectable sweat in the production of the music.
The villagers never seemed to tire. The music lasted all night and
not nearly long enough. I can still hear it.

22

AGE AND GENDER

Dear Dr Kilngott,

Relevant to one of the proverbs in this section concerning *ngon* pumpkin seeds is the drawing I have enclosed. It is not very well drawn, but I have tried to capture an important activity in the village. Women and children often spend several hours shelling *ngon* seeds in preparation of a well-liked Ntumu meal. A special metal rod is used to crack open the seeds on a rock. The seeds are small and it is an arduous task which requires nimble fingers. Children are frequently deployed to do it. Several thousand *ngon* seeds must be individually shelled to make a meal for a small family. Because this activity is long and boring the participants pass the time in singing or gossip. The result of their work is truly fantastic. Once shelled, the seeds are ground on a flat rock until a paste is formed. Water and a small portion of dried fish are added for taste and then the mixture is cooked in a closed pot. The *ngon* swells and produces a flan or souffle-textured dish. It is very agreeable to a European palate and is often offered to the Greek buyers as a kind of tribute when they come during the cocoa season.

Continuing on with human personae, the Ntumu language makes use of at least four age-designating nouns. These form a group of terms which are outside of the Ntumu generation-designator in their kinship terminology. In descending order, these name certain age groups more or less absolutely:

Nyamboro: 50+ years old
Mo'o: 15-45 years old
Monomo'o: 10-15 years old
Mon: Birth to 10 years old

I have only heard these titles used in relation to males and they often appear to be relative to the age of the speaker. These age designators become figurative generation-designators when used in other than a general sense. It is perfectly correct for a sixty year-old Ntumu *nyamboro* to call some upstart whippersnapper of forty a *monomo'o*. I have not found any equivalent set of titles for Ntumu females.

For the Ntumu, the acquisition of age is the acquisition of wisdom and social status. The following proverb conveys this:

(034) "An old man's face never gets wet by the rain."

Here, by analogy, the *nyamboro* old man is shown never to be the fool, but rather someone who cannot be hoodwinked. In the following, both "young" and "old" adjectival markers are used:

(035) "What you do to old Abossolo, young Abossolo sees."

Abossolo here is the name of a specific individual. Basically, the message here is: "Respect is something learned from observation."

Both sexes figure in Ntumu proverbs, but most often the gender distinction is made in adult personae and not in references to

children. In the following, a female vanity is shown not to have a place in horticulture:

(036) "A woman with long fingernails never grows *ngon.*"

The *ngon* pumpkin is one of the Ntumu's main seed staples and the process of hand planting, harvesting, drying and shelling the seeds is hard on the nails. Unbeknownst to the women of the village, a labour-saving device exists. Far to the north, in the town of Nkongsamba on the border between anglophone and francophone Cameroon, a Peace Corps volunteer has invented a crank driven machine that looks like a Gatling gun which shoots out shelled pumpkin seeds at a rate of several hundred a minute. It may take years before this machine reaches Ntumuland.

Similar to the proverb above, man's "pride" of his horticultural efforts is shown:

(037) "A man never walks bent in his farm."

In the light of the last two rather sexist proverbs, I have a suspicion that the men write the proverbs. There seems to be a dearth of proverbs which portray women as the bearers of admirable qualities.

After many weeks of asking the elders of the tribe about the meaning of their name "Ntumu", I have collected enough of a consensus for a possible etymology. It seems that among the tribesmen the universally accepted etymology of the word *ntumu* is derived from a folktale common to most tribes in this part of Cameroon. It is the epic etymological tale of *Afirikara,* the ancestral father of all Africans. The story has been written down and appears in Bulu as *"The Journeys of Afri Kara".* Unlike Bulu, the Ntumu language has no "fr" consonant cluster, hence the extra syllable in the name. According to this well-known tale, *Afirikara* had six sons and these are the origins of the Fang, Pygmy, Okak, Bulu, Ewondo and Ntumu tribes. As the epic explains, upon hearing of the birth of his last son, *Afirikara* who was by then a very old man, declared that this son should be named *Ntumafiri,* "the staff of *Afirikara".* The *ntum,* "staff or walking/working stick" was the symbol of his age, rank and wisdom. Although *ntum* is the most likely root of *ntumu,* the name of the major river in the region, *ntem* is clearly related.

A LEAF OF HONEY

The fact that the upper Ntem River Basin is the predominate homeland of the Ntumu and that phrases like:

> *munumotyuntem,* "male progeny of the Ntem" and
> *munumotyuntum,* "male progeny of the staff"

are minimal phonemic pairs and considered equivalent statements, is significant.

Sincerely yours, Joseph

23

SENSIBILITY AND CULTURAL SENSITIVITY

The work on the hut was progressing very well. Thanks to the efforts of both Robert and Sylvain, the spindly structure of raffia and bamboo was now recognizable as a possible dwelling-place for humans. However, time was running out. The date Robert and I set for his return home was almost upon us. We now worked long hours in collecting building materials from upstream. I wanted to have a good stock of bamboo poles and raffia fronds so that I could finish off the construction after he had gone. The day came when I realized that we had collected enough material and that I needed some tools which could only be obtained in the town of Ebolowa. It was time to say goodbye. Robert and I started packing for the trip back to Ebolowa. I left my hammock, most of my clothes and the rest of my personal belongings in Sylvain's hut in Meyo-Ntem. I put all my research papers in the backpack and took them with me. Everything else was expendable, but my fieldnotes were irreplaceable. Robert figured that he would have enough time to go to his own village near Ebolowa and visit his family for a few days before it was time to return to school in the town. Robert and I hiked along the now familiar trek to Ma'an.

The prospect of continuing my fieldwork on my own was daunting. Robert's assistance had been invaluable. He had helped me linguistically through the initial stages of meeting the Ntumu tribesmen and learning their language. Robert had also become my best friend. Our time together had been roughly divided among three main activities: my linguistic research, hut building and conversation. For me, the latter was the most enjoyable. Robert had a bright and clear mind and he was articulate in

124

several languages. He had an insatiable appetite for knowledge. His ability to quickly grasp new concepts was truly admirable. He never wasted time stating the obvious and found meaning and nuance in whatever he saw or heard.

We were a perfect match. I was ignorant of his world and he was ignorant of mine. In the beginning we discovered that we both held some surprising misconceptions about each other's race. We were both anxious to replace this ignorance with knowledge. At the end of a couple of months of sharing the same experiences and our constant truth-seeking discussions about virtually everything, we grew to know the insides of each other's culture, beliefs and characters pretty well. It was a rare opportunity and we both knew it. It isn't often that representatives of two diverse races and cultures live together in such egalitarian and isolated surroundings which allow them to examine beneath the superficial skin of one's personal exterior. Our conversations systematically peeled away the shiny veneer of cultural protective packaging and we looked long at the real product of each of our civilizations. The trying conditions under which we lived tested the veracity of our stated values and mores. Our tacit deeds and spontaneous reactions to difficulties were weighed against our voiced ideals and beliefs, day after day. The memory of his companionship and the days spent in the jungle working with Robert define for me the racial unity and cultural understanding possible in this world. This is my point of reference when I try to encourage others to work harder in bringing different races together in unity.

Robert and I walked silently along the path to Ma'an and passed the sites of a dozen adventures, passed the memories of gorillas and dugout canoes, of council meetings and cunning chiefs, things which are indelibly inscribed in our minds. Ma'an was different from when I had first seen it. Robert and I had visited it several times and had met the district Commissaire and his Chief of Police. We had also been interviewed by the Commander of the six Cameroonian Gendarmes stationed there, who had asked us what we were doing in Ma'an. I had made friends with some of the tribesmen who owned the rickety shops that opened on market days.

The only way to get to Ebolowa from Ma'an was to wait until a vehicle came along. There was no scheduled transport. Usually people had to wait for days until something rolled in, but we were in luck. On the morning we walked into Ma'an a green van was parked in the market square. There was a young boy on top of the roof of the vehicle pulling baggage up on a rope. We asked him when the van was leaving and the boy said he didn't know. Robert and I went to look for the driver. We found him sitting in a nearby mud hut which had been converted into a bar. The bar consisted of a counter and ten bottles of Cameroonian Guinness on a shelf behind it. The driver was sitting on one of the two stools in the place. We asked him when he was planning to leave and he looked at his watch and said that it would be a few minutes. We negotiated the price of two places and paid the man. The driver put most of the money in his pocket and bought another bottle of beer with the rest. Nine bottles of beer on the wall. He leaned back against the wall and told us to find our seats in the van because he was leaving momentarily. We went and sat in the van expecting the driver to follow us. The van had open air windows and two wooden benches along the sides so that the passengers sat facing each other. The space between the benches was reserved for baggage and livestock.

The villagers said that this van was the first vehicle to reach Ma'an in a week. It was packed. We sat in the van and waited for the driver to finish his beer. It took him a while to go from nine bottles of beer on the wall to no bottles of beer. We waited seven hours to leave. It seems the driver also had a girlfriend in Ma'an. At about three o'clock in the afternoon the driver appeared. He wasn't legless but he was definitely feeling no pain. All that time sitting in the van I couldn't stop thinking about my family. I had not seen my wife and daughter for more than eight weeks and now that I was finally going to see them I couldn't wait. I had sent them a few hand-carried letters with people who were going to Ebolowa, but I had received very few answers. The ones I did get were written with love and encouragement.

The trip to Ebolowa took two days. Three hours down the road it got dark and the driver decided to spend the night in a village he knew "just off the main road". The driver had more than one girlfriend. He parked the van in front of her hut. Robert and I and the rest of our band of travellers spent the night propped up in our seats swatting mosquitoes who were in a feeding frenzy. No one could sleep, including the goats and chickens under our feet. By the morning I just didn't care anymore. I was so tired and bitten I would have exchanged my soul for a pillow and a mosquito net. Just after dawn the driver got into his seat, whistled a cheerful little tune and started the engine. I don't remember the rest of the trip.

A LEAF OF HONEY

Later that day we rolled onto a patch of paved road and I woke up from the sudden lack of potholes and dust. A sign alongside the road informed us that we were just five kilometres from our destination. The man next to me wanted to talk and I didn't. He pointed to a sign and said that *Ebolowa* meant "the place of the stinking gorillas". I just nodded and thanked him. I was too tired to ask him how the town got this name. I never did find out. It was good to know that I was so near to seeing my family. The van unloaded its passengers in the market square. Robert and I said goodbye and he went off to look for a vehicle going to his village. I knew I would see him again. He was a student at the school that Tohu Elaka taught at. I put on my backpack and walked to the Elaka's house and knocked on the door.

My two-year-old daughter took one look at me and hid behind her mother's skirt. Fanny didn't seem to mind what I looked like and gave me the kind of hug that comes straight from the heart. It was good to see my family again. I just stood there with my arms around them in the doorway. The first thing my wife said to me was that I had lost a lot of weight. Frankly, I had been too busy to notice. She took me to a full-length mirror in the house. I had almost forgotten what I looked like. What I did remember looked nothing like this. My hair was a bit too long and my beard ragged and redder than I remembered. Under the dirt and dust, my face and the backs of my hands were dark from sunburn. The palms of my hands were a series of cuts and scrapes at different stages of healing. My wife was right about the weight loss. My stained and faded jeans hung loosely on my hips. The once blue cotton shirt I wore had two buttons left and part of a sleeve missing. She insisted on giving me a haircut right then and there. The Elakas heated up some water and I took my first hot bath in two months. I was suddenly so tired that I fell asleep in the bathtub. When I woke up, the water was cold and reddish brown. I was cleaner but not clean. I refilled the tub and scrubbed until I was.

Fanny handed me some clothes which were not only clean, but dry, even the socks. My wife traded the heavy leather climbing boots I had been sleeping in for weeks for a pair of real shoes, shoes I had forgotten that I owned. Fanny and Fariba cooked a Persian meal of rice and sauce. Tohu bought some bread and we ate off plates instead of out of a tin or frying pan. We sat at a table you could get your legs under and rest your elbows on. The Elakas had

127

an aqua-filter and for the first time in weeks I drank a glass of water with nothing swimming in it.

The best part of all was after dinner. There was a bed waiting for me which had never been rained on, with sheets. No swinging hammock, the bed had legs that were actually attached to the ground. A hammock is fine in a pinch but a bed is better. For the next week I did nothing but rest, heal and recuperate. The Elakas wanted to hear all about my research. I couldn't have cared less. I was sick of it. Linguistics, anthropology and research were the last things I wanted to talk about. I wanted to hear myself and others speaking English for a while. On the second day back in Ebolowa, I discovered Tohu's library. Tohu had studied English literature at the University of Yaounde and he had books, real books, not anthropological books. He had shelves full of novels, epics, sagas, biographies, histories, science fiction, things that had characters and plots. The only books I had taken with me into the jungle were anthropological texts and a Baha'i prayer book. My mind was dying for a story line. I also discovered that the Elakas had a Scrabble board and a two-volume Unabridged Oxford Dictionary, the one that has print so small it comes with a magnifying glass.

One evening after Tohu and I played Scrabble, I broke down and talked about my research. The conversation drifted onto the subject of sensibility and cultural sensitivity. He told me a great story about an occurrence that demonstrated a lack of both. It was something that had happened to a friend of his called Francois who worked for a governmental ministry in the capital.

One day Francois was asked to accompany a Canadian lady who worked for the World Health Organization in Cameroon. The lady wanted to visit a particular village some distance from the capital, Yaounde, where she worked. There was a United Nations project planned for the village and Francois was to escort the WHO representative to the proposed project site. The village was only a few hours' drive from the capital, so the lady decided to take her own car. Francois and the lady talked as she drove through the dirty streets of the capital out into the cleanliness of the rural countryside. Francois watched her as she spoke. She was an immaculately disinfected elderly white lady who was very health conscious and sincere in her wish to improve the African's state of hygiene and sanitation. They visited the village and Francois translated for the lady when some of the villagers who couldn't speak French asked questions.

A LEAF OF HONEY

On the way back home, they drove through a stretch of jungle. Francois saw a small hut beside the road and asked the lady if he could buy a handful of bananas from a villager for his lunch. The lady stopped the car and Francois bought his bananas and proceeded to eat one. When he had finished, he stepped to the side of the road and threw the banana peel out into the jungle. When he tried to get back in the car, the lady told him that she had seen what he had done and told him he shouldn't be a "litter bug". She told him to go immediately and get the peeling and bring it to her. Francois felt demeaned but submissively went into the jungle to look for his peeling. He finally found it and brought it to her. She gave him a condescending lecture on the evils of littering and poor sanitary practices as she took out a clean white Kleenex from her purse. She wrapped up the peeling and put it into the glove compartment of her car. For the rest of the trip back to Yaounde, Francois sat quietly as the lady spoke at him about things like sanitation, cause and effect, public education and the difficulties of raising underdeveloped countries to a developed state. As she drove, the rural clean green scenery gave way to the squalor and trash of the capital's surrounding build-up of cardboard shantytowns.

When they arrived at her apartment block in the European *quartier* of the capital, the lady asked Francois to come upstairs. She took the Kleenex-wrapped peeling between two fingers and climbed the four flights of stairs to her modern apartment. She took Francois into the kitchen to show him the proper way of disposing of litter. She stepped on the foot lever of her shiny sanitized chrome dustbin and the lid obediently flew open. Looking to see if Francois was paying attention, she dropped the Kleenex-wrapped banana peeling into the bin and lifted her foot. The lid closed heavily with a gratifying clunk.

"Now, that's what you do with litter," she said, bringing to a close her object lesson. The irony of the story was what happened next. The lady said that her cook would arrive in a few minutes and asked if Francois would like to stay for a cup of tea. Francois agreed. The lady went off to wash her hands and change her clothes. Francois sat patiently and looked around the room. The apartment was filled with the memorabilia of the countries to which the World Health Organization had sent her. After a few moments, the lady's cook arrived from doing the shopping in the market. Francois introduced himself and followed him into the kitchen to chat while he brewed some tea and started supper. When the cook found that his dustbin was full, he unhesitatingly knew what to do. Francois watched as the cook took the dustbin to the rear balcony and emptied its contents over the side. The contents, including the tissue-wrapped banana peel, settled onto a very large and still growing pile of rubbish in the alleyway behind the apartment block, four stories below. The sanitation expert had obviously never wondered where her refuse went or noticed the pile of rubbish in her own backyard. The lady soon finished changing her clothes and sat down with Francois to have her cup of tea. She continued lecturing him on the subject of sanitation. Francois just sat there, sipped his tea and smiled. He never told her what he knew on the subject.

I laughed until my sides hurt at the irony in Tohu's story and wondered how my own actions would be seen by the tribesmen with whom I lived.

24

PUTTING THE KEN IN KINSHIP

Dear Dr Kilngott,

The children of the village have been showing me their variations on cat's cradles. This game of making patterns with a loop of string between the fingers is played by children almost everywhere I have travelled. The two patterns I have drawn for you are of pieces of tribal furniture. The top one depicts a raffia bed and the lower one that of a chair. Because the second configuration is less obvious, I have included a drawing of an actual three legged chair cut from the branches of a tree.

This week I will address the terms of kinship which often occur in Ntumu proverbs. Used in analogy, kinship terms are sometimes applied to animal and plant personae. In the following proverb the term *nga*, "wife", is figuratively applied to *okbwa*, a partridge-like fowl which is also called the "bush chicken".

(038) "The male *okbwa* said to his wife that she should sit on the eggs fast because the dry season has many things."

The nesting season for the *okbwa* is during the rainy season. During this time most predatory animals of ground-fowl seek shelter and don't roam about as much. When the dry season returns, so do the predators of the ground nesting *okbwa*. The message here is simply: "Hurry, before it is too late".

The general term *mvong*, "progeny", is a kinship and plant-related term which figures in the following:

(039) "It always starts with progeny and finally reaches the trunk."

131

A LEAF OF HONEY

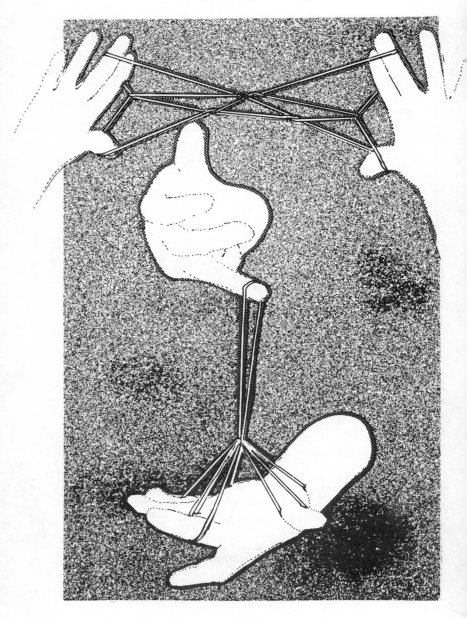

132

When used in conjunction with specific plant terms, *mvong* can be translated as "seed", with a meaning closer to "seed corn" rather than "corn seed". In this conjunction, *mvong* connotes "the seed which is saved for replanting". When not presented in conjunction with specific plant names, it retains the above connotation but is figuratively applied to the progeny of humans: "the human offspring which is saved for replanting". The above proverb is further enhanced by the analogous term *nkuk* for "trunk" which shares the same ambiguity as it does in English for either "tree

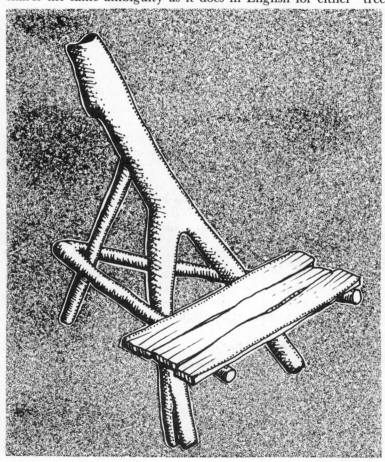

trunk" or the human torso "trunk". This poetic proverb warns that things that start between children can escalate into involving the parents and that the "my father can beat up your father" scenario is to be avoided.

As applied to humans, several other kinship terms are found in Ntumu proverbs:

ka: "sister" and other female relations of the same generation.

monyang: "brother" and other male relatives of the same generation.

eisa: "father", mother's brother, father's brother, mother's sister's husband, father's sister's husband, and ascending males.

nya: "mother", mother's sister, father's sister, mother's brother's wife, father's brother's wife, and ascending females.

nkia: "parent-in-law", wife's mother, wife's father, wife's father's mother, wife's father's brother, etc. This term describes wife's older sister, but not wife's younger sister.

nga: "wife". This is used to make reference to wife's younger sister's potentiality of becoming a second wife, and occasionally to wife's older sister, but with regard to certain rights other than marital.

As representative of kinship terms applied to human personae the following proverbs are presented:

(040) "If you refuse to do a favour for your *nkia,* don't you know it will rain?"

Here, the message is universal: one should always do the favours one's mother-in-law asks, because if one refuses, she will never forget and sooner or later make one wish one hadn't refused. And again using *nkia*:

(041) "If you want to know what your wife will look like when she is old, look at your mother-in-law."

This proverb is undoubtedly borrowed from the French:

"Regardez la mere de votre epouse
et vous pouvez imaginer comment elle sera."

The mother-in-law seems to be the butt of as many jokes among the Ntumu as she was in Colombia, where I once saw a bit of Spanish graffiti that read,

"Adam was lucky, he had no mother-in-law".

The Colombian youth often used the term in their *piropos*, "flirtatious street remarks". Upon seeing an attractive young lady walking with her mother, an appreciative man would call out in a loud voice, *"Hola, suegra"*: "Hello, mother-in-law." This expression plays upon the ambiguity of sexual relationships potential and past.

Sincerely yours, Joseph

25

THE *PUSH-PUSH*

After a week of rest and Fariba's good Persian food at the Elaka's house, I was mentally prepared to return to Meyo-Ntem and the next stage of my research. Being away from the constant pressures of learning a new and difficult language and from the discomfort of living rough gave me enough time to evaluate my work so far. I looked through my fieldnotes and saw that my first two months among the Ntumu tribesmen had been a successful cultural introduction. Dr Kilngott would be proud of me. However the real work lay ahead. Learning the tribesmen's language was not an end in itself. There was a more important reason to learn it. The Ntumu language was one of the cultural keys which I hoped would unlock some of the hidden beliefs and world-view of the Ntumu people. I knew that I would never be able to know all there was to know about their culture. That was a never-ending task. Even a basic understanding would take more than the year I had allocated for my research. It would take a lifetime. Culture must be inherited, assimilated, lived and passed on for even the rudiments to be truly understood. Maybe I would get lucky and find something in the proverbs I was collecting which would allow me to write an accurate, if only basic, description of this people's world-view. In any case, my fieldnotes were a good start and I was full of enthusiasm again and ready to continue.

There were, however, practical matters to consider. I wanted Fanny and Anisa to join me in Meyo-Ntem and I had the well-being of my family to think of now. The hut on the island was near enough to completion to plan for my wife and daughter to come with me. Fanny was uncertain about living in the middle of a river but said she would give it a try. The prospects of having my family with me were exciting. I drew up a check list of things we would need to take with us to survive for the next six months. I spent part of the week buying and packing things. I bought the tools I needed to finish the hut and organized the remaining equipment for my research. In consulting with my wife, we agreed that what we needed more than anything else was not on the list: a more reliable mode of transport than the occasional bush-taxi or moonlighting Land Rover. The villagers in Ma'an told me that sometimes during the rainy season no vehicles reached Ma'an for two or three months. Clearly this was a condition I had to do something about if I was going to take my family into the jungle away from hospitals, doctors and medicine. My wife and I decided to take some of the money we had saved and buy our own means of transport. A four wheel drive jeep would have been ideal but the stipend that the University of California gave us wasn't enough by a long shot.

The only means of transport we could afford was something with half as many wheels and that meant a motorcycle. The town of Ebolowa had several resident expatriate merchants and I asked Fariba if I could borrow Tohu to come with me and help negotiate buying a motorcycle. There were a few hardware and machine shops in town and we walked around to all of them. No one had a motorcycle for sale. A few of the merchants had some glossy brochures left, but informed us that it would be several months before the next shipment of motorcycles came in.

Finally Tohu took me to meet one of the Greek businessmen he was acquainted with in the town. The Greek's business was buying cocoa beans from the tribesmen of the surrounding area and exporting them to Europe. I wondered if this was the same Greek the chief of Ma'an had referred to. Tohu spoke in French with him and translated for me. I learned that to increase his profits the Greek imported manufactured goods like hardware and cloth and sold them in the town. This type of import-export business was very common in Africa.

The Greek imported for wholesale several types of motorcycles and usually stocked Suzuki, Kawasaki, Honda — all of the Japanese models. He said that many years ago he had been one of the first merchants to introduce motorcycles into this part of Cameroon. As a result, the Bulu tribesmen had adopted *suzuki* as their word for "motorcycle". He laughed and commented that the villagers now distinguished the different types with words like *yamahasuzuki, kawasakisuzuki, hondasuzuki,* and, of course, *suzukisuzuki.* Today, however, the Greek had only two bikes left, both of them small Yamahas. As the wholesaler, he was the one who supplied the rest of the merchants in the town, and he knew that everyone else was sold out. I looked at the price tags and mentally counted the money I had. I discovered that there was just enough money for the fire engine red Yamaha 100 street-bike. The more powerful Yamaha 125 trail-bike next to it would have been more suitable to ride in the jungle, but I didn't have the money. Although the small street-bike was very impractical, I had no other choice.

The Greek merchant also sold a contraption commonly known as a *push-push.* It was a box-like frame with two bicycle wheels on either side and was originally designed to be pulled as a cargo trailer for bicycles. It acquired the *push-push* name from pidgin English speakers on the coast where it was first produced because it ended up being pushed by hand rather than pulled by a bicycle. The Cameroonians found it lightweight and strong and useful in transporting goods to and from the market, but after buying one, few of them could afford the bicycle to go with it. For me, it was comparatively inexpensive and would be handy both on the road and in the village. I had seen them being pushed in several villages. I tried to haggle for a lower price for both the Yamaha and the *push-push,* but the Greek was firm, knowing full well that no one else in town had them for sale.

Of course there was another problem I had momentarily forgotten about. I had never ridden a motorcycle before. Knowing how to ride a bicycle, I asked myself, "How difficult can it be?" I was to find out many times. I paid the man, trying not to think about the exorbitant price and what the equivalent amount would be in dollars. The Greek pocketed my cash and stripped away the protective shrink-wrapped plastic sheeting around the Yamaha 100. He started the engine for me to prove that it worked and asked if I wanted to ride it home. I said no, not yet. It was obvious that I didn't know how. I thanked him and pushed it around the corner to the only gas station in town and filled up the tank. There were many children around and they began to follow me and help me push it. It was obvious that the motorcycle was brand new. Nothing in Africa was that clean and bright but once. The children were in a playful mood and kept motioning me to get on it and ride. I was embarrassed to try to ride it home. I wasn't even sure I could restart the thing. I decided to wait until later and learn to ride it in a less

138

public part of town. We pushed my shiny new red motorcycle back to the Elaka's house and I said, "*akiba*", "thank you" in Bulu, to the children. I showed my wife my new toy and began to teach myself how to ride it.

The first thing I did was to read the instruction booklet that I found tucked under the seat. It was written in English, French, Portuguese, all the other colonial languages of Africa and in what I assumed was the motorcycle's mother tongue of Japanese. The English section was typical of technical translations. The grammar was a bit odd and some sentences lacked verbs, but the worst part was the strange vocabulary. Some of the words I had to look up in Tohu's dictionary, not because they were technical, but because their assigned meanings were so uncommon. It was as if the translator didn't speak English but had just used a Japanese-English dictionary and translated the text word by word. I was intrigued by the general unintelligible style of the text until I discovered that the translator was obviously unaware of a fundamental feature of English dictionaries: that multiple meanings of words are listed in the order of common usage. Some of the words which the translator had employed carried their rare, obscure, archaic or even poetic meanings and were found tenth or eleventh in the dictionary listing.

The booklet introduced all the features of the machine and showed how to maintain the engine and repair tyre punctures, but nothing about how to ride it. I had trouble starting it. Everytime I kick-started it, it would lurch forward. I soon learned what the "N" position on the gear foot lever meant. It's so easy when you know how. Once I figured out how to put the gear box in neutral, it started very nicely. I took my life in my hands and got on it. I soon mastered the skill of letting out the clutch slowly and changing gears without killing the engine. I imagined that it would be like learning to drive a car. The slower the better. Of course, the slower you go on a motorcycle the more unstable it is. I practised riding it up and down the dirt streets for a few days. I never fell off and my confidence and speed grew. I soon found myself riding along in second gear, wind in my face, singing a silly Arlo Guthrie tune:

"I don't wanna pickle,
I just wanna ride my motor-sickle.
And, I don't wanna die,
I just wanna ride my motor-sigh . . . icle."

I shopped around the town and bought the cheapest crash helmet I could find. It was an Italian piece of moulded orange plastic like an upside down salad bowl that fitted on top of the head with leather flaps that covered the ears. It had no visor. I went back to the Greek merchant and he sold me what had to be a pair of World War Two army surplus goggles. They weren't expensive, but then you get what you pay for.

After a few days of practising my leaning when going around corners and third gear, I felt I was ready for a test run to one of the villages just outside of town. I reached the edge of the pavement and ventured out into the world of dirt roads. It didn't seem as bumpy as sitting in the back of a bush-taxi. I had never dared to open it up before. There wasn't that much pavement in Ebolowa. I found a relatively smooth stretch of road and decided to go through all the gears. It was great fun. However riding a motorcycle in Africa has its drawbacks. On the way back home I was riding along in fourth gear when something smacked me in the face. It felt like I had been hit with a baseball bat. I didn't lose control of the bike but I immediately slowed down and stopped. I touched my mouth and found that my lip was cut and bleeding a bit. I felt something moving on my chest and looked down inside my jacket. I found a very large and slightly stunned stag beetle. It was the size of my palm and must have weighed 200 grams. The huge beetle had been flying along minding its own business when I had run into it at about 80 kilometres an hour. It was a shock for both of us. It didn't look damaged and I laid it in the undergrowth beside the road and it crawled away. When I returned to Ebolowa I rode directly to a shop and invested in a real helmet with a visor which covered the whole face. I presented the Italian salad bowl to Fanny to wear because she always sat behind me and if I ever met that beetle again it would have to go through me before it got to my wife.

The *push-push* came with a trailer hitch attachment that was supposed to bolt onto the back of a bicycle seat. Of course it didn't fit on the Yamaha. I took it to a panel beating shop and had it welded onto the carrier rack. I could not go very fast with the *push-push* on the back because it would jump around whenever I hit a rut. It pulled better when it was loaded. I bought some long strips of rubber in the market which had been cut from old inner tubes. These were elastic and ideal for tying down the load on the *push-push*.

26

SOCIAL STATUS AND STEREOTYPES

Dear Dr Kilngott,

I was doodling the other day and I decided to draw a picture of the daub-and-wattle wall of my hut. I know that the subject matter is about as exciting as watching paint dry, but it reveals the structure which supports the mud-huts of Ntumuland. The upright poles are slit logs spaced evenly and set in the ground. These are tied together with a latticework of raffia strips and mud squished by hand into the openings. There are a few places in my hut where the external skin of plaster has fallen away to reveal where all the cockroaches live.

The terms descriptive of the Ntumu *bang* or "social status" occasionally occur in Ntumu proverbs. In the following hyperbolical proverb, the bachelor is portrayed as worse off than if he were married:

(042) "A bachelor doesn't eat or wash everyday."

An age old verity. 600 years ago Chaucer wrote:

> *"Bacheleres haue often peyne and wo"*.

Several Ntumu social institutions such as the *aba* provide for the feeding of unmarried males. The above is humorously exaggerative in conveying the message "better wed than unfed". In the following, bachelorhood and matrimony are contrasted in respects to male comportment:

(043) "Why do you act like a bachelor who visits a woman sometimes."

Prescribed roles for Ntumu males are different during bachelor-hood and matrimony, often the transition from one role to the other is long in coming.

Life for the widow is difficult in Ntumu society. The treatment of a widow by her late husband's family immediately after his death may appear vengeful and cruel. It is a complex social institution called *akus*, which loosely translated means "the squaring of debts". The following two proverbs deal with widows:

(044) "*Akus* has come to the elephant's nest."

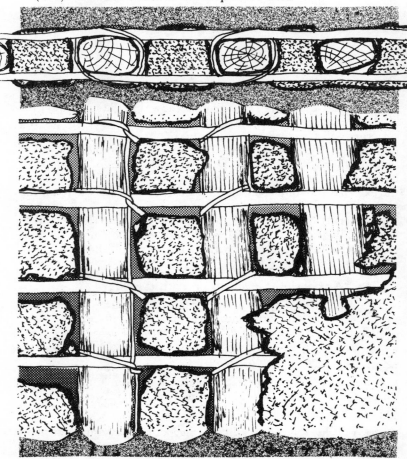

A LEAF OF HONEY

First of all, let me explain what an "elephant's nest" is. Elephants are believed to build shelters from branches they break off or small trees they uproot. These shelters protect and camouflage a female elephant while she bears her young. Now regarding *akus*, the death of a Ntumu male is a time debts and inheritances can be collected by seizure by any male relative of the descending generation except his own progeny. This means that the deceased's sister's sons, his brother's sons, his mother's brother's children's sons, etc. may claim inheritance but not the dead husband's son or daughter. It is also a time, even during the husband's funeral, when any of the aforementioned males relative's are allowed to "mistreat" the widow. This often vengeful treatment sometimes entails requiring the widow to lay down next to the casket during the funeral and accept verbal abuses and accusations of guilt in the death of her husband. These males have the unquestionable right to order the widow to perform any labour in payment of unpaid debts and surrender any of his possessions. Because of such seizures, disputes often arise in the village among the menfolks who often have to replace items taken:

(045) "The house of the widow is open, the house of disputes is open."

A few tribes with which the Ntumu have minimal contact are mentioned in their proverbs. The following refers to the Hausa, with whom the Ntumu have occasional mercantile relations:

(046) "You refuse the Hausa and you like their necklaces. But who made the necklaces, is it not the Hausa?"

The relationship between objects and the makers of objects is used to express the relationship between acts or gifts and the giver of such in the Ntumu society. To the Ntumu, it is hypocritical to accept a gift in kind or help from someone without likewise accepting the individual's friendship.

Pygmies are viewed as primitive in the eyes of the Ntumu. A tribe of Bayele Pygmies live near the Ntumu region but very deep in the jungle and they are rarely seen. Although looked down upon as being less civilized and less Christianized, the Ntumu readily confess that the Pygmy are superior in the "ways of the rainforest". The following proverb intimates the tree-climbing ability of the

143

Pygmy. This is no small skill when some hives are located fifty metres above the jungle floor on trees with no branches to climb on.

> (047) "If you want to drink honey from the tall tree, free the Pygmy."

Here, the idea of paying for a favour with a favour is communicated: "You scratch my back and I will scratch yours." This Maussian concept of equalized reciprocity pervades all of the Ntumu's interactions. It applies to both material and exchanges of service. It, in some ways, is the backbone of their tribal economy. The Ntumu live in an area and condition which does not provide many ways for the individual to save for the future. There are no banks or facilities to store food or other commodities effectively for long periods of time. The above proverb presents the philosophy behind a very complex Ntumu social device: the unsolicited distribution of one's excess. By giving away each day those commodities which one cannot use but which will perish if not consumed, a kind of rotating fund or savings account is established between each individual and the rest of the Ntumu village. An individual can deposit in times of personal plenty his excess, banking on the knowledge that when a personal lean period strikes him, he can withdraw from his social account by collecting the excesses of others to meet his own lack.

Members of the Hausa and Bamileke tribes are famous, or perhaps notorious, as traders. Each major population centre in Cameroon has a number of resident Hausa and Bamileke often forming their own ghetto or *quartier* of the town. The Ntumu call the Bamileke tribe *englafis,* "the English", for some unknown reason. Traders from these tribes often visit villages in the Ntumu region bringing with them items which are usually unavailable to villagers.

Sincerely yours, Joseph

27

THE CONVOY

The morning came to set out on the trip to Meyo-Ntem. I attached the *push-push* to the back of the motorcycle and Fanny loaded the carry rack and front handlebars with backpacks. The *push-push* was loaded with the heavier things like a 20 gallon drum of gasoline for the motorcycle, my fieldnotes, books, a portable Brother typewriter and other supplies. I had made friends with some carpenters in a workshop next door to the Elaka's house and constructed a wooden box that opened into a lap writing table. Everything was wrapped in plastic to make it waterproof. We had a hot breakfast and thanked the Elakas for their hospitality. The three of us got on the motorcycle. Fanny and I wore our helmets and Anisa sat sandwiched between us with a bandanna around her head. We couldn't find a helmet small enough for Anisa. Tohu and Fariba took some photographs and they wished us a good trip. We said we would be back in about six months.

I figured it would take us a day to get to Ma'an and another half day to reach Meyo-Ntem. I didn't calculate in variables such as road conditions, inclement weather and a border skirmish. The first stretch of road was flat and dry, but I still found that I had to ride slowly because of the weight we were pulling. Soon we came to some hills. To climb them we had to get off and help the engine pull the load. Going down hill was worse. The *push-push* would try and race the motorcycle to the bottom. We would again have to get off to ease the load down. The hours crept by, it became dark and we had not even reached the half way point. It had begun to downpour and we decided to keep moving until the next village. Sleeping alongside the road in the middle of the jungle was not an option. It was raining so hard, that it was difficult to see the way ahead in the light from the motorcycle.

The rain didn't let up and between the noise of the rain and the engine we couldn't hear what was approaching us from the rear. All of a sudden, I noticed that the road ahead was lit up. I looked over my shoulder and pair of very bright headlights was coming up fast behind us. The road was narrow and the vehicle was as wide as the road. A few glances backward convinced me that whatever it was, it hadn't seen us and wasn't going to slow down. I tried to find a smooth area to pull over and let it pass, but there wasn't one. There was a deep water-filled ditch along both sides the road. Unfortunately there wasn't enough time to stop and lift the bike and *push-push* over the ditch. As the truck was just upon us, I shouted, "Hang on!" and aimed the bike at a gap between the trees. We left the road flying and crashed through the ditch and up a bank into the undergrowth. My family stayed on the bike behind me until we hit a tree stump and fell over. The *push-push* broke loose and followed the bike into the jungle. We came to rest just as the truck careened past. It didn't stop. I wasn't sure that the driver had even seen us in the torrent. The truck was followed by a fast moving convoy of a dozen or so similar vehicles. They looked like military personnel carriers. They came up the dark road one by one and passed us without noticing. Each vehicle seemed to be moving as fast as it could. Fanny and Anisa were shaken but apparently unharmed. They had landed on a soft spot. We were covered in mud. As we lay there watching the military roll by and wondering if there was a war somewhere I discovered that I was injured. The mud on my right hand felt warm and I looked down and saw that I had cut it open pretty badly. It didn't hurt but just felt numb. I wrapped a handkerchief around it to stop the bleeding. It was too dirty to try to dress properly.

We waited until we were sure that all the vehicles had passed before we attempted to get the motorcycle and *push-push* back onto the roadway. We wanted to avoid being run over again. We discovered that the trailer hitch on the *push-push* had broken. I took some of the strips of rubber and attached it as best I could. It stopped raining, but the tires of the heavy trucks had pounded the road surface until it was about a foot deep in mud. It was now imperative to find shelter for the night. My hand had begun to throb. The next village couldn't be far off. We struggled through the thick mud. It was impossible to ride and we had to push. We were exhausted, bruised and soaked in mud. The mud was too deep for Anisa to walk, and we had repeatedly to carry her a few paces forward, leave her there and push the bike up to where she was waiting. At one point Fanny fell face down in a puddle and her hair was matted with mud that ran down her neck into her clothes. This was a test of character. I remember looking at her and feeling so proud of her inner strength. She never once complained, gave up or broke down and cried.

We were, however, nearing the limits of our energy. We hadn't eaten since breakfast and we had been doing hard labour for some eighteen hours. We couldn't find the village. We came to another hill. Fanny had to push and guide the *push-push* from the rear as I walked next to the motorcycle and tried to power over the ruts in the road. In my exhaustion, I slipped and the bike fell over on me. The engine stalled, the headlight went out and then it was dark. I was pinned and the hot manifold on the engine was slowly burning my leg. I struggled to get free. This time my hand really hurt. Fanny tried to move the bike off of me. Suddenly, dozens of lights appeared out of nowhere. I had fallen over in front of a village without knowing it and the villagers had come out with their kerosene lanterns to see what had happened. They helped Fanny lift the motorcycle off me and get it upright again.

My family and I spent the night in some kind-hearted tribes-man's man-house. We washed as best we could and bandaged my hand from our first aid kit. The next morning we ate as much as we were able under the circumstances and started out again. The road surface was still terrible. We pushed as much as possible but the spokes of the wheels clogged with mud and we had to stop several times and clear the wheels. In the light of day, the villages became familiar and I could see that we would reach Ma'an that night.

Tired and battered, we finally arrived at our destination in the middle of the night. I felt like I had run over by a freight-train. I went to look for the chief. I should have been excited about arriving, but after the hardships and suffering of the trip, it seemed so anticlimactic. All I wanted to do was sleep. I could feel excited about starting a new life and continuing my research later. Sleep first. It was hard not to notice the many military vehicles parked in the market square when we rode in, the same ones which had nearly run us over. Luckily the chief was still awake and he offered us a place to sleep in an adjoining hut. I asked him about the trucks and he explained what had happened. Unbeknownst to us, the

Cameroonian and Equatorial Guinean governments were having a disagreement over the boundary line between the two countries and there had been some fighting. The military had been sent in to show the flag.

We spread a blanket out on the dirt floor, rigged up a mosquito net and got ready to sleep. We thanked our host for his kindness, and I put my head down and closed my eyes.

Two seconds later my eyes were open again. Mysteriously it was dawn. I had been dreaming that a soldier was prodding me with a gun barrel. For a moment nightmare merged with consciousness. Someone was shouting and poking me with something hard through the netting. I muttered something as I tried to find the edge of the net to lift and see what was the matter. Two armed soldiers in camouflage uniforms stood over us motioning us to stand up. At gunpoint they took us to a hut occupied by their military commander and several officers for interrogation. The commander's facial markings were typical of the far north of the country and he obviously wasn't from any of the tribes in this part of Cameroon. He didn't speak English. He spoke French. I didn't. He asked us many questions and became quite angry because we couldn't or wouldn't answer. As far as he was concerned, all whitemen spoke French. I tried to explain in English who we were and what we were doing in Ma'an. He pointed to one of his soldiers to translate. The soldier was very afraid of his superior and asked us questions in Pidgin English. His words were difficult to understand but I tried to answer. The translations into French were suspiciously and considerably longer than my answers. I listened to what he was saying. Even with my very limited understanding of French I could see that the soldier was totally misrepresenting what I said to him. He wasn't translating, the soldier was just telling the commander what he thought the officer wanted to hear. It seemed as if he was afraid to admit the limitations of his translating ability. After the soldier spoke, a large man I recognised as the local *Secretaire du Commissaire,* whispered something in the commander's ear. The commander demanded to see our papers.

I showed the commander a letter of introduction from Dr Kilngott at the University of California and our passports. He couldn't read English and found it unlikely that one family could have members of different nationalities. Usually the wife's nationality was the same as the husband's; however, Anisa and I were Americans and Fanny was Colombian. He looked at the clean-shaven man in the photo and then at me with a beard and asked if this passport was mine. Communication between us was impossible. I tried speaking Spanish to see if someone else in the room might be able to translate. There was no one. This only exacerbated the situation. I tried what little Ntumu I knew but again no luck. Finally the commander became frustrated at my babbling and shouted at me to shut up. I shut up. We were made to understand that we were arrested. The fact that I claimed I was an American but had some clean-shaven man's passport, and could apparently speak fluent Spanish but not French, made the commander suspect me of being on the wrong side of the border with Equatorial Guinea. In short, a spy.

Most of our belongings and the *push-push* were seized and locked in a room. Fanny and Anisa were ordered to sit in the back of the military commander's jeep. I was about to get in the jeep with them when I was told to stay where I was. The commander shouted some orders to his men and got in the front next to his driver. As they drove off Fanny looked tearfully over her shoulder at me and clutched Anisa tightly to her chest. I asked the soldiers where my wife and daughter were being taken but no one would answer. I watched the jeep speed away and disappear around a bend in the road. I was terrified. My family was being abducted, and there was apparently nothing I could do about it.

"Oh yes there is," I said to myself. I ran to my motorcycle, kick-started it and took off after the commander's jeep. Some soldiers ran after me and shouted at me to stop. I put my head down, didn't look back and rode like the wind. I didn't know what I was going to do if I caught up with the jeep, but I wasn't going to be separated from my family. The jeep had a few minutes' head start and was faster than my motorcycle. I pushed the engine to its limits and rode with it flat out, but I still couldn't catch up with them. I was especially worried for Fanny's safety. For the next six hours I followed the jeep's tracks to make sure it hadn't turned off in the jungle somewhere.

28

A HOOP TOO BIG

Dear Dr Kilngott,

Animal personae in Ntumu proverbs is highly analogous and more diverse than any type of personae. Some fifty-one different species and several more generic animal terms appear in the proverbs so far collected. These include most of Noah's Ark:

> ants, caterpillars, flies, larva, millipedes, bloodsuckers, snails, crabs, three types of antelope, bats, boas and four unidentified snakes, wild canines, domesticated dogs and cats, cape buffaloes, elephants, goats, chimpanzees, gorillas, panthers, wild and domesticated pigs, two species of rats, three kinds of squirrels, chameleons, crocodiles, frogs, and four types of lizards, tortoises, four unidentified birds, chickens, hawks, hummingbirds, parrots, partridge-like fowls, and the ubiquitous sparrows.

With the possible exceptions of one type of antelope: the *zip*, the panther, the cape buffalo and the wild boar which are nearly regionally extinct, all of the above are found in the Ntumu rainforest. These animal names far outnumber the terms found among the human or plant personae in the proverbs. The total number of proverbs which incorporate animal personae also outnumber those proverbs of other types of personae. I have decided to divide these into the following groups:

1 GENERIC ANIMALS
2 SPECIFIC MAMMALS
3 SPECIFIC REPTILES
4 SPECIFIC BIRDS
5 SPECIFIC INSECTS

The animal characters in these proverbs appear in two different modes: natural and pseudo-human. In certain proverbs animals figure normally, manifesting natural animalistic characteristics and limitations. In others, however, animals emulate human abilities such as articulate speech.

GENERIC ANIMALS:

The word *tsit*, in isolation, is a generic term meaning "any animal" but when used in conjunction with a specific animal term, for example, *zok*, "elephant", *tsit* takes on the meaning of "meat". *Tsitzok* or "elephant meat" is an example of this.

(048) "If a hoop is too big for a elephant, what animal then will it fit?"

This is a round about way of saying "the matter is obvious". There are several different proverbs which communicate obviousness. I will assemble them and look at them separately later.

The elephant is the largest animal in the Ntumu jungle and the example is used when a maximum size is needed to compare something to. The other extreme is the *soso*, "hummingbird". The hoop in the proverb is a special apparatus for climbing tall oilpalm trees. It is made of *nlong*, a hefty vine which is tied in a circle. I have enclosed a drawing of one. The *nlong* is really two lengths of vine tied together. Note the knots. The *nlong* are used to support the climber while he is tapping the sap in the palm to make a quick-fermenting drink called "palm-wine". The "hoop" is portrayed as too big for the largest of animals hence it is obvious that it, likewise, will not fit any other animal. Other Ntumu proverbs use terms

151

which are generic but for sub-categories of animals. The following is one such example:

(049) "The *kunuk*, though it is also very smart on the branches, does not look like a monkey."

The central idea here is, "Things that are different sometimes share similar qualities". Both the large-billed blue *kunuk* bird and the monkey are arboreal animals but they are nevertheless different.

Like the whippoorwill of North America, the *kunuk* bird has an onomatopoeic name. It gets its appellation from the sound it makes with the bulb-shaped acoustic bell on the top of its bill: "*Kooooo-nuk, Kooooo-nuk, Kooooo-nuk*". Another related bird, according to Ntumu taxonomy, is considered rare and mystical. It is forbidden to kill the *mzakunuk* because it tells the time of day for the tribesmen when they are in the bush working. It is believed that the *mzakunuk* bird gives its distinctive call at 0600, noon, 1600 and 1800 hours.

The word for "monkey" in the above proverb is *kweng*. It would be better translated as "generic primate". It is a term which is applied to all primates in the Ntumu region except humans. Aside from this, all the primate species also have their own specific term in the Ntumu language. However Ntumu taxonomy does not label a distinction between "apes" and "monkeys".

I am told that palm-wine is a common beverage throughout West and Central Africa. The palm tree from which the juice is extracted grows freely in the Ntem basin and I have watched the villagers tapping palms several times. Palm-tapping is dangerous work and several of the villagers have admitted with some embarrassment to falling out of palm trees. They explained that their *nlong* hoops sometimes slip. Perhaps it is for this reason that I have noticed another method used to obtain palm-wine. A small palm is cut down and the base of it wrapped so that all the sap runs into a large container. This technique produces a much higher yield but, of course, kills the tree. My friend in Ebolowa told me about the works of a Nigerian storyteller called Amos Tutuola who writes about Yoruba village life and palm-tapping. He didn't have any of his books, but from his description it doesn't sound so dissimilar from the practices of the Ntumu tribesmen.

A LEAF OF HONEY

Being an abstainer from such things, I am unable to tell you what palm-wine tastes like. Some of the American Peace Corps volunteers in Ebolowa, however, describe it as a cross between down-home moonshine and jet fuel.

Sincerely yours, Joseph

29

PALLIATION AND POWER

I hammered on the Elakas' door in desperation and hammered again. After a moment Tohu opened the door. He looked startled to see me.

"Have you seen my wife?" I blurted out frantically. Tohu just stood there, blinking, dumbfounded by the question and the implications it carried. He looked me up and down in disbelief. I can now imagine what was going through his mind. Just two days before he had waved goodbye to a happy and excited family as we rode out of his front gate. He hadn't expected to see us again for another six months. What could have gone so wrong in so short a period of time that I would ask that kind of question? But there I was, filthy and obviously injured, desperately seeking a misplaced wife.

"Tohu, please answer me. Have you seen Fanny?" I pleaded.

"No. No, I haven't," he said in a bewildered voice. "Why? What has happened? What's the matter?"

Suddenly, I became aware of how very tired I was and the pain in my hand. I quickly told him about being arrested and the military commander abducting Fanny and Anisa. I explained that I had followed the jeep tracks as far as I could, but when they reached the paved segment of road outside of Ebolowa I couldn't tell which way they had gone. In the middle of my story, Fariba came to the door to see who it was. They asked me to come in the house and sit down. My legs were shaking from fatigue. Tohu tried to reassure me that everything would be all right. He said that if they had been arrested they were probably at the military camp just outside of town.

A LEAF OF HONEY

I couldn't sit down; panic was sweeping over me. Every minute that passed was filled with increasing fear for their safety. I couldn't just sit and wait for them to turn up. I had to keep looking for them. I decided to go to the military camp. Tohu pointed out the general direction and I rode off. I was now living on adrenaline. I hadn't slept more than six hours in the last sixty, and hadn't really eaten. I rode to the camp but found nothing; it was nearly empty. I rode up and down the streets of Ebolowa looking for Fanny or the jeep. I tried the police station, the immigration office, everywhere. My family was nowhere to be found. I prayed they had not been taken directly to Yaounde.

After about an hour, I returned to the Elakas' house and found Fanny and Anisa sitting in the living room, drinking a cup of tea, quite safe and unharmed. The military commander had taken them to the home of his superior, the *Prefet du Ntem*.

Fanny told us that the *Prefet* had been very kind and spoke good English. He had asked her what we were doing in Ma'an and Fanny had explained why we had come to Cameroon and the linguistic research I was doing. She told him we were Baha'is and that she and Anisa were staying with the Elakas while I found a place for us to live. The *Prefet* seemed to know about the Elaka family and asked Fanny if she meant the Persian radiologist who had married one of the Cameroonian teachers at the *Lycee*, the state secondary school. Fanny had said yes. He had examined the passports and papers the military commander had taken from us and then looked at our two-year-old daughter in Fanny's arms and said that it was obvious that we weren't spies. No mother would ever allow her child to be endangered like that.

The Prefet gave our papers back to Fanny and said that if we had come to see him when we had first arrived in Ebolowa this would never have happened. He and the military were unaware that there were foreigners living in the *District de Ma'an*. However, he told Fanny that even though our visas and passports were in order, we still needed to obtain a research permit from something called *ONAREST* in the capital. He then instructed the commander to drive Fanny and Anisa to our friend's house.

While Fanny was telling her story, a truck pulled up outside and someone knocked at the door. Tohu answered it and then called me over to speak to a man in an officer's uniform. It was a military man I had not seen before. Reading from a piece of typed paper, he asked me in French if I was Joseph Roy Sheppherd. I said I was.

Tohu translated. He informed me that I should report to the *Prefet's* Secretary at the Government Offices the next day. The officer was formal and direct but not angry, and after he had delivered his message, he politely said goodbye and drove away. I had been worried that riding off on my motorcycle might be interpreted as trying to escape. I was relieved that at least they knew where I was. We all sat down and finished our tea.

I looked at my wife and child and felt so thankful that they were safe. I had never been so frightened in my life. Not knowing where they were had been unbearable. We took turns in the bathroom washing off the dirt and grime of the last two days. Lord, it seemed like a month since we had left Ebolowa. All that suffering and for nothing. It was like a nightmare in which no matter where you ran, you always ended up right back where you started. We were still in Ebolowa, but now most of our belongings were somewhere in Ma'an. Fortunately, many of our clothes were still strapped to the back of the Yamaha. The clothes were soaking wet, but at least we had something to change into. After we washed and ate, we went straight to bed.

My hand felt much better the next day when I woke up. I wondered when all this chasing around would end and we could settle down to a normal life in Africa. This couldn't be normal. Fariba had hung out some of our clothes and by noon they were dry enough to wear. I dressed as smartly as I could and rode the Yamaha to the Governmental Offices of the *Prefet*. The insides of my thighs were bruised and saddle-sore from riding the motorcycle for so long. The Governmental Offices were a left-over from the time of French colonial rule and were palatial in size. There were several *fonctionnaires,* civil servants carrying papers back and forth. I parked my motorcycle in front of the main stairway and stopped the first one that came by. Armed with Tohu's oversized English-French dictionary, I awkwardly asked for directions to the office of the *Prefet's* Secretary.

"*Ou... etre... le... Secretaire... de... Prefet?*" I asked, flipping from page to page in the dictionary, looking up every word. The *fonctionnaire* just stared blankly at me. I repeated the last three words several times and finally he said something in very rapid French and pointed. Now, it was my turn to stare blankly. It wasn't much use trying to construct a question if I wasn't able to understand the answer. The man beckoned me to follow him and lead me to a door. I knocked but no one answered. I opened the door a little and peeked in to see if there was anybody in the room. Behind a large desk in the middle of the room, sat a young man in a dark suit. As soon as I saw him, I opened the door the rest of the way and walked in. He watched me coldly as I boldly approached his desk and stuck out my bandaged hand to shake his. The young man slowly stood up and reluctantly shook my hand over his desk with a frown.

"*Secretaire . . . de . . . Prefet?*" I asked, pointing at him with my other hand. The young man let go of my hand and stepped back. He had the expression on his face of a person who had discovered a bad taste in his mouth. I repeated the grammarless question: "*Secretaire . . . de . . . Prefet?*". The young man sat down again and picked up his pen to resume work, but didn't answer. "*Sec-re-taire . . . de . . . Pre-fet?*" I pronounced slowly, trying to make myself understood by articulating each syllable.

"*C'est: 'Secretaire DU Prefet', non 'DE Prefet'* " he shouted angrily. He pointed his pen at a chair across the room near the door and motioned for me to sit in it. I went and sat down obediently and didn't say another word. It was plain to see that I had insulted the young man in some way. I might have made friends with the Ntumu tribesmen, but I wasn't doing very well in establishing good relations with the military or government officials. The young man continued his work in conspicuous silence. He never once looked at me. After awhile, I began to feel uneasy. I hadn't even been able to tell him why I was here or what I wanted. An hour went by like this with the young man signing letters, occasionally answering the phone and in general ignoring my existence. Finally, he got up and left the office without a word. As I sat in the room by myself, I didn't know what to do, if I should stay or leave. A few minutes later, another man entered the room and told me in English to come back tomorrow morning.

Tohu came home from work at the Lycee in the afternoon and I told him what had happened with the *Prefet's* Secretary. He put his hands to his face, shook his head in despair and asked me to sit down. He told me that if were going to meet the *Prefet*, I had a lot to learn and, very quickly, before tomorrow morning. The first thing I needed to learn was a few polite and useful phrases in French, such as "*Pardonez moi, je ne parle pas francais*": "Pardon me, I don't speak French."

Tohu also briefed me on the position of the *Prefet* and advised me on how to behave in his presence. He explained that the Prefet was the chief administrative officer of this *Departement*, the *Departement du Ntem,* and one of the sub-governors of the Cameroonian Province of *Centre-Sud.* He explained that the *Departement du Ntem* was a state, like the state of California, and that the *Prefet* was like the Governor. Tohu asked me candidly if I would have behaved the same way if I had been in the offices of the Governor of California.

I felt very ashamed and realized that what Tohu was saying was true. I had not understood the rank of the man I was to see, and this had affected the way I had acted. I had been brash and arrogant. I thought about this for a moment. Sometimes it is so tempting to try to justify ignorant behaviour like this by saying to one's self, "It's not my fault, I hadn't intended to be rude." Palliation is an insidious cultural stigma that is difficult to overcome. Tohu pointed out that a foreigner often unconsciously puts the onus on the people around him to adapt to him, instead of the other way around. The truth is that the people around him don't care about his "intentions" if his actions are seen as offensive, disrespectful or rude. It was humbling to realize that I had been guilty of the same kind of cultural unconsciousness which I had so often seen and condemned in others. Perhaps this was the real lesson of anthropology: to study others to learn about yourself.

I was beginning to understand that people in their own homeland have basic cultural rights. These are as important to them as the personal freedoms which an American finds in the Bill of Rights. Cross-culturally, however, these American "unalienable" rights are not as fundamental as Americans might think. When an American travels abroad to other countries, he no longer has those rights and should be submissive to new cultural laws, expectations and customs. People expect to be treated in a manner they are used to. A stranger should not impose his standards on others.

I saw I was acting like a tourist and not an anthropologist, and tourists are a country's worst ambassadors. Informality was the standard I had unintentionally imposed on the *Prefet's* Secretary. Respectful formality was the cultural standard here and therefore expected. This was the root-cause of it all. Thinking back, my overriding American sense of easy informality had affected my whole demeanour. My gestures, stance and voice level had all reflected a mental attitude inappropriate to the circumstances. Little wonder the man didn't want to speak to me. He saw me as unbelievably contemptuous and impudent.

A LEAF OF HONEY

Tohu said that there were some things that I must, and must not, do tomorrow. First of all, I had to be prepared to wait. Bureaucracy moves a little slower in Africa and waiting was part of the process. I probably would not be given a fixed time for an appointment and would be expected to sit in an outer office and wait until the *Prefet* wanted to see me. It might be hours or days, depending on how unimportant the *Prefet* felt I was. Tohu advised me to take a book to read. Even if the *Prefet* was not busy, he might have me wait for several hours for no other reason than to cool my heels. This was his way of letting me know my place. When I was called in, I was to stand humbly and patiently at the back of the room near the door and wait until I was invited to move closer. The *Prefet* might choose to finish up what he was doing before acknowledging my presence. If the *Prefet* offered to shake hands with me it would be a good sign, but I should not oblige him to shake my hand by sticking mine out like most Americans do. Under no circumstances was I to put my hands in my pockets, fidget or look at my wristwatch to check to see what the time is, as it was impolite to look bored or impatient. Tohu cautioned me never to point, give or receive anything with the left hand. In cultural terms, such an act was tantamount to spitting in someone's eye. I must always remember that the occasion was an *audience* with an important person, not an *appointment* with an equal, and that the *Prefet* had the power to terminate our presence in his country at the slightest provocation.

I was awed by Tohu's good advice and sagacious understanding of how things worked. He knew more about my cultural behaviour than I did. Over dinner that night, I discovered that Tohu also had a deep insight into the social dynamics of bureaucracy in Africa. He explained that what had happened at the Government Offices was partly to do with the fact that the concept of hierarchical power was subtly different here in Cameroon. Here, "power" was defined as simply the ability to inconvenience someone else, and "authority" basically boiled down to the right to impede, complicate, hinder or make things problematic. The greater the ability to do these, the greater the power. In America and Europe bureaucracy has been long-established and civil servants there enjoy that sense of power which carries with it prerogative, privilege and liberty. These were rather limited here, he explained. Most government bureaucracies had been established under colonial administration and most civil servants were of a generation that remembered colonial rule. Old ways still

A LEAF OF HONEY

continued. Here, hierarchy existed to formalize a pecking order within a bureaucracy and not to delegate responsibility in decision-making. This often left a bureaucrat with the authority only to control the processing of pieces of paper which crossed his desk. Decision-making was restricted to deciding when a paper was processed, not what was written on the paper. This meant that the only remaining aspect of power left to a civil servant was his ability to process things quickly or slowly. In short, either to facilitate someone or to inconvenience them.

People like the feeling of power and power needs to be perceived by others to be felt. In Africa, demonstrated power was more readily perceived than potential power. If a *fonctionnaire* had the ability to inconvenience someone and exercised it, then others would know he had power. If he did not demonstrate this ability in some way, then they would not know he had this power and therefore not respect him. This was the way the system worked. Individuals like me had to be prepared to allow a person in authority to show his power, and making people wait was the easiest way of exercising one's ability to inconvenience.

30

TO KILL AN ELEPHANT

Dear Dr Kilngott,

The elephant appears to occupy an important position in Ntumu folklore. This must spring from a time when the elephant was more numerous and the Ntumu tribesmen more dependent upon it as a food source. In most of the proverbs so far collected the elephant usually figures in a hunted or slaughtered condition. In the following group, each proverb presents the elephant as a food source at some stage of procurement. The message conveyed in each of these differs despite the situational similarities. "Be prudent in times of prosperity" is the underlying message of this antithetical question:

> (050) "Is it that if you kill an elephant,
>   you uproot your eggplant?"

This is an example of Ntumu "rhyming". In English, a rhyme consists of the close similarity of sounds in words or final syllables, especially at the ends of lines of verse. Whereas this is possible to achieve in the Ntumu language, it is not as aesthetically correct in verse as ending phrases in alliterative monosyllabic words. The two phrases above demonstrate this. In Ntumu, "elephant" is *zok* and "eggplant" is *zong*. The difference between these two words is not only phonetic but phonemic: *zok* and *zong* are minimal pairs. This kind of alliteration is the basis of the Ntumu sense of "rhyme".

These two food sources have another relationship which is less poetic and more pragmatic. In times when meat is scarce in an Ntumu village, the women will prepare something called *mindjim*

162

zong, "eggplant or aubergine water", to satisfy the hunger for the taste of meat. It is a soupy drink served hot and made from *zong,* eggplant; *osang,* an aromatic graminaceae also called "fever grass"; *ondondo,* chili peppers; *musup,* another aromatic leaf; and *okum,* a smaller plant similar to the eggplant. All of these are cooked together, but the final liquid has had the fruit of the *okum* removed before serving. When this drink is served, it is typically a sign that times are lean — an antonymous situation to that after an elephant kill. Here, the proverb warns, by substituting familiar objects and conditions, that "having plenty now does not mean that there will be plenty later". It is a reminder to the Ntumu to maintain a minimum to fall back on.

The Ntumu society fluctuates between cash-crop and subsistence economies. Each year after the harvest of cocoa beans, the Ntumu farmer is relatively rich. But the harvest is also the time when the Ntumu region is inundated with travelling merchants, on foot or on bicycle, peddling their wares, and soon the farmer's money is spent and he and his family are forced to return to a subsistence agricultural and hunting economy until next harvest.

In the Ntumu equivalent of the English proverb "Where there is smoke there is fire", the setting of the elephant hunt is also employed:

(051) "The elephant goes and leaves the blood."

This proverb uses a literal example of cause and effect and shows that although an elephant is not seen, it can be tracked and located by following the bloody trail it leaves after it has been shot. By analogy, it conveys, "You can know something by its effects". In the same hunting setting:

(052) "One never jumps on a tortoise's back to go and shoot an elephant."

Here, the message is clearly "there is a time for expediency". And finally, the elephant kill is again used as the setting to form the Ntumu counterpart of the English proverb, "Rome wasn't built in a day":

(053) "An elephant (carcass) cannot get rotten in only one night."

A LEAF OF HONEY

In both these proverbs, patience is the message and each in its own culturally relevant way effectively communicates "little by little, big things are accomplished". In the case of the English proverb, the analogy is additive and in the Ntumu proverb it is subtractive. An elephant carcass requires several days to butcher and carry back to the village.

Sincerely yours, Joseph

31

THE RESEARCH PERMIT

After yesterday, I was anxious not to repeat the same cultural mistakes I had made. I got up early, put on the best clothes I had with me and borrowed a tie from Tohu. When I arrived at the Secretary's office, I was prepared for a long wait. In my pocket, I had an interesting paperback. I gently tapped on his office door and waited. A moment later a voice inside the room commanded: "*Entrez.*" I entered and quietly closed the door behind me. I stood beside the door and waited until the Secretary put down his pen and looked up from his work. He silently nodded at me and smiled.

"*Bon jour, monsieur le Secretaire DU Prefet,*" I said nervously in obviously well-rehearsed French.

"And good morning to you too Mr Sheppherd," he said in flawless English. "How can I help you?" I felt really embarrassed at having butchered his language yesterday for nothing.

"I have been told that I need to see you," I said.

"Won't you please have a seat," he said politely, gesturing to the same chair I had sat in yesterday. "You seem to have had some trouble, haven't you?"

"Only a little," I lied.

"The *Prefet* would like to speak to you." The Secretary picked up his phone, said a few words in French and put it down again. "The *Prefet* is busy now, but if you will wait outside, I will call you when he can see you." He opened the door for me and indicated a wooden bench in the hall. I thanked him and sat down and read my book.

The paperback was one that Tohu had lent me. When I had described my proposed research and interest in proverb analysis, he asked me if I had read any of the works of Chinua Achebe,

Cyprian Ekwensi or Gabriel Okara. I had to admit that I had never even heard of any of them. Tohu said that they were among the best and most well-known African writers. Each had woven tribal proverbs into his novels. I was beginning to realize that there was an Africa-shaped hole in my liberal education. The book Tohu had lent me was *Things Fall Apart* by the Nigerian writer Chinua Achebe. It was great. It was the kind of book you read, sigh and say to yourself 'if only I had written that'. The story was laced with wonderful sayings. There was even a proverb about proverbs:

"Proverbs are the palmoil with which words were eaten".

Palmoil is a vital food in West Africa and it is part of every meal, even among the Ntumu. It is obtained from a kind of palm and is used as both the cooking oil and the sauce. Palmoil made the dry cassava roots go down easier.

"Mr Sheppherd." I looked up from my book and saw the Secretary standing over me. "The *Prefet* will see you now. Please follow me," he said politely. I was surprised that I hadn't been made to wait very long. I glanced at a clock on the wall as the Secretary led me through his office to another door. A whole hour had passed without my noticing I had been totally enveloped in the story. The Secretary knocked once and then showed me into the *Prefet's* office. It was spacious and panelled in African hardwood with attractive pictures and carved artwork along the walls. The *Prefet* sat behind a massive desk beneath a large framed photograph of the Head of State, the President of Cameroon. The *Prefet* was shorter than his Secretary and about forty-five years old. He was dressed in a well-tailored, pin-striped suit. He did not get up when we entered. His Secretary directed me to a seat in front of the desk and then sat down himself in one of the chairs that lined the walls.

"Mr Sheppherd, what are you doing in the *District de Ma'an?*" asked the *Prefet,* getting directly to the point.

"I am an anthropologist studying the Ntumu tribesmen and their language," I said.

"Who has sent you here to Cameroon?" he asked.

"The University of California ... in the United States of America," I said.

"I know where California is. Is that where you teach?" he asked.

"No sir. I mean I don't teach, sir. I'm still a student," I said.

"I see. Then, is this research part of your doctoral dissertation?" he asked.

A LEAF OF HONEY

"No sir," I said.

"Your Master's thesis?" he asked.

"No sir. It is for my Bachelor's Degree in Anthropology," I admitted. The *Prefet* did not look happy at my answer.

"Are you telling me that the University of California sent you all the way to Cameroon unsupervised to do undergraduate research by yourself?" The interview was not going well. He looked perturbed. I couldn't tell if he was perturbed at my lack of academic degrees or that he had never heard of such a thing and doubted me. I wanted to explain, in consolation, that it was Senior Honours Research, but he didn't pursue the matter and asked me some questions which I couldn't really answer.

"Why do you whitemen always come to Africa to do your research? Is it because you think we are primitive or interesting savages? Don't you have any people to study in your own country?" he asked accusingly.

"I am interested in studying culture and African is more interesting. The American culture is very young," I said lamely. In my mind, I was trying to find the simplest comparative explanation that would suffice. The last thing I wanted was an ideological confrontation. "The Ntumu have an old culture and their wisdom has been carried in their heads for many generations. I would like to help write some of this wisdom down on paper." I hoped he would not complicate my simplistic reasoning by mentioning the native North American Indians.

"Do you realize that we are much more tolerant than you Americans?" demanded the *Prefet*. "What if a group of Cameroonians went to your hometown in California and asked to come into people's houses and ask them questions? What do you think they would feel about that?" I thought about this for a second. He was absolutely right. Projects of academic cultural research were practically unilateral. I tried to picture the average conservative resident of Victorville opening up his front door and finding several African tribesmen standing there with spears and clipboards, wanting to come in, to ask questions, nose around and stay for a year.

"To tell you the truth, I don't think they would be as well received as I have been here," I admitted. "I appreciate the kindness and tolerance your country and people have shown me."

"When you say that you want to write things down, does this mean you intend to write a book about the Ntumu?" he asked.

A LEAF OF HONEY

"Yes sir," I said.

"What kind of book?" he asked.

"I am not sure yet," I answered honestly.

"I hope it is not the kind of book which is, how do you say, *pejoratif* and belittling to our country. In Cameroon we are concerned with what other countries say about us." He then told me that several years ago a Frenchman had filmed a group of crazy people with no clothes on. He had paid them to jump up and down and stick out their tongues. The Frenchman had then gone back to Paris and sold the film to a movie-maker who distributed it to many cinema theatres of Europe as part of a short movie. The film-maker had added a soundtrack which falsely stated that this was normal Cameroonian behaviour. By chance a Cameroonian diplomat had happened to go to a cinema in Paris and had seen the film. It had been very humiliating for him to sit there and hear the audience howling with laughter at the falsely portrayed behaviour of his compatriots on the screen. Since that time foreigners wishing to document Cameroonian life for any reason were required to apply for an *Autorisation de Recherche,* a research permit. The *Prefet* informed me that I needed to apply for one before I could continue my fieldwork.

I asked whom I had to see to request such a research permit and the *Prefet* replied that the only governmental organization who could issue a permit was *ONAREST* in Yaounde. *ONAREST* was an acronym for <u>O</u>ffice <u>N</u>ational de la <u>RE</u>cherche <u>S</u>cientifique et <u>T</u>echnique and the *Prefet* gave me their address. He also informed me that as soon as I obtained a research permit from Yaounde I must deposit a copy of it with his Secretary and that until I had this permit, my wife and I were forbidden from returning to the *District de Ma'an.* With the news of what constituted a setback in my scheduled fieldwork, the *Prefet* stood up and ended the meeting with me. I thanked him for his time and he shook my hand. His Secretary, who had been taking notes, showed me the way out.

During the next two weeks I made four trips to Yaounde on my motorcycle to the offices of *ONAREST.* The research permit required photos, photocopies and a dozen supporting documents from the Immigration Department, Police and the American Embassy and, above all, a detailed research proposal. This last item gave me the most trouble and I had to make a special trip to Yaounde as a result of the choice of a single word in my proposal. At first reading, *ONAREST* turned down my application flat because I had used the word "folklore" in my description of methodology. Although the proposal was written in English, to the francophone reviewers of my application this word was highly insulting. Unfortunately, the French *folklore* does not mean the same as "folklore" does in English. I had used the word to mean "the traditional legends, beliefs and customs" of the Ntumu, not knowing that the word carried a pejorative nuance in French of "myths, superstitions and primitive practices". I had to travel to Yaounde to explain my choice of word. By borrowing an eraser and rubbing out the offending eight-letter word, I was able to write in the less offensive word "culture" instead and resubmit my proposal. The removal of this single word satisfied the officials at *ONAREST* and seemed to exonerate me from being accused of a number of things including a cultural elitist at least and a racist at worst. It is amazing the power one word has. This semantic change, of course, did not affect my methodology but did soothe sensitive ruffled academic and bureaucratic feathers.

A few days later I was finally given authorization to carry out linguistic and anthropological research under the aegis of the *Institut des Sciences Humaines* (*ISH*) of *ONAREST* in the region of Ebolowa-Ambam-Ma'an in the *Department de Ntem*. The permit was valid for one year. Before leaving the offices of *ONAREST,* I read the conditions carefully:

a) The researcher or research team shall be required to contact the headquarters of *ONAREST* in person, immediately on arrival and before proceeding to any part of the United Republic of Cameroon where the research is to be carried out.

b) At the end of his/her activities and before departure from the United Republic of Cameroon, the researcher or research team shall in addition to this authorization deposit two copies of report of field research work (typed) with the Director General of *ONAREST,* and thereafter, at least two copies of all subsequent publications from the fieldwork effected in the United Republic of Cameroon.

c) Under no circumstances shall the researcher or research team be allowed to carry away objects of cultural value or documents of national interest to the United Republic of Cameroon without a covering letter or approval from the competent authorities.

d) Researchers with research permits exceeding three months shall present quarterly reports of their fieldwork to the headquarters of *ONAREST.*

e) The researcher or research team shall be obliged to recruit a Cameroonian counter-part or collaborator or assistant in his research team.

f) This authorization loses its validity once the researcher or research team leaves the United Republic of Cameroon before the date of its expiration. In this case the competent authorities shall have to be contacted anew for a fresh authorization.

I made a dozen photocopies of my hard won *autorisation* to have on hand, and got on the Yamaha and started toward Ebolowa. Armed with this I could now begin the process of getting my family back to Ma'an and restarting my research.

32

DUMB DOGS AND
MYSTERY-MEAT STEW

Dear Dr Kilngott,

Dogs figure in several of the Ntumu sayings I have thus far collected and in the context of these proverbs the canine personae are portrayed as rather unintelligent. Whereas this idea is supported by conversations on the subject with several elders, I find this somewhat inconsistent with what I have seen in village life. Dogs are domesticated, valued, well looked after and not usually allowed to run wild. When a truck approaches a dog and its owner on the road, the owner will invariably reach down and hold the dog's front legs, or pick up the dog altogether, to keep it from being run over. As you will see, each of the following examples reflect an attitude which considers dogs as a little dumb.

(050) "The dog is not clever in searching out other animals, it only knows its brothers' houses."

It is said that a dog only knows how to find the burrows or lairs of its "family", and that this is nothing great. Any animal can find its way home. When a dog is commanded to hunt, it simply takes its master to its "brothers' house". The above proverb is used when someone is bragging about doing something that is considered commonplace.

Interestingly, the Ntumu tribesmen do not see the ability of an animal to be trained and obey humans as a sign of its intelligence. Quite the contrary. Because of its independence they attribute greater intelligence to the cat than to the dog. Surprisingly they see the tortoise as having the greatest intelligence of all.

The Ntumu do not appear to keep pets and from what I have observed, the tribesmen keep dogs for three basic reasons: to protect personal property as watch dogs, to assist hunters in the procurement of fresh meat as hunting dogs and to be occasionally cooked as a meat source themselves. The first two purposes are by far the most common. Dog and groundnut stew is not a daily meal and dog-meat is not a basic commodity found in the market-place. As far as I know, no one raises dogs as meat on the paw.

I am often invited to share a bowl of stew in the villages I visit. Usually I am unable to recognize the meat by taste. I have discovered that whereas it may be culturally acceptable to ask the host what kind of meat is in the stew, it is not polite to ask where it came from. Because of this, I have not been able to determine if the few dog-meat stews I have had were the result of a dog being run over by a vehicle or intentional butchering.

The Ntumu tribesmen are aware that the whitemen have their own personal food aversions and cultural culinary taboos. The Christian missionaries they have met are very didactic on the subject of what is fit to eat. This is one of the religious cultural impositions you told me about. Consequently the Ntumu are a bit self-conscious about their traditional foods and refrain from eating certain things when strangers are around. It has taken my hosts a few months to stop identifying me with other whitemen who have condemned the kinds of food they eat. The fact that now I am openly offered dishes which would nauseate one of these missionaries on purely doctrinal grounds is a comforting demonstration of their acceptance of me.

I do not have strong objections to what I am offered to eat and the Ntumu respect the fact that I may graciously decline to accept it. They appreciate the open-mindedness which allows me to try almost anything and understand that I may prefer to eat some things rather than others because of taste. As an anthropologist, I cannot make those kinds of value judgements which would condemn or restrict what others eat. Personally, as a Baha'i, I have only one food taboo, not to eat game if it is found dead in a trap or net. This is not dogmatic (pardon the pun), but rather common sense with regard to eating things which may have been dead for a long time and may have become putrid. I do not have the Islamic notion of *halal* meat or the Judaic standard of *kosher*.

A LEAF OF HONEY

To me the "cleanliness" of food is not spiritually intuitive or mystically intrinsic but rather a matter of simple hygiene. Didn't Christ say, somewhere in Matthew, that "it isn't what goes into the mouth that defiles a man but what comes out of the mouth".

Back on the subject of dogs, in reference to asking for things and getting a favourable response, the following analogous proverb prescribes:

(051) "One never calls a dog with a stick in his hand."

Here the message is pan-cultural: kindness and a soft approach are the most effective ways to persuade someone. This Ntumu saying demonstrates the least effective way. Threatening someone is the worst way to get someone to do something for you. The old Italian proverb is the one we often hear in Europe and America: "Honey catches more flies than vinegar."

Appeasement is illustrated in the following proverb in which the dog figures:

(052) "If you take a bone out of a dog's mouth replace it with a cassava."

When something is taken away or lost in life, replacing it with something else will help to lessen the loss. A stick of cassava is similar in size, shape and colour to a bone.

In the following, the dog and several other domesticated animals are cast as analogous members of an Ntumu village:

(053) "Two chickens were fighting and the rooster, the dog and the goat were asked to separate them. But they all refused because they knew that if two members of the same village are fighting, their problem won't last long."

Although rather long for an Ntumu proverb, this clearly states what I have mentioned before. When arguments arise, they are short-lived and followed by apparently complete reconciliation.

Sincerely yours, Joseph

33

FRIENDSHIP AND THE GORILLA FIST

Riding the motorcycle over long distances back and forth to Yaounde gave me time to think about the things that were happening to me. I recalled that in the beginning two basic objectives motivated my going to Africa: academic achievement and personal development. The academic objective was far more describable than my perceived need for personal growth. I knew that the opportunity of going to Africa would allow me to utilize and expand the observative, technical, analytical and descriptive skills I had thus far acquired, but more importantly, I felt that the practical experience of living and working in a rural environment would nurture the development of my character. I was old enough to see that the lack of diverse cultural interaction was cementing me in the morass of narrow-mindedness. Social inertia is difficult to overcome. Without intentionally breaking loose and broadening my experience, I could easily fall victim to the routine of a comfortable and affluent American life-style and eventually become socially unable to understand the needs and the potential of our emerging planet-nation.

In a very practical way I had chosen to become a kind of pioneer. Mankind was the last great unexplored frontier. To search for that frontier, my family and I had decided to move to a new land and settle. I hoped that, in the process we would have the opportunity to explore a new part of the social world and break new ground in contacting new peoples. In the same spirit that urged my forefathers to move west in a covered wagon in search of fertile farmland in California, my family and I journeyed through equatorial Africa on a motorcycle in search of people and a share of the wealth of human culture. Pioneering was a good word for what we were doing. There were hardships, discomforts and unfamiliar ground to cross, but there were also the benefits of new experiences, discoveries and understanding. I felt it had been well worth the effort.

Distance on the back of the Yamaha also gave me time to think about other things. Ever since the *Prefet* asked me what kind of book I wanted to write I found myself asking the same question and looking around in my mind for the answer. First of all I had an academic obligation to write about the Ntumu people. Anthropological research would be a waste of time if I didn't make any cultural information I collected available to others. One of the ethical and intellectual duties of research and discovery is to pass it on. More importantly, living in Europe, South America and now Africa, outside of the cultural environment of my native United States had taught me an uncomfortable fact about the present condition of us human beings: we are basically a race of mutually ignorant peoples. The book would have to be written in such a way to help overcome this.

An important factor to consider was who could benefit from such a book. There is a large world outside of academia, and anthropologists don't have a patent or copyright on cultural matters. Anyone who seriously works in the areas of social and economic development is interested in cultural beliefs and values. In fact, cultural awareness is vital to the success of any international or intercultural project. The book could be aimed at the modern day pioneers. Those who initiate development, prepare new ground, and open up new means of cultural exchange are as much pioneers as the settlers who moved west across America in the eighteenth and nineteenth centuries.

The potential worth of a book about the interaction of two cultures would be to show the effect that a new culture has on the person. To do this, it would have to be partially autobiographical. Culture would be the major theme: the context of the culture to its environment and a meaningful description of the beliefs and practices of a tribe of people. Ethnographically this would be valuable because in all likelihood the Ntumu as a people would not exist inside two generations. Urbanization and post-colonial social pressures had already started to take their toll. There was already a tendency of the young tribesmen to move to the capital in search of work. Once there, they rarely came back.

175

A LEAF OF HONEY

The book would have to be a story and cover a time span so that the readers' attention could be kept. It would have to be a story about the people themselves, of individual characters and not just pages filled with sweeping cultural generalizations. The proverbs would be the focus and pivotal point of the book. It would be important to reveal the context, setting and the use of the proverbs I collected. I wanted to convey to the reader a sense of the flavour of the Ntumu culture so that others could see what it was like to live in the village. This would mean describing the tribal activities and including a smattering of Ntumu words and expressions. Above all, I would have to convey the fact that whatever I discovered about the Ntumu culture would always just be a drop in the ocean of what was really there.

I knew that I was not a good or natural writer. I had no false modesty about my ability. Words did not flow from my pen like magic. Writing was a struggle. Thought flows faster than words and words link faster than one can write. I didn't believe that a book would miraculously appear before my eyes if I wished hard enough. I wasn't surprised that when I sat down to write occasionally, all of a sudden, nothing would happen. It was a process of trying to articulate vague understandings in the mind.

Writing was a means of clarifying things and bringing them up from a fuzzy intuitive level. The mind was vast enough that it could hold contradictory concepts. The written word was not so vast. Writing separated the gold from the dross and the valid from the unsubstantiated.

Another thing to remember was that books tend to outlive their authors who cannot always be there to explain them. They end up as independent of the personality and understanding of the author. The methodology of my research would be as important as the content. I decided that the most efficient way would be to include the letters and reports I had sent to my supervisor as a chronicle of the kind of work I was doing.

Of course, I would have to change some of the names of the people to protect the peace of mind of both the innocent and guilty, not to mention the continued physical well-being of the author.

These random thoughts filled the time. With experience, riding the motorcycle became a reflex and the bends and ruts in the road were approached almost instinctively. However since the night when my family and I were nearly run over by a military convoy, I had become somewhat paranoid about trucks, especially logging

176

trucks. I was beginning to suspect that the first basic rule in the tacit Cameroonian code of driving was

"Mass makes might".

Anything having a greater mass should be treated with a healthy deference. Any second rule regarding questions of vehicle right of way was simply: "Reread the first rule".

Logging trucks had the unconditional right of way by virtue of their intimidating size and weight. I discovered this rule on the way home from Yaounde with my Research Permit.

I was zooming down hill at the Yamaha's terminal velocity. The wind was rushing round my helmet and the scream of the over-taxed engine drowned out all other sounds. I had my head down to reduce the wind drag with a calculated hope that I would somehow develop enough inertia to make it to the top of the next hill without having to down-shift into second gear. It was sort of a game I played. In this crouched position I happened to glance in the sideview mirror. The road behind me had disappeared. I shook my head and looked again. All I could see was a shimmering metallic wall that shouldn't be there. For a second I couldn't make out what it was. But just when I was about to look over my shoulder and see where the road had gone, a deafening blast from an air-horn reached out and smacked me in the back of the helmet. I almost jumped off the bike from fright. I turned around and looked. A few feet behind me, breathing down my neck, was a huge chrome grill and bumper followed by about forty tons of truck and African hardwood. A logging truck. It was thundering along with no intention of slowing down. Apparently the driver the driver played the same sort of games and had the same hopes for topping the next hill as I did. He gave me a few more blasts on the horn to remind me he was serious. Not interested in slowing down one bit, the driver finally succeeded in pushing me off the road.

I had always wondered what "soft shoulder" meant. I had this thought as I left the asphalt, the sand grabbed my wheels. The bike came to rest before I did. I flew over the handlebars and fell badly, mostly on my head. I was thankful I was wearing a real helmet instead of the Italian salad bowl. The motorcycle ended up on its side with a long scratch and dent on the fuel tank. My sideview mirror was smashed. The damage wasn't much and I wasn't injured, but what pain I did feel was numbed by indignation and anger. I was livid. I got back on the bike with vengeful determination and continued along the road just daring the logging truck to show itself. According to my odometer it took me twenty kilometres to catch up with it. The driver had pulled off the road just outside the town of Mbalmayo and parked beside a hut which had been converted into a bar. The owner had added an extension which served as a dance floor. The scratchy notes of an old Jim Reeves record could be heard as I stopped beside the door. Inside were several tables with checked tablecloths, the kind you see in restaurants. There was only one customer in the bar. I had cooled down a bit by that time and I greeted the proprietor and drew up a stool at a table in front of the driver. He had a young lady sitting on one knee who was refilling his glass with beer. After unsuccessfully trying what I knew of Ntumu and French, I found that he would respond in Pidgin to my English.

"Look at my face. Do you know me?" I asked.

"No," he said in a suspicious way.

"You are mistaken! I say you know me," I insisted.

"I say I no know you," he said, giving the girl a squeeze.

"You must know me!" I wasn't going to go away.

"Why you say I know you?" he asked.

"Because you cannot hate me unless you know me," I said cryptically. The man frowned at me and whispered something to the girl who then got off his lap and left the room.

"Hate you?" he asked carefully.

"It is obvious you hate me," I assured him.

"I no hate you," he stated calmly.

"I know for certain that you hate me," I said. He turned to the barman who shrugged his shoulders.

"I no hate you. Why you say I hate you?"

"Aha! Because it is impossible for you to want to kill me unless you hate me first," I said calmly. I could see that he was trying to decide if I were trying to provoke a fight or just plain crazy. I was keeping him from his rendezvous with the young lady in the back and he was becoming annoyed.

"Na me, I no di hate you, and I no di know you. Na what kinda palaba dis?" he asked in a bewildered way.

I leaned forward and said quietly: "If you don't hate me or know me, then why in the hell did you try to kill me back there on the road?"

"Pardon?"

"You ran me off the road with your truck." I pointed outside. "I was the one on the motorcycle." There was a moment of silence and then he raised his eyebrows and began to laugh. Now he knew what I was talking about.

"Oh, na dat you?" he asked with a malicious smirk.

"Yes, it was me," I replied dead serious. There was a long silence.

"Na look dis, I say sorry trouble fo you," he said at last and offered me his hand in friendship.

"No. I will not take your hand or accept your words. You are still laughing and do not see that I am serious. You do not understand how I feel," I said adamantly.

"Please, accept my ap-o-lo-gy." He ordered a beer for me from the barman. I remained silent. The proprietor came and opened the bottle and placed it in front of me. I folded my arms defiantly.

"I refuse it," I announced, knowing full well that it was highly insulting to refuse a gift.

"Why you refuse my gift?" he asked.

"I don't drink beer," I said.

"You no drink beer?" he asked in amazement. I could hear him saying to himself "Maybe he is crazy."

I saw a bottle on the shelf of a foul-tasting pineapple flavoured soft drink called *ananas* which no one liked. I ordered a bottle and the barman placed it in front of him.

"Drink this, this is *my* gift to you," I challenged him.

"I no drink *ananas,* it gives worms and tastes like sick," he said and then spat on the floor to emphasize his point.

"Nevertheless, it is my gift to you. Do you refuse my gift?" I asked, daring him to refuse it. Impasse, the two bottles faced each other like chess pieces in stalemate on the checked cloth.

"There is only one thing left to do," I said. "Stand up and come over here if you want me to solve the problem for you." The driver stood up, squared his shoulders and walked around the table. He was taller than I thought and he was ready for a fight. I held out my hand to stop him and with a mischievous grin I hugged him around the chest the way two tribesmen do to make peace.

The driver was very surprised. I moved to where he had been sitting and said: "Now sit down in my place. I will be the big bad truck driver and you will be the almost dead motorcycle rider for a while. Now you will see how I feel." We both sat down in the opposite positions we were before. The driver laughed as we now drank, he had his beer and I sipped the *ananas.* He seemed content but he was right, it did taste like vomit. We made friends and laughed and talked about many things. The driver said his home village was near here and that several years ago he had gone to the city of Douala and learned to be a driver. That is where he learned his Pidgin English. Now he was back driving over the roads he used to walk beside. Instead of getting out of the way of passing trucks, other people now got out of his way. He proudly confessed that once he had lost a rear wheel on the logging trailer and hadn't noticed. He had driven quite a distance before he had stopped to see where all the sparks came from. The axle had plowed a furrow in the asphalt for seven kilometres. The wheel had ended up crashing into the hut of some villager who locked it up and held it for ransom.

I was about to continue on my way to Ebolowa when I jokingly asked him to promise me that he would not try and kill me again. He became serious and agreed only on the condition that I stay and have something to eat with him to seal this verbal contract. I sat down again and recognized this as the custom the Ntumu called *avuzo'o*. The man was not just being polite. What he was offering was tantamount to becoming blood-brothers. More than that even, he was offering that our children and their children would be blood-brothers. I took his offer seriously. He gestured to the owner of the bar and asked what there was to eat. The owner said something I didn't understand.

"It's not *zo'o* antelope, is it?" I asked. *Zo'o* was the traditional meat used to seal an *avuzo'o* pact.

"No," he said. "Is stew." That is all he would say. Before it arrived the driver asked me if I were going to refuse it like the beer. I said I couldn't refuse a friend who had just offered me *avuzo'o* and promised not to try to kill me again. The barman laid out two plates and brought a covered dish with our dinner in it. The driver paused before he lifted the lid.

"Sure you no refuse?" he asked with a strange smile trying to stifle a giggle. "Na dis one eh no whiteman chop," He said. "This one is not whitemen food".

"A deal is a deal," I said. "Whatever it is, we will eat it as if it was *zo'o.*" He lifted the lid. In the bowl was the cooked hand of what I feared and then hoped was a gorilla. The driver reached in the bowl, plucked off a finger and offered it to me ceremoniously. I knew that all would be lost if I hesitated. I accepted the offered portion and we ate as brothers.

A LEAF OF HONEY

"*Avuzo'o*," I said, trying not to think about what I was eating.
"Na so we deh," he replied. "That is the way we are."

I saw him on the road many times after that and we ate better things together. We remained good friends and, true to his word, he never once tried to kill me again.

34

DEAD LIZARDS, SUCCESSION AND ACQUIESCENCE

Dear Dr Kilngott,

As personae, reptiles have an important role in Ntumu proverbs. The Ntumu rainforest environment abounds in many reptilian species and some of these have invaded the tribesmen's folklore. The most predominant of these are the lizards.

Judging from my conversations with both the young men and the elders of the village, lizards are a complex phenomenon in Ntumu culture. At certain times and under certain conditions they are feared, avoided and even taboo to eat, while at other times, they are sought after, trapped and consumed. This shifting condition is especially true of one lizard in particular. The *nka'a* is a large lacertian reptile and the subject of several ominous proverbs:

> (054) "A dead *nka'a*, taking it to the village is bad, leaving it in the forest is also bad."

Here, the knowledge of another Ntumu saying is required to understand the analogy and the purpose underlying the dilemmic situation in the proverb:

> (055) "If you find a dead *nka'a* in the forest and you don't know what killed it, then it is a sign that something bad will happen to you."

The tacit "not knowing what killed the lizard" is implied and understood in the first proverb and refers to the situation where an *nka'a* is not found in a snare or trap but dead of unknown causes. To the Ntumu, this occurrence is a bad omen. When this proverb was explained to me, the "something bad" was described as synonymous with the death of a relative. The inferred meaning of the proverb is that you cannot nullify the bad omen of finding a dead *nka'a* in the forest by taking it to the village as if you had trapped it. An omen is immutable. In general, the proverb states: "That which is, is". Besides the *nka'a,* another lizard, the *ebumakukwing,* a smaller lizard but with a longer name, and the *kwe si* ground-dwelling rat are also considered bad omens if similarly found.

In proverbs which describe someone who cunningly stirs up sedition and then effectively "plays possum", the *nka'a* lizard again appears:

(056) "Hiding like an *nka'a.*"

This is an attributed character trait of the *nka'a* because of its behaviour in nature. To escape a predator, the *nka'a* will first move quickly in a noisy and active show of fear and flight from danger and then stop still and wait, lying in the undergrowth. The lizard's survival strategy is effective in avoiding becoming the prey of animals which could easily outrun it. The natural camouflage of its green skin and the lack of eye-attracting movement helps it to survive. The predator pursues the *nka'a* in the direction of the initial movement and usually by-passes the unnoticed lizard. The analogy here compares the *nka'a* tactics, to the behaviour of someone who slyly remains silent to avoid involvement or accusation. The proverb especially refers to the kind of person who brings up a problem in the council of elders and then withdraws from the conversation and sits silently, allowing others to point the accusing fingers of guilt around the hut. Subsequently others have to defend the accusation.

Succession of responsibility is the subject of several proverbs. In the following, two lizards figure, *jiugo* chameleon and the above-mentioned smaller lizard:

(057) "If *jiugo* dies, *ebumakukwing* takes over the load."

Another proverb conveying the same message of succession but by another means, analogizes:

(058) "If the load falls from the head, it falls on the shoulders."

A LEAF OF HONEY

These two proverbs illustrate the Ntumu ideal of the necessary succession of authority and the personal acquiescence to the greatness of the past. Succession of responsibility, namely the chieftaincy of the tribe or the family leadership, is usually passed from father to eldest surviving son and is seen as passing from greater to lesser and not from greater to potentially equal. The two proverbs on this subject demonstrate this by presenting examples which show a load passing from larger to smaller and from higher to lower. The analogies of lesser size and height are employed intentionally to maintain that although the mantle of leadership has passed to another, that new leader will never equal the rank and achievements of the previous leader.

Many other reptiles populate Ntumu proverbs but they will not be included here. There is one reptile, however, I would like to tell you about which I thought was mythical until quite recently. No, I have not found the legendary brontosaurus of the Congo. I have finally come across the *twi* snake, which several of my Ntumu hosts have been telling me about for months. They informed me that the *twi* is black and has two white heads, one on either end of its body. To say the least I was incredulous at such a story. They further described this snake as having eyes and a mouth at both ends and being able to move in either direction, forward and backward or backward and forward. With two heads it is hard to tell. They even told me a proverb about indecision and greed in which featured the two-headed snake:

(059) "The *twi* slept hungry because of its two heads."

I asked them many questions about the *twi* because, frankly, I didn't believe such a snake could exist. I knew that "two-headed snakes" occasionally occur in nature. As a child, I remember visiting a glass walled "snake-house" at a zoo and seeing a two-headed snake. It was born with the abnormality of having a second head growing out of the side of the first. At first I thought that this was the explanation for the *twi* snake. The Ntumu tribesmen, however, told me that they had never heard of a snake with two heads on one end and assured me that the *twi* had one head on each end. They were able to draw a picture of the snake and referred to it as a commonplace and distinct species. I told my Ntumu friends that a species of snake could not exist which had a head at either end of its body. Mother Nature doesn't know that kind of joke. Further conversations revealed that it wasn't a single individual

184

freak which had been seen by them because several people claimed to have seen more than one at a time and over a period which exceeded the normal lifespan of a snake. For months the problem of the *twi* was left unresolved. Until last week.

As it turns out, the *twi* actually does exist. I was walking along with an Ntumu elder when he stopped me and pointed to something moving in the grass near the path. It was a snake. He told me it wasn't poisonous and after chasing it for awhile we caught it. He informed me that this was a *twi*. It did seem to have two heads. However, upon closer examination, it did not have two real heads but rather the end of its tail was blunt and marked almost exactly like its head. The tail-end of this snake had eye-like markings and a thin line of a mock mouth. The *twi* had probably evolved these features as a successful ruse against predators trying to attack them from behind.

Sincerely yours, Joseph

35

A MOTORCYCLE BUILT FOR FIVE

Lately we had been through one testing problem after another. But now it looked as if the last obstacle to our work had been lifted. With an optimism tempered by experience, we set out, yet again, towards Ma'an. This time we were in no hurry. We decided to wait until my wife and child could go by public transport and when there was a bush-taxi available, I would follow behind it on the motorcycle. After the hardships of the last trip, it was a good decision. It would be slower but more comfortable for them.

This time the trip was mercifully uneventful. When we arrived in Ma'an the first thing we did was to present a copy of my research permit to the *Commissaire*. He was pleasant but not overjoyed to see us again. He released the *push-push*, which was exactly where we had left it. It had been searched but it was a relief to find nothing was missing, especially my fieldnotes. As part of our baggage, the bush-taxi had transported a large drum of gasoline. I calculated that with the smaller drum we had left in the *push-push* there would be enough fuel for the motorcycle for an entire year.

There wasn't enough daylight left to continue on to Meyo-Ntem so the chief of Ma'an gave us a place to sleep for the night. It was the same hut that we were arrested in. In the evening many of the villagers came by to greet us. Everyone we met, including the resident *gendarmes*, were apologetic about our trouble. We were told that during the time I was shuttling between Ebolowa and Yaounde getting my research permit, the border skirmish had subsided and the military and the convoy of vehicles had returned to their camp. There had been no mention of the incident in the state-run national newspaper, and here in Ma'an the villagers had been told not to talk about the conflict. A few months later some Spanish-speaking Okak tribesmen from over the border told us that the Equatorial Guinean and the Cameroonian forces had shot up a village near Micomeseng.

Early in the morning we loaded up all our belongings on the *push-push* and set out very slowly on the final leg of our interrupted journey to Meyo-Ntem. As was always the case, word of mouth in the jungle travelled faster than our motorcycle and trailer. As loaded as we were, almost anything could move faster. By the time we arrived the entire village of Meyo-Ntem was back from the fields waiting for us. The villagers were dressed in their best clothes. The women wore matching cotton prints with the Cameroonian flag and a portrait of the Head of State on it. Bolts of cloth of this design were periodically distributed to villages across the country by the government. Everyone was lined up along the road and they greeted us with the syncopated clapping and song that usually greeted a visiting government official. Very ceremoniously I introduced my wife and daughter to each member of the village in turn as we walked down the line. I taught Fanny the appropriate manner of greeting: a handshake for the men and a clasp of the wrists with the women. I had told the villagers a lot about my family and from the way that they were received I could tell they would be welcome. After the struggle of getting here it was gratifying to be wanted. The chief of Meyo-Ntem offered us a hut next door to my friend Sylvain until we could move to the hut on the island in the river.

For the next few days we settled into a new life. We unpacked our few household items and Fanny set about nest building and turned the cramped one room hut into a home. The women took Fanny under their wings and showed her where to find drinking water and firewood for cooking. They flat-plaited Fanny's hair the Ntumu way and fitted a basket with shoulder straps for her to carry her loads from the fields. Within days my wife was transformed, she looked entirely different and blended well into the sisterhood of the village.

Anisa made friends with the neighbouring huts' children and wandered from hearth to hearth around the village during the entire day. She had a dozen mothers and scores of brothers and sisters. For the first few days Anisa was always surrounded by children who wanted to touch her straight hair and fair skin. Some of them were convinced that it was some kind of white paint and would try to rub it off to reveal her true colour underneath.

Anisa learned to play the Ntumu children's games and especially loved the clapping dance. It was a game which only the girls played. Two girls would face each other and begin a short dance in which the fall of the feet corresponds with a complex clapping beat of the hands. One girl would lead and try to trick the other. With every fourth clap the leader would raise either of her legs. The challenger must be able to anticipate her rhythm and raise the same leg. After four rounds, the leadership is won and a new challenge begins. Anisa could be found playing this between the huts all day and well into the evening. In the usual silence of the village during the day the little girls' rhythmic clapping became a reassuring background noise indicating that Anisa was all right.

Another game was called *jinji'i* or "catching the goat". The girls sometimes allowed the boys to play this one. A group of children would hold hands in a large circle and sing a song which imitated the bleating of a goat: "*Maa maa ma, zudabianuzu*". It was a game of tag in which two of the children, one on the inside of the circle and one on the outside, would take turns being the goat and being chased. The object of the game was for one child to get inside the circle and catch the goat. It was the job of the children holding hands to try to keep her from passing through. As they sang they would hold their hands high in the air offering entrance and then lower them quickly if she tried to get in. The game was full of feigning movements and tricks to pass under their hands and catch the goat inside the ring.

A few days after we arrived I took my wife to see the hut I had built for her. We strolled the two kilometres to the riverbank opposite the island to see our new home. I was very happy. It was a gift I had worked hard building. We held hands and chatted as we went, the way good friends do. We had been married four years now and had travelled to five continents during that time. We now lived in a place that was very different from her native South America. She had changed dramatically since we got married in her home town of Bucaramanga. I loved her and was very proud of her progress and her ability to adapt. In the beginning we spoke only Spanish together but now that she had learned English, we spoke about half the time in her language and the other half in mine. Fanny had a natural facility for learning languages. While she was staying in Ebolowa, she had been learning French and now she was beginning Ntumu. She was on her third new language in as many years. Not many people could do that. And to think that when I first met her in Colombia she spoke no English at all.

Remembering back, it had been heartwarming to watch her attempts to learn my language. In the beginning she tried so hard. Every new word was an achievement she wanted to share with me. Shortly after we moved from Colombia to California I remember coming home from the university one evening and being met at the door with an excited smile. She couldn't wait to show me what she had learned that day in English.

"You'll wonder where the yellow went when you brush your teeth with Pepsodent," she pronounced proudly. American television is the best and worst educator. The excitement of the morning game shows and the melodrama of soap operas in the afternoon were her daytime language teachers. In the evenings she went to classes at a nearby high school to try to continue the education she had to forego as a child in Colombia. We had just had Anisa and there were several other Spanish-speaking mothers in the class studying English as a second language. She loved it. At the age of twenty Fanny was finally going back to school after eight long years. Before we were married she told me the story of how her education had come to an abrupt end. It was a day she had never forgotten.

The morning she was to begin secondary school, she had got up early and eagerly dressed in her school clothes ready to go off to her first day. But when she went into the old kitchen for the usual breakfast of *arepas* and *caldo*, her mother told her what she had been putting off telling her for some time. There was no money for another year of school. There was no other way to say it. Her mother had tried to find another way, less cruel, but there wasn't any. Fanny was heartbroken. She loved school and studied hard. She, like everyone else in Colombia, knew that education was the one key to breaking out of the endless circle of poverty. One educated child could find a good job and support the entire family. Her mother said that Fanny had to stay home and work in the house and help the family earn enough money so that they could eat. Fanny had cried bitterly, not only from the immediate disappointment, but from the realization that at the age of twelve her formal education was finished. There was so much more to learn, but the realities of being female and poor in a social system of *machismo* and *oligarquia* had caught up with her. These were realities that would continue long after her crying stopped and resignation set in. She knew she was trapped. She went back to the corner of the bedroom she shared with three sisters and a baby brother and took off the school clothes she had put on with such anticipation. She folded them neatly and put them away. Someday she might be able to wear them again. Fanny put on an old dress and went back to the kitchen. Instead of school books, her mother handed her an apron and helped her to tie it in the back the way she had done a hundred times before. This time, however, the little girl knew it was for real. It was forever. Fanny picked up a broom and began her life of work in the home, the endless chores and the hopeless scrimping that were her responsibility to the family's survival.

Although in marrying me Fanny had escaped that, I was conscious that she still felt that responsibility.

At the riverbank, my wife silently stood for a long minute looking across the water at the raffia and bamboo structure I had been referring to as "our home" for so long. It looked smaller and less glorious now that I had been away from it for a while.

"Is that it?" She said. It was the kind of question which answered itself and said a lot more than three words. I felt a little disappointed that she was not as excited as I would have liked. But, after all, she had given up a real house in California and suffered greatly to get here. She deserved to feel a little let down. Fanny turned to me and hugged me and whispered "Thank you. It looks very nice, dear." In her embrace I new that this lady was made of better stuff than I.

As it turned out, she never even set foot on the island. A few weeks after we arrived in Meyo-Ntem, just before we had planned to move, the *Secretaire du Commissaire* drove up to our temporary hut and informed us that the *Commissaire* had decreed that we could not live on the island. He said that it was too close to the border with Equatorial Guinea and that this was for our own safety. The *Secretaire* informed me that the *Commissaire* was the head of police and the senior appointee of the Cameroonian government in the *District de Ma'an* and it was his responsibility to look after foreigners living in the district. His injunction was final. With that he drove away.

190

A LEAF OF HONEY

Although there was a crowd assembled the *Secretaire* had not even greeted the chief or any of the other villagers. Not being an Ntumu he had little regard for the tribal hierarchy and its authority. It was impossible to know if this constraint on where we could live was instigated by him in the name of the *Commissaire* or actually came from his superior. Because of this *Secretaire*, the district administration was aloof and oppressive. Knowing his reputation, I had made a point of giving the *Secretaire* a wide berth. The restriction he was now imposing was not a good sign. He seemed to want to show me he had clout and although he couldn't block my cultural investigations within the Ebolowa-Ambam-Ma'an triangle in the *Departement du Ntem,* he was able however to restrict where I could live. I am sure he was annoyed that I was back under his feet. I suspect that he thought he had seen the last of me when we were dispatched with the military commander. The reason behind this prohibition was obviously other than the one stated and this troubled me. This was a warning. The border may have been only forty kilometres from the hut, but it wasn't the neighbours to the south that I had to look out for, it was him.

The *Secretaire* here in Ma'an completely lacked the polish and ethics of his counter-part in Ebolowa. This one was someone you would cross the street to avoid. I had met the *Commissaire* of the district several times while Robert was translating for me and had been treated well by him, but the arrogance of his underling was impenetrable. The *Secretaire* was an unusually tall and massive man who sported a large and ostentatious moustache. I couldn't help but be reminded of Eric Campbell, that villainous character in early Charlie Chaplin films. Sometimes first impressions endure. Unfortunately for us, he would later prove to be quite dastardly himself.

I was extremely disappointed that after all the hard work building a hut for my wife we wouldn't be able to live in it. The temporary hut the chief of Meyo-Ntem had offered us in the village became the only place left for us to stay. It was small and cramped with the three of us and our belongings, but we settled in and began a daily routine of getting up before dawn, gathering firewood, carrying water, bathing, eating and collecting proverbs.

Not living in a surplus society, we saw that it would be best if we grew some of our own food to eat. The chief gave us a little plot of land to grow our vegetables on. We planted some of the seeds we had brought with us from America alongside Ntumu staples like

191

manioc roots and yams. Later when they sprouted and grew the tribesmen were just as repulsed by our vegetables as we were by some of theirs. Planting and tending the plot was hard work. The days had become very hot and it rained less now. The planting season meant that the weeds and undergrowth had to be cleared and burnt. The ashes were spread over the ground and hoed in as fertilizer. The days were going by quickly. I continued my research and made periodic trips to villages around Meyo-Ntem.

One day I was called to the office of the *Secretaire* and informed that Fanny, Anisa and I would have to move from Meyo-Ntem to a hut in Ma'an. This further restriction was justified again by the same excuse that it was for our own safety. "Safe from whom?" I asked myself. Somehow the closer I lived to the *Secretaire* the less safe I felt. When the villagers of Meyo-Ntem learned of this the men were sympathetic and the women cried openly. We had been living in the village for several months and we had become part of the activities of the village. They insisted that they each carry one of our belongings on their heads all the way to Ma'an. This was a brave act. It was clearly a passive protest against the forced move. The long silent line of villagers marched into Ma'an under the observation of the *Secretaire*. In a region where his command was law, this was an incredible act of condemnation and dissension.

The room which had been commandeered for our use was part of an old hut that had fallen into disrepair. We weren't given the main hut but an annex around the back. It had one window and a door that would not lock. Somehow we never felt the human warmth in Ma'an that we enjoyed in Meyo-Ntem. The people were somewhat afraid to associate with us under the noses of the *Secretaire*, the police and *gendarmes*. Nevertheless, after a few weeks we made new friends and were able to fix the places in the thatch roof that leaked the most and build a clay stove and oven just outside the door under the overhang of the roof. To tend our fields and continue my anthropological work, we had to walk or ride almost daily to Meyo-Ntem.

Months passed, and in April we received an invitation to come to a party at the Elakas' house in Ebolowa. It was going to be a potluck. It was about time we took a break. Fanny and I had very little we could bring to a potluck dinner. Food was scarce, especially the kind that other people would eat. About a week before we had bought a pair of medium-sized crocodiles from one of the local snare trappers. We had eaten one already but still had one tied to the leg of the bed with its mouth wired shut. One crocodile that size didn't seem enough to take to a potluck so we negotiated to buy a goat from the chief. The chief of Ma'an owned all the goats that roamed the village. After agreeing on a price he pointed one out and all the children of the village helped in capturing it. It was great fun to watch. The whole village took part. They circled round it and a few of them chased it until it was cornered. I could see where the game Anisa played with them originated.

On the day we wanted to leave there was predictably no public transport so we loaded up the Yamaha for the long trek to the land of hot running water and plenteous food. We tied the crocodile to the carrying rack at the back and the goat over the fuel tank in the front. Fanny, Anisa and I sandwiched ourselves between them. We looked strange as we rode through the villages on the way. I will never forget the look on the Elakas' faces as we rolled up to their front door with our contribution to the potluck. We grilled the crocodile and stewed the goat. The potluck was a great success and about thirty people of all colours and nationalities came. Some of the newer Peace Corps Volunteers who weren't as used to bush-meat as we were tried the strong-flavoured crocodile as a novelty but didn't eat much. As one young lady politely commented: "A little croc' goes a long way."

36

CHICKENS, CHILDREN AND CLANS

Dear Dr Kilngott,

Of the proverbs which feature birds, those with chicken personae are the most numerous. It is an odd coincidence that the Ntumu word for chicken is *kup*, pronounced "coop" as in "chicken coop". The *kup* occupies a special place in Ntumu culture and, aside from the duck, it is the only bird which the Ntumu have domesticated. By domesticated I mean animals which are accustomed to living with the Ntumu tribesmen and which are dependent upon the village for food and safety. Chicken meat is served on special occasions and to special people. What happens to all the ducks I have not yet determined. I have so far never seen anyone eating a duck.

Among the tribesmen, the gift of a chicken is a sign of high regard. And to a lesser degree, the gift of a chicken's egg is also a sign of respect and friendship. It is customary to give a chicken to a friend or family member upon his return from a long trip. It is one of the presents given to a suitor from the family of the maiden he has come to ask the hand of.

Not only among the Ntumu, but among many West African tribes, the presentation of a chicken is accompanied with an almost ritualistic exchange of action. When a guest arrives, the head of the family will send the children out to capture a specific chicken. He describes the fowl in detail in "stage whispers". The guest is supposed to hear what is being said. He can see the children running about in the yard, but the guest sits and continues with whatever he is doing and gives no sign that he knows what is happening. Soon the children succeed in running down the particular hen or rooster and binding its feet together. The chicken is then presented by the host to the guest for inspection. The guest receives the chicken with the two hands of gratitude and feigned surprise. At this point it is the recipient's duty to scrutinize the bound bird, commenting on its size, weight and health. In the end the recipient compliments his host on his generosity and on having raised such a fine and fat bird. The guest is then asked if he would like to have it cooked there and then or if he would like to take it back to his own village. The bigger the bird, the greater the sign of respect.

The value of an individual chicken is high within the Ntumu tribal economy. Although in monetary terms a four-pound chicken costs a little over four dollars, in barter value, it is worth as much as the material and labour of replacing an entire roof of a hut. This is often about a week's work. The following proverb deals with the gift of a chicken:

(060) "One never eats a spoilt chicken when he has a friend."

This, plus the next proverb, is the Ntumu equivalent of "a bird in the hand is worth two in the bush". The intimated message here is that the promise of a chicken is a sure thing: it is domesticated and therefore easily caught; whereas the promise of an *okbwa*, a wild partridge-like fowl sometimes called a "bush hen", is not so certain:

(061) "One never promises an *okbwa* to one's mother-in-law."

As has been shown in another proverb, the Ntumu believe that good relations are to be maintained with one's mother-in-law at all counts. The following proverbs, in which chickens figure, all concern the rearing of children:

(062) "When the rooster dies, the eggs get rotten."

Here, in analogous terms, the lack of parental guidance is shown to lead to poorly-disciplined children. "Spare the rod and spoil the child". I think that my mother would subscribe to this proverb. When I was a toddler she used to point at me and whimsically proclaim, "Babies are born with their brains in their butts and every so often you have to drive it towards their heads".

When one child is punished sometimes other children seeing the punishment feel glad that it is not happening to them. The following two proverbs deal with this:

(063) "Hawk catches chicken, but *nguleyeyebe* is the one who is happy."

Nguleyeyebe is a small non-descript bird which is preyed upon by the hawk, as is the chicken. Similarly, when punishment is being doled out to one child, it is painful to those who are watching, especially if they know that their turn is coming:

(064) "When you cut up the chicken, antelope looks at you."

What is tacitly implied here is that the antelope knows that the same thing will happen to him.

This particular antelope, the *zo'o*, is the basis of a complex Ntumu social institution called *avuzo'o* which literally means "sons of the antelope". *Avuzo'o* is like an ancient treaty which links and joins certain *ayong*: "clans" together in eternal friendship. The elders of the village explained that many generations ago two adversaries from unrelated clans made a pact of friendship by hunting a *zo'o* antelope together and eating it. This act established an everlasting noncombatant relationship between their two clans and descendants which gave them certain rights and privileges. This special relationship also encouraged intermarriage. I have thus far been able to isolate almost thirty of these clans. The elders further explained that some of these clans were unable to establish *avuzo'o* bonds because they were too closely related by blood and such a uniting treaty would have resulted in "clan incest". Since then several of the other clans have entered into *avuzo'o* with each other. These allegiances are only binary, that is, between two clans. One clan maybe *avuzo'o* with more than one other clan, but the others need not be linked together. There is a reason for this. The Ntumu must marry outside of his own clan. Whereas *avuzo'o* may be a social device which maintains peace and unity, the absence of it tends to restrict families who may be related too closely from intermarrying.

When two strangers meet, one of the first things they do is determine their clan membership, to see if they are traditional adversaries, neutral or allies. If they discover that they are *avuzo'o* they become very happy. It is as if the two of them, themselves, had sat down to this treaty-meal centuries before. They regard each other as long lost friends. These are some of the Ntumu clans I have isolated:

azok	esatolo	yemvan
eba	ese	yemvang
esakoe	esebeng	yemveng
esakotan	yekombo	yengap
esala'ane	yekomto'o	yendjok
esambita	yemekak	yesok
esamengon	yemeyema'a	yevol
esamvak	yeminsen	
esangbak	yemvam	

These are like the clan-totems of the North American Indians and translate with names of animals and personal attributes such as sons of monkey, sharing, camping, gates, sins, rain, scars, beauty, kindness, etc. Because I was born outside of the Ntumu homeland I was without clan designation. This was clearly an impossible condition for someone who lived among them. Clan identity is vital. The elders set about to rectify this. Because I first lived in the upper village of Meyo-Ntem, I was adopted, without ceremony, as a member of the *eba* clan. However when I was forced to move to Ma'an, the people there insisted on referring to me as a member of the *esambita* clan. The *eba* are not *avuzo'o* with the *esambita*. Subsequently a rivalry has developed over my clan affiliation which has resulted in a new proverb. I have heard this used several times:

(065) "If there were no Meyo-Ntem, Ma'an would not have known Joseph."

I am flattered, but I suspect that this saying is doomed to be short-lived and will vanish from the Ntumu folklore and be forgotten as soon as my year is finished and I leave.

Sincerely yours, Joseph

37

THE PYGMY AND THE MAGIC
WATERFALL

It was Anisa's third birthday. We wanted to give her something special but there was no place to buy her a birthday gift. I sharpened my machete and knife and carved a high-backed chair for her from logs of a smooth-grained wood called *iroko*. Fanny helped weave the seat out of an extra hammock rope we had. In the end it looked like a proper chair.

We bought a tough old rooster in the market for an exorbitant price and cooked it for Anisa. Compared to her last birthday, it was a pretty pathetic meal but it was special because every ounce of it was a true sacrifice. We tried to dress up the hut as best we could but there is only so much you can do with a dirt floor and walls. Before we sat down to eat, however, Fanny and I said grace for the first time in a long time and then we sang *Happy Birthday* to Anisa. She was very happy as she sat proudly in her own little chair and ate her birthday dinner. The clay stove couldn't bake a cake so, as a real treat Fanny made some drop doughnut pastries fried in the last of the cooking oil.

It was the cocoa harvesting season around Ma'an. The cocoa trees behind our hut were laden with ripening pods which we had watched change from green to purple to golden yellow. The Ntumu did not have the technology to turn cocoa into chocolate. They just harvested the pods and sold the dried cocoa beans to the Greek buyers. This process involved splitting open each pod and scooping out the beans by hand. There were about fifty beans to a pod and each bean was surrounded by a soft white fruity sheath. The sheath was removed by allowing the beans to ferment in special wooden containers under the overhangs behind their huts.

A LEAF OF HONEY

After a few days in these vats the white sticky sheath disintegrated and only the brown bean remained. It was the bean that the Greeks would buy, but only if they were dried enough not to rot in transport. While some large plantations around Ebolowa could afford to build firewood heated driers, in Ntumuland the sun was the only economical way to dry the beans. The cocoa beans were spread onto large woven drying trays made of raffia. These had retractable roofs on bamboo rails which could be slid over the drying platform in a hurry if it started to rain. It was strange to think that a plant native to Central America and cultivated by the Aztecs could dominate the lifestyle of a village of Ntumu tribesmen up a river in far-off Cameroon.

It was hard to imagine how the confectionery gnomes of Switzerland processed these less than aromatic dried cocoa beans into the chocolate products we were used to seeing in candy stores in America. Being born a chocoholic and cut off from my normal daily fix, I tried in desperation to make chocolate a couple of times over the fire in our hut. It was more difficult than Iímagined. I first took some fermented and sun-dried cocoa beans, roasted them and then ground up enough to fill a small pan. It made a dark brown sticky powder that looked a lot like instant coffee. I added some sugar and water and cooked it until it was thick and bubbly. We poured it out on a metal tray and cut it up into squares after it cooled. Although it looked like fudge brownies, it tasted awful, nothing at all like the Mars bar I craved. I had always loved chocolate and wondered where it came from. Now it seemed ironic to be living in the middle of a vast region of cocoa production but unable to make chocolate. Whenever I really craved for a chocolate bar, I would look around me and sigh, "Cocoa, cocoa everywhere and not a bite to eat".

Our next-door-neighbour finally showed us what part of the cocoa plant was good to eat. He gathered a few of the ripe pods from the backyard and cut one open. He extracted a white coated bean and popped it into his mouth. He sucked on it for a few moments and then spat out the remaining brown bean into his hand and showed us. He said the brown part didn't taste very good and threw into one of the wooden fermenting boxes. I didn't tell him I already knew that. The white sheath however had a delicate and subtle sweet flavour like vanilla ice cream. It was a real treat after months of a diet of bush meat, roots and tubers. We gave Anisa half of a pod for her own. She loved it. We told her to suck the

199

white part and then spit out the bean. She didn't listen. Fanny and I sat down and consumed two or three pods each before we noticed that Anisa wasn't spitting out the cocoa beans. She was just swallowing them when she was done. By that time she had eaten about ten beans. She didn't become ill exactly, but that many beans contained enough caffeine to keep her awake for two days and nights. We didn't get much sleep either. She kept waking us up and wanting to play.

Because it was the cocoa season, most of the villagers were busy bringing in their cash crops and didn't have much time to talk with me about proverbs. I found that I had free time on my hands to do some exploring. I worked with Sylvain and helped him harvest his small crop, and as a vacation we decided to take a trip into the western jungle to find the Pygmies. Sylvain had seen Pygmies a few times before but he had never travelled to where they lived. In the middle of their homeland to the west was also the convergence of the different branches of the Ntem river and a series of large waterfalls. Sylvain had heard about the waterfalls. They were magic. From the legends of his tribe Sylvain believed that the forces of nature were mysteriously different there. He told me stories that had been told to him, stories which said that wristwatches, clocks and radios would mysteriously fail to work near the falls. The legends also claimed that birds would avoid flying over the area and if they did they would fall to the ground dead. Even stones were reported to fly upwards if thrown over the falls.

With all these stories, I was determined to see the waterfalls for myself. Because the trip would involve a considerable amount of walking, Fanny and Anisa elected to stay home. I took my watch, tape recorder, camera and compass with me to verify if there were any static electric or magnetic anomalies. Sylvain and I packed a couple of backpacks for a week's trip and set out westward. We rode the motorcycle through many small villages which neither of us had ever seen or heard of before.

Travelling with Sylvain, however, had certain disadvantages. He was very tall and gangly, and his long legs were just not designed for sitting in the pillion seat of the motorcycle. When he had his feet on the ground we looked like a Polynesian canoe with outriggers. But when he put his feet up on the foot rests, it was worse. His knees came up almost as high as his shoulders. Sitting like this with the bright orange helmet and bulging goggles my wife loaned him made him look like an enormous grasshopper perched behind me. His height and weight on the back made the centre of gravity of the bike dangerously high. It was difficult for me to make him understand that his every movement had an effect on the stability of the bike.

Sylvain also had a disconcerting habit of getting off the bike without telling me. If he noticed something interesting alongside the road he wanted to stop and take a look at, he would simply put his feet down and stand up. This was not so bad if we were stationary but the first time he did this when we were moving, he found himself lying in the road with his face full of mud puddle. Sylvain was a fast learner though. From then on he would wait until I was going relatively slowly and then stand up. The bike would surge ahead and I would stop to see if Sylvain was all right. More often than not he would be alongside the road examining some new tree species or plant.

On the Yamaha mud puddles and potholes were the bane of my existence. They caused me endless trouble. I was always careful not to splash anyone standing beside the road. Aside from being incredibly offensive, it was also illegal. The advent of the personal car and the thoughtlessness of mainly European drivers had forced the Cameroonian government to impose heavy fines on drivers who carelessly soiled the clothing of bystanders. The dirt road that ran through the village of Meyo-Ntem was a minefield of potholes as a result of the heavily laden cocoa trucks that plied between the river and Ma'an. Just one truck could take a small rut and turn it into a miniature Grand Canyon by the end of the cocoa season. There was no way of predicting where these potholes would develop. The road had so many bends in it that I could never see very far ahead of me as I rode. I had to memorize the position of these muddy potholes whenever I found them. They usually consisted of two long ruts which were widened and deepened each time the truck wheels went through them. When it rained it was impossible to guess the depth of these muddy puddles. There usually wasn't any way to avoid the puddles because the jungle grew straight up at the edge of the road. I found that it was safer to ride through one of the puddles than attempt the steep and slippery ridge between them.

You never knew what might be at the bottom of these holes. If a truck driver got stuck, he would try to fill the pothole with sticks, twigs, lumps of hard laterite soil or rocks if he could find them. I had to ride slowly through every puddle the first time to know just how deep it was and what lay hidden at the bottom. I had to remember what each puddle was like for the return trip. Sometimes, I could follow my own tyre tracks back the way I came and avoid any surprises.

One day on the way back from a short trip I came to a long puddle which I remembered as being very shallow. Instead of crossing over and going through it on the same side of the road as before, I kept to my side of the road. You would think that both ruts would be the same depth. They weren't. This side was somewhat deeper. As I went through the puddle the bottom dropped out from under me. When I came to rest I found myself still sitting on my motorcycle in the middle of the puddle with only my handlebars above the water. The motorcycle gasped and spluttered somewhere underneath me and a large smoky bubble broke the surface and the bike died. Muddy water is not good for an internal-combustion engine. It took me about three hours to pull it out of the puddle, push it back to a stream I had passed, wash the mud off, tear the engine down, flush out the intake and exhaust manifolds, reassemble and start it. By the time I got underway again and returned to "the pit", the shallow puddle on the other side of the road was almost dry.

The road Sylvain and I took west ended in a village called Nyabessan. This was the heart of the Mvae territory. There were some Mvae villages near Meyo-Ntem and Sylvain could understand their dialect. He jokingly said that it was like speaking Ntumu with a mouth full of cassava. The villages looked different in the design of the huts and their layout. Many of the trees had glass wind-chimes hung in them to scare away the birds that fed on the crops they planted. These were the same square green-glass bottles that the Ntumu used for so many other things. We left the Yamaha beside a hut where the road ended. We would have to go the rest of the way on foot.

We walked some distance westward until we came upon a small man curled up asleep beside the path. As we approached he suddenly woke up and ran away and hid behind a tree. Sylvain called to him and the man answered in Mvae from behind the tree. He asked us in the equivalent of four-letter expletives just what we thought we were doing scaring the living daylights out of a peacefully sleeping hunter. Sylvain apologized and explained that we were looking for the waterfall near here. The man said that if he showed us where it was, would we go away and leave him alone?

A LEAF OF HONEY

Sylvain agreed. The man stepped out hesitantly from his hiding place. He looked strangely old but about the size of a ten-year-old child. He carried a short handled machete at his belt and carried a crossbow. I was very surprised to see so ancient a weapon. It could have come straight out of a museum. In the fifteenth century the Portuguese had explored the coast of this part of Cameroon. In fact, it is believed that the name of the country came from *camaroes* the Portuguese word for "prawns" written as notations on early navigation charts. Five hundred years ago this crossbow design must have been borrowed from the *besteiro* soldiers who accompanied the Portuguese exploration and trading ships.

The small man talked with Sylvain for a few minutes and then told us to follow him. The man walked with a swagger and all his movements seemed to begin with a jerk. He said he was of the Bayele tribe. *Bayele* is the indigenous word for Pygmy. The man didn't say much to us but he grumbled a lot. He talked to himself in a low voice which sounded like an endless string of profanities and complaints. He reminded me of the dwarf Grumpy. From the deference which Sylvain gave him, I could tell that he thought the Pygmy was magic. This area between the falls and the ocean still belonged to the Pygmies, but only because it had not yet been penetrated by roads or other tribes. The Pygmies were the only ones who had access to the coast from here because they were the only ones who knew the paths. They occasionally traded salt inland from the coastal towns of Campo and Kribi.

We were never able to ask the man his name. He was too anxious to get rid of us and with his machete cut a path through vegetation that was otherwise too thick to move through. After about an hour of blazing a new trail through the undergrowth we began to hear a distant roar.

The sound became deafening as we approached. A fine mist fell through the leaves overhead and below the thick moss underfoot the ground shook. The forest ended abruptly at the river edge. I left my backpack on the ground and carefully approached the brink. I held tight onto a tree and leaned out to look over the edge. Below us the Ntem river rushed by, white with the froth of its rapids. Looking upstream I saw that at this point the river ran straight as a line drawn against a ruler. I sighted along my compass. The river was flowing south-west and must be following one of the parallel geological fault lines common in this part of Cameroon.

A LEAF OF HONEY

With the spectacle of the mighty river beside us, we hiked for several kilometres through the jungle at the edge of the descending torrent. Our diminutive guide still led the way. The river ended at the lip of a steep plateau. This was the magic waterfall. We were bathed in the mist and cool spray of the Ntem as it crashed onto the lower part of the river. The Pygmy showed us a way down. At the base of a long stairway of fragmented stone we came to a floor of granitic bedrock worn smooth with the ages of water abrasion. Beside the waterfall there were bathtub-sized cavities carved in the mother rock. The shallow ones were empty but some of the deeper ones were filled with round stones which had been washed downstream and trapped. Periodic flooding had spun and tumbled the stones in the hollows until they were spherical and polished smooth.

Sylvain stood in amazement as he stared up at so awesome a demonstration of nature's power. I checked my equipment and showed him that my watch, tape recorder and compass still worked perfectly well. Sylvain posed with our guide as I took a photograph of them with the falls as a backdrop. Sylvain grinned from ear to ear and Pygmy looked bored. Before we retraced our steps to where we had found the Pygmy, Sylvain picked up a few of the polished stones as souvenirs. These would be his proof when he returned to his village and recounted his adventure. Unable to resist the temptation, he threw one of the stones up at the water. The stone appeared to rise at an unnatural angle before it disappeared into the falling spray. I couldn't believe my eyes. I threw some stones myself and the same thing happened each time. They certainly didn't appear to behave like a normal thrown stone. I could not resolve this occurrence and it worried me all the way home to Ma'an. Sylvain wasn't perplexed at all and explained it in one word: "magic".

A few days after we returned home I hit upon a plausible explanation. I showed Sylvain that if you take two stones and throw one high up in the air and as the first comes down throw the second one at it, an interesting optical illusion happens. The second stone appears to rise sharply upward for a while before it falls. It was the same with the waterfall. There was no way to translate the words: "optical illusion". I explained that because the waterfall was moving downward, the eye was fooled. Instead of having a static background as a plane of reference for the stone's flight, the downward motion of the background made the stone in the foreground look as if it flew upwards. In short it was simply a "trick of the eye". I felt quite satisfied with my deductive logic and saw it as the scientific explanation to a phenomena that was the basis of a very old tribal belief. Sylvain listened silently to my laboured explanation and finally said that it wasn't simple at all, that it was contrived and over-complicated. He dismissed it entirely by saying that it was much easier to believe in magic.

38

BIRD LEGS AND SOCIAL JUSTICE

Dear Dr Kilngott,

Grouped below are several interesting but unrelated proverbs in which different kinds of birds figure. A few of these birds have never been pointed out to me in the jungle and I only have the Ntumu terms for them. Even if they were pointed out to me, what I know about ornithology is so limited that it would still be impossible for me to identify and find English equivalent names for them. It is for this reason that these birds are referred to by their Ntumu names.

The bat is included here along with the birds because Ntumu taxonomy classifies it as both a mouse and a bird. As I continually discover, the Ntumu are very wary of those things which do not fall neatly into one mental category, especially if those mental categories are mutually exclusive. In trying to explain this, one Ntumu elder said that a bat had to be a kind of mouse or a bird but not both. If something is a bird it cannot also be a mouse. Things which are ambiguous like this are difficult to understand and treated differently. I believe that this ambiguous status in classification is the cause of the bat being seen as taboo among the Ntumu. Another strongly tabooed bird is the *du'u* which figures in the following riddle-like proverb:

(066) "With one *du'u* you break three taboos."

The *du'u* is referred to as an inedible and an extremely ugly bird which lives in the Ntumu region. It is considered so ugly that a common insult among the Ntumu is "You are as ugly as a *du'u*".

A LEAF OF HONEY

Specifically, the three taboos mentioned against this bird are as follows:

1) Pregnant women are forbidden from looking at it for fear that the unborn child will be born looking as ugly as a *du'u*.

2) Unmarried women are forbidden from looking at it because if they do it is said that no one will marry them.

3) The trapper is forbidden to harm the bird because if he does it will bring him bad luck in trapping.

The riddle of this proverb is to guess what kind of person can break all three taboos with only one *du'u*. The answer, of course, is a female trapper who is both pregnant and without husband, who has been unlucky enough to have killed a *du'u*. This proverb is used in other than this riddle context and carries the message that simple actions can sometimes have complex consequences.

The Ntumu jungle and folklore are full of several beautiful species of hummingbirds. The *soso* hummingbird figures in this analogous proverb:

(067) "Is it that if hummingbird has an abscess on its leg, you pierce bat's leg instead because it is fatter."

Soso, being a hummingbird, is considered the smallest bird. The bat is seen as only a little bigger. According to several long conversations around the evening fires with Ntumu tribesmen, this proverb, in analogous terms, deals with the issue of responsibility for one's own actions and states that culpability is not comparative. For the Ntumu, innocence or guilt is judged individually, on the basis of one's own behaviour and is not determined by comparison with the other people's relative compliance to the laws of the tribe. This has a subtle impact on the Ntumu concept of collective hypocrisy. Christ's teaching of "Let he who is without sin cast the first stone" is not seen as relevant when the accusing body is not an individual but rather the council of Ntumu elders. This would be an interesting test of Durkheimian "contract" theory. In the proverb the bat is naturally suspect and perhaps even guilty of a greater crime, but the hummingbird's crime, symbolized by the abscess, stands independent of the bat's reputation or actual offence. This concept of absolute personal accountability seems to permeate both Ntumu tribal jurisprudence and the teachings of their Christian-based religion where culpability is equated to sin. The message here is "No matter how big other people's faults are, each person should be treated according to his own actions". There is a non-relative standard of behaviour to be followed. The presence of this proverb and others in Ntumu folklore states a profound concept underlying their sense of social justice and perhaps helps to explain the absence of the use of legal precedent in the judicial decision-making of the tribal council of elders. There are no fixed punishments for fixed crimes. Each case is tried according to the specific circumstances of the individual.

Another proverb featuring sparrows deals with comportment and wastefulness:

(068) "Sparrow never praises the one who cuts down the plantain tree."

Here, by presenting an analogous negative example, the message of "Be prudent and not wasteful" is conveyed. This is the Ntumu equivalent of "Waste not, want not". The following proverb says: "When in doubt, don't do it":

(069) "If you wonder about a bird when it is still very young, leave it in the nest."

The Ntumu tribesmen see the passage of time as beneficial to understanding. One of the prerequisites of wisdom is age. Time gives every problem a new perspective and solutions are often revealed by waiting. This proverb advises patience when faced with the unknown.

Regarding how a stranger in an unfamiliar place should be wary of being fooled or tricked:

(070) "The bird that comes from far away is easily caught in the glue."

The glue referred to here is the sticky resinous sap which some trees produce. Birds which are familiar with this kind of tree avoid it and know where to perch away from the sap. Others, however, do not seem to know it is dangerous and subsequently die, stuck to the resin. This analogous proverb is an equivalent statement of the English "Far from home, near thy harm".

208

A LEAF OF HONEY

Many other birds appear in Ntumu folklore but conspicuously absent from the proverbs collected so far is the owl. Owls are more frequently seen by Ntumu villagers than some of the birds which do figure in the proverbs and this absence may be due their hatred of this particular bird. The owl is one of the most feared of all the animals by the Ntumu and is seen as an omen of death. The sighting of an owl is an event which is often spoken about for days in speculation of who might die. Sometimes at night an owl will sit in a tree near the village and hoot. In the relative silence of the night, the noise can be so loud that the villagers are kept awake. It is seen as especially ominous if an owl alights on the roof of a hut. Every sort of verbal abuse is employed to move the bird off the roof. Shooting the owl or throwing something at it is said not to be wise because this will assuredly result in the death of someone. Like an unwanted guest, the only way to get rid of an owl is to make it feel unwelcome and shout insults at it. These insults begin as rather civil requests to move on, but if after several minutes the owl takes no notice, the insults become more and more abusive. Finally, if after all this the owl still refuses to spend the night somewhere else, a villager may have to resort to the ultimate curse: "May you have *tenea* on your head". *Tenea* is the Ntumu word for a scalp disease like mange which results in the loss of hair and feathers. The villagers explain that often the prospect of this disease is so horrible to the owl that it will fly away.

The owl as a symbol of knowledge and wisdom in American culture is quite opposite to the Ntumu belief of it being the embodiment of evil. I wonder what my Ntumu hosts would assume about a culture like mine in which "cute" characterizations of owls are commonly worn as jewellery, act as motifs on clothing and hung as artwork on the walls of our houses.

Sincerely yours, Joseph

39

THE INHERITORS OF THE EARTH

Insects are by far the most numerous of the ambulant creatures on this planet. I am sure that if census-taking aliens conducted a head-count of animal life here they would conclude that the third planet out from the sun was firmly controlled by creatures with six or more legs. Cameroon and the tropical rainforest belt of Africa seem to have a higher than normal population density of insects and anyone who has ever lived in this jungle area is full of horror stories about insects. Each newcomer to the rainforest copes differently with the environment and the limited access to the comforts he once took for granted. Each person tries to take along with him his own personalized life-style support system.

When I first arrived in Ma'an I saw myself as a relatively well-adapted person and was unmolested by the bugs. This soon changed. I discovered that there was an entire ecosystem of insects living in our hut. The worst of these co-habitants were the cockroaches. At first I believed that, theoretically, we would rarely get in each other's way. After all, cockroaches were basically nocturnal and, if left alone by them at night, I would hopefully remain diurnal. All that was required was a little basic respect and tolerance. However what is tolerance to some is down-right infestation to others. The old wattle and daub walls of the hut were home to a myriad of the little beasties. Most of the wood in the walls had been eaten away by the termites, leaving a labyrinth of cosy passages and chambers for the cockroaches to live in. The cockroaches in Africa are not the small household variety found in Europe or America; these are large gnarly-looking critters weighing in at about an ounce each. To distinguish them from the ones we knew in California my wife and I called them "whoppers". Some of them were so frequently encountered as to be given individual names like pets.

Objectively speaking, there is nothing intrinsically offensive about cockroaches: they occupy a necessary niche in the ecological workings of nature. Knowing this, however, was of no comfort and did little to rid me of an acute aversion to them. Living with them in a small hut was a constant battle for niche supremacy. They seemed to have a misconceived belief that my abode was part of their niche. I disagreed with this viewpoint and reasoned that the hut had been built by humans for humans and this was a clear-cut invasion of my niche. I adopted a simple philosophy: a niche for every creature and every creature in its own niche. Human tenets and bipedal tenants are easy to ignore when you live close to the ground. The cockroaches had their own counter-philosophy: mankind is temporary, cockroaches were here first and will eventually inherit the earth.

I found that cockroaches could eat things bigger than their own heads and they weren't finicky either. Anything left open was fair game. Because of this, every single item in the hut had some kind of protective device against the cockroaches. All of our dry goods were put into the squarish green glass bottles we found in the bush. We would spend hours locating unbroken bottles, washing them in the stream, carrying them the two kilometres back to the hut and drying them out. We would then carefully pour our rice or sugar through a funnel into the bottles, stop up the openings with plugs of candle sticks and dip the ends of the bottles in melted wax. This would keep out the moisture and air and would probably safeguard the contents from cosmic rays, but not from cockroaches. Somehow they would eat their way in and wait for us. One wall of our hut looked like a wine cellar, with row upon row of square green bottles stacked against it. The bottles were organized into sections. There were individual rows of rice, sugar, beans and lentils. Even matches were stored in bottles. We had one table in the hut from which we usually ate. The legs of the table were set in tin cans filled with kerosene to discourage the insects from climbing the legs and having dinner with us.

One evening my wife opened a tin of condensed milk. This was an imported luxury. Sometimes we had some in our tea or coffee. She poked two small holes in the top so the thick milk would pour better. Before going to bed she placed the tin in one of our bug-proof containers. The next morning she took it out and tried to pour some into the coffee. It wouldn't pour. She shook it. It still wouldn't pour. To start the flow, she put the tin to her lips and sucked at one of the tiny holes. She gave out a mournful whimper and put the can down.

"What is the matter?" I asked. She gulped and stared at me for a second with anxious eyes.

"Ask me later," she muttered and ran out of the hut with her hand over her mouth. A moment later I could hear her vomiting.

Later she told me that when she sucked the tin it tasted strange, sort of bitter. She looked at the tin and saw a huge hairy cockroach leg projecting out of the hole. She realized that she had just sucked the stuffing out of the cockroach into her mouth. It was at that moment that she had whimpered and I had turned around and asked her what the matter was. She had been distracted by the question and had swallowed without thinking to answer. I think that this was a major turning point in her life.

Whenever I see a cockroach I recall one of the worst experiences in my life. It was a very hot day and I had just returned from a long ride from Meyo-Centre. I remember arriving tired and sweaty, with only sleep on my mind. I pulled off my helmet and hung it on a peg in the wall on the way to my hammock. I fell into a long sleep and awoke in the afternoon. I glanced at my wristwatch and suddenly remembered that I had promised to see Sylvain in Meyo-Ntem and I was late. I jumped up and grabbed my helmet on the way out. I got on my motorcycle and kick started it into life. I put my helmet on, pulled the chin strap tight and took off. I roared off down the road trying to make up for lost time. I didn't want to keep my friend waiting. I had just reached the end of the village and fourth gear when all at once hundreds of huge whoppers streamed out of the lining of the helmet and poured across my face inside the visor and down my neck. I was travelling at about fifty miles per hour and couldn't even take one of my hands off the handlebar to push them out of my eyes. In the horror-filled seconds it took to slow down, jump off the bike and tear my helmet off, the cockroaches had invaded every inch of my clothing. I had to strip down, shake and examine all of my clothes before I could compose myself, dress and continue. The memory of it still makes me shudder.

Cockroaches have a natural enemy, far more efficient than man: the *nsuluk* army ants. One night when we were about to go to sleep we heard the eeriest sound. The cockroaches were screaming. I had never heard a sound like it. It began in one corner and soon spread around the hut. We listened. Inside each wall was a chorus of screaming insects. At first we could not imagine what it could be but then all of a sudden a few cockroaches began to pour out of the walls and fly around. I had never seen a cockroach fly. I was in my hammock and Fanny and Anisa quickly got in with me and we tucked the mosquito netting tightly around us. In the light of our kerosene lantern we watched as thousands of roaches streamed out of every crack and crevice in the walls. As soon as they emerged they took to the air. It was like a black snow storm of cockroaches inside the hut. A plague of biblical intensity.

At first we couldn't figure out what could have caused them to behave like that. It was obvious they were fleeing something, but I didn't know what. Then we saw it. An unimaginable number of deadly *nsuluk* ants followed the cockroaches out of every crack. They swarmed and covered literally every inch of the walls, floor and roof of our room. It was as if someone had spray-painted everything brown. There was no way out for us. We had to just stay put and watch. The *nsuluk* were merciless. Every time a cockroach landed the ants attacked it. Some of them would land in desperation on the hot lantern, crackle a moment and fall off dead. The sound of the ants eating the cockroaches was audible above the diminishing screams. We were lucky to be protected by the netting and suspended by two ropes from the rafters. We stayed very still and the *nsuluk* never ventured very far down the ropes. The battle lasted more than an hour before the screaming stopped and the ants left. If the lamp had not been lit when this all started we probably wouldn't have been able to remain calm. We decided it would be safer to sleep exactly where we were and not risk the ants returning. The next morning the floor of the hut was brown on brown, strewn with a layer of cockroach remnants.

40

THE BLOODSUCKER

Dear Dr Kilngott,

The *osun*, "tsetse fly" or "bloodsucker", is a large fly-like proboscis-bearing insect which can fly without being heard and land without being felt. It is greatly disliked by the Ntumu who take great pains to pursue and kill it once it is seen. The hatred of this insect stems from the tribesmen's knowledge that the *osun* somehow causes infection of the blood, blindness, sleeping sickness and elephantiasis. From conversations with the tribal medicine man, I don't think the Ntumu understand that the *osun* carries filarial parasites which are the real causes of such ailments. It doesn't matter: the accomplice is as guilty as the criminal among the Ntumu and the *osun* is swatted whenever spotted. The following proverb concerns the indiscriminate behaviour of the *osun*:

(071) "The bloodsucker never cares about the social status of anyone."

This proverb is used when describing a certain kind of individual who has no apparent regard for rank or station and is analogous of the thief who isn't choosy and steals from high and low alike. To combat the *osun* the tribesmen make flyswatters which they wield against this and other types of flying pests. I have enclosed a drawing of one. It is called an *akbwa* and is a little less than a metre in length and made of the stiff fibres running down the middle of a palm leaf. These fibers are easily collected from the palms which the weaver birds have stripped to make their nests.

Several hundred of these tapering fibers are bunched together and bound with a strip of raffia bark. The drawing shows how the excess raffia bark is woven around as an ornament. The following proverb incorporates both the *osun* fly and the *akbwa* flyswatter:

(072) "The bloodsucker is now on the hand that holds the flyswatter."

Here the message is simply "the worm has turned" or "the shoe is now on the other foot."

Ground snails are large and common in the Ntumu region. They are eaten and considered a great delicacy. To prepare the snail for cooking it is separated from the shell by knocking a hole in the side, cutting the anchoring muscles, and pulling out the meat. The claw on the end of the foot is cut off and the meat is cleaned by rubbing it with halved lemons to remove the unpalatable slime. What it tastes like requires being very hungry and much getting used to. It is similar to clams or mussels.

The empty shell is not used other than by children and is usually discarded in the jungle. Large piles of these shells can be seen. Some snail shells end up as toys for children. The blunt-nosed conical end of the shell is separated from the rest and the thin spiral internal walls removed, leaving a cup-like cone. This is spun on a hard surface with a snapping motion of the fingers and is played with like a spinning top. The following proverb employs the analogous snail shell in describing an aspect of self-determination:

(073) "Empty snail shell
        face to ground
        collects dirt,
        face to sky
        collects the rain."

This poetic and epigrammatic proverb explains that if a person seeks evil he will find it and if he seeks goodness he will find that. The syllable count and content of this proverb is almost Japanese *haiku* in style and is of a syntax which suggests that it is older than others I have collected. In an opportunistic way some of the missionaries have exploited this proverb to describe the Christian doctrine of free will. Apparently it has been employed as an effective means of discrediting any cultural traces of the concept of fate or some Calvinistic belief in predestination from rival religious missions.

This analogy of a cupped receptacle is similar to several sayings among the North American Indians which employ an empty basket to make the same statement about good and evil. If I remember correctly, one prophetic story described a basket with a woven design of a cross with the ends of each arm bent at right angles counter clockwise on the inside. It was called the basket of goodness. Because the pattern was woven through to the other side, a mirror image was produced on the outside of the basket. The inside design was a symbol of goodness. Ironically when turned upside down, on the convex side, the side which could hold no goodness, it showed a Nazi swastika.

Sincerely yours, Joseph

41

A LITANY OF FAMILIAR WORDS

The threat of malaria is one of the unfortunate things we had to live with in the rainforest. Everyone had it, but most of the time the medicine we took kept us from feeling the symptoms. The medicine against malaria was called Chloroquine and we had brought with us a couple of tins of 1000 tablets each. I figured that this was a sufficient supply for the three of us if we survived the rigors of my year of fieldwork and a lifetime supply if we didn't. The concentrated bitterness of these tiny tablets is indescribable. If you think of how nauseatingly sweet one small saccharin tablet is on the tongue then you can begin to understand the bitterness just one of these tablets of Chloroquine has in it. Fanny and I dreaded the daily ordeal of finding some way to quickly swallow the tablet without it touching the tongue. We never found one, the pill would always leave a bitter aftertaste. Anisa, on the other hand, insisted on chewing them. Watching her do this would make me shudder but she said she liked the taste.

This drug was definitely one of those remedies which was almost as bad as the disease it was supposed to cure. It had several non-therapeutic side-effects. It affected my eyesight with occasional but distressing little flashes of light and had a devastating effect on the short-term recall part of my memory. For a medicine that demanded consistent and conscientious consumption, this particular side-effect was self-defeating. It was easy to miss a daily dosage because you couldn't remember if you had already taken one. I finally changed to another brand called Flavoquine which didn't have these side-effects.

A LEAF OF HONEY

As far as I remember, my long-term recall wasn't affected by Chloroquine. But then, if it was, how would I know? Memories about being forgetful are not very reliable. Events in the recent past were definitely a problem. I became absent-minded. I would walk out of the hut with my clipboard, full of determination to go somewhere and do something and not be able to remember where or what. I would sit, frustrated, for a few moments on my motorcycle trying to remember where to go.

As time went on I began to worry about this. I started to write down my ideas about Ntumu culture not as part of efficient field methodology but more out of a fear that I might not remember them later. I felt like one of the inhabitants of Macondo in Gabriel Marquez's *A Hundred Years of Solitude.*

This side-effect reminded me of the joke about goldfish.

Goldfish are said to have the shortest memories in the world because they are never able to remember what they were going to say. They think of something, but just as they open their mouths to say it, pop! they forget it and close their mouths again in bewilderment. Goldfish spend their entire lives swimming around slowly opening their mouths, forgetting, and then closing them. Opening, closing, opening, closing.

Even though we all took our anti-malarial medicine everyday Anisa woke up one morning with a headache, the shivers and a little fever: all the signs that she had contracted malaria. She said she felt tired and wanted to stay in bed. I reread the instructions on the package of Chloroquine and increased the "prophylactic" daily dose of one tablet to a "curative" dose of three tablets. At that point, I wasn't too worried: I had had the symptoms of malaria several times and the curative doses had always worked.

That afternoon I saw the an elder called Papa Akong and I mentioned to him that Anisa had malaria. He invited me to sit in the *aba* while he smoked his pipe. He asked me what my culture saw as the cause of this illness. Papa Akong sat quietly puffing his tobacco while I explained that the word "malaria" came from two Latin based words: *mala* and *aria* which meant "bad air". This was because for hundreds of years people used to believe that the disease was caused by the foul-smelling and unhealthy air near the stagnant water of swamps. I told him that medical science had

219

proved that it wasn't the air at all. It was the mosquitoes that bred in the swamp water. I paused to see if Papa Akong was still interested.

"What do the Ntumu medicine men say about malaria?" I asked. Papa Akong replied that illnesses were largely due to the presence of evil spirits. Subconsciously I believed that my scientific explanation was more reliable than the superstitious reasoning of the old man. In that smug assurance that only technology can breed, I challenged this idea. The conversation which followed taught me a much-needed lesson in cultural humility. In trying to dispel what I saw as superstition and replace it with scientific knowledge I revealed how my ethnocentric air of technological superiority had blinded me to the reality of the things that I myself took on faith.

"Why do you say that evil spirits are the cause?" I asked.

"Because a medicine man told me and I have understood what he said," replied the man.

"The American missionary doctors in Ebolowa would disagree. Couldn't this medicine man be wrong?" I asked.

"Everyone is wrong about everything," he said philosophically. "Some people know something, but we never really know anything. We are always learning more about the things we are sure we know everything about, just as we are always learning about things we know nothing about. Isn't this true with European doctors?" he asked. To the Ntumu, all whitemen were Europeans regardless of where in California they came from. I said that in a philosophical way he was correct but that this didn't help me to understand evil spirits. I asked him to describe these spirits.

"When you say 'spirits' do you mean that they are the departed souls of men and women?" I asked.

"No, they are spirits because most of the time you cannot see them," he said.

"Have you ever seen these spirits?" I asked.

"Not everyone can see them. A medicine man can sometimes see them because he knows where to look. The spirits are carried by certain people and things," he added.

"What do you think of the European doctors at the missionary hospital in Ebolowa?" I asked.

"They are like Ntumu medicine men. Sometimes they cure the sick and sometimes they don't, it depends if they are stronger than the bad spirit. If the spirit is young or weak then the medicine man or doctor will win and the sick person will get well. If not, the person will die," he said.

"But these doctors have been to school and learned much about healing and medicines," I said.

"Do you think medicine men are born medicine men? They also learn from the older generation about herbs and plants that help healing," he said.

"But the doctors have special medicines for malaria," I insisted.

"The medicine the European doctor gives for malaria fever at the hospital tastes very much like the bark of the tree the medicine man uses." The Ntumu had obviously discovered a quinine substitute from a local cinchonic tree.

"But the doctor knows what causes malaria," I said.

"What does your science say causes malaria fever?" he asked.

I explained in simple terms that there were different types of mosquitoes and one of them, called the "anopheles", carried the microscopic protozoa or "little animal things" that were transferred into the bloodstream when the mosquito injected its needle-like sucker into our skin.

"How do they cause the fever? Have you ever seen these 'little animal things'?" he asked.

"Well, personally no," I confessed. "I think they attack the blood. But I don't know exactly how this causes the fever. I am not a doctor."

"Then how do you know that they exist? Why do you believe that they cause the illness?" he asked.

"Well, because a doctor told me." I was beginning to see where Papa Akong was leading this conversation.

"So you believe that something you cannot see is carried by something else and attacks the body, and you believe this because you trust a medicine man called a doctor who sometimes cures people if these invisible things aren't too strong. We seem to believe in the same things." Papa Akong put his pipe back in his mouth with a click of the teeth and grinned around it. It was all very humbling.

Anisa's temperature went up and down a few times but after two days the fever was clearly much worse. It became painfully obvious that our daughter was not going to get any better in Ma'an under our own care. Fanny and I decided to take her to Ebolowa and the hospital there. Predictably, there was no transport to be found in the market square. It was Sunday morning and the village was almost deserted. Even the military was gone. The only people around were the village Baptists and the Catholics who were trying to out-sing each other in their thatched churches on either side of the road. We decided not to wait any longer and prepared the Yamaha for a long trip. We placed Anisa between us on the motorcycle and started off. I had to ride slowly because Anisa was so sick that she kept drifting into unconsciousness. Mercifully the road was dry and it only took us eight hours to reach Ebolowa.

However it was nearly dark when we arrived and we found the hospital was closed and locked. I couldn't believe it, it was criminal. How could an entire hospital be closed and locked? We went to the resident doctor's house but the doctor wasn't home. Finally, we went to the Elakas' house. By then Anisa was in a very bad condition. Our only hope was to locate the two German volunteer nurses that worked at the hospital. Neither Tohu nor Fariba knew where the nurses lived. While our wives stayed home with Anisa, Tohu and I went out and asked everyone we met until we found the nurses' house. We knocked on their door, but they were out. No one knew where they were. I was frantic. It was like a nightmare. Wherever we turned there was no one to help us. Time was running out. All we could do was to go back to Tohu's house.

There is nothing more soul-rending than watching your own child die. Anisa would cry the way only a dying child cries. Her voice was soft and faraway. Pleading. She had uncontrollable shivers and every minute that passed she became worse. Beads of cold perspiration clung to her skin. Then all of a sudden the shivers stopped. She didn't cry anymore. Anisa was beyond the pain. Long minutes would pass with her lying quite still and then she would open her eyes for awhile and ask for water. I held her tiny limp body in my arms and watched the light in her eyes grow dim. I would have given my life a thousand times to save hers. I would have done anything, but all I could do was cry. I cried at my helplessness. I cried from the depths of my soul. Fanny and I held her and each other and silently cried at the realization of losing her. Tears streamed down our cheeks and dropped on her placid face. She didn't even notice. She was slipping away.

There was nothing left to do but pray. Fanny and I began to say a Baha'i prayer:

A LEAF OF HONEY

"Is there any Remover of difficulties save God?
Say: Praised be God! He is God! All are His
servants and all abide by His bidding!"

A litany of familiar words. We said it over and over and over again. Time stood still. We watched Anisa's every breath and breathed with her as her respiration became shallow and irregular. Her lifeless eyes stared out of half-opened lids. She didn't ask for water anymore.

At that moment the two German nurses we had been searching for rang the doorbell. They came in and saw Fanny and me sitting on the floor holding Anisa in our laps. Through grief-numbed senses I heard them tell Tohu that they knew where the doctor was. They just came from him. God, there was hope! They rushed out and got the doctor. He took us to the dispensary of the hospital in his car, unlocked the door and gave Anisa an injection. She was going to make it.

If my faith in prayer ever peaked, it was at that moment. Later the two nurses said that they were on their way to a party when all of a sudden they got the idea of stopping by the Elakas' house to say hello. Anisa had to stay in bed but she steadily recovered and we were able to return to Ma'an in a few weeks.

223

42

PLANT PERSONAE

Dear Dr Kilngott,

One of the proverbs this week talks about a particular kind of Ntumu trap, so I thought I would enclose a drawing of a typical monkey and squirrel trap. Because these animals are swift moving arboreal dwellers, they are difficult to catch. When a trapper sees several of these animals habitually crossing a path in a particular location, he will construct an elevated ramp of cut branches between the trees on either side of the path. In the middle of the ramp he places a configuration of sticks such that the animal using this overhead causeway must run through them. In this he arranges a wire snare which is secured to a bent branch. When the animal steps on the trigger the bent branch swings back and snares the animal around the neck.

Plants of all kinds figure heavily in Ntumu proverbs and are nearly as numerous as proverbs containing animal personae. This week, I have selected plant personae from two groups: generic plants and plant-related products. I will send some examples of specific plants next week.

A few generic plant terms appear in the proverbs collected but by and large most proverbs which feature plant personae employ specific plant terms. As with the animal personae presented above, plant personae appear in both natural and humanistic roles.

The generic Ntumu term for tree is *ele*. This is also a term used to describe "wood" in general. It is generic in the sense that *ele* translates as "unidentified tree species". The generic term "tree" in English carries a slightly different meaning. In English taxonomy a "pine" is a "tree". Not so in Ntumu: a "pine" is a "pine" because you know the name of it. An unidentified conifer is a "tree" because you cannot identify the particular species. If someone comes along and identifies the conifer for you, it ceases to be a "tree" because now you know that it is a "pine". The following is the only proverb collected in which the term *ele* figures:

(074) "The tree is born with a hole, a man is born with wisdom."

Here, the proverb employs an analogous format in which an element from the jungle environment is compared with an attribute of man. As with many Ntumu proverbs, the analogy is implied and requires additional information to be understood. Not all trees grow and develop a hole through their trunk. Such a tree is novel and rare. In like manner, wisdom is not something which is commonplace and inherent in everyone. A man whose character manifests wisdom is just as rare to come upon. The point of the analogy is that a tree with a hole through it, like human wisdom, is a natural occurrence and not something attained by those who are not born with it. Analogies which compare wisdom and trees

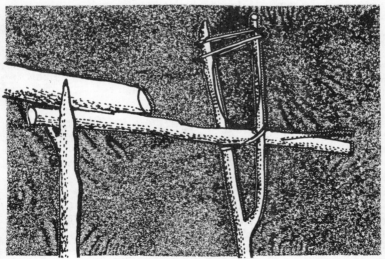

appear in other West African tribes. Among the Ibo of eastern Nigeria this comparison exists:

> "Wisdom is like a (certain hardwood tree),
>> it grows where it wants to grow,
> it is not something that can be cultivated."

Another generic term is *eza,* "plant". This term refers to non-tree plants. The following proverb employs a specific plant name which is sometimes given to strong and healthy children as a title.

(075) "*Okbwate* never stands on other plants' roots."

The message here is to be self-supporting and strong like the free-standing *okbwate* herb. Several Ntumu proverbs use plant-related terms, terms which describe specific plant parts or groupings. The following are a few examples of these:

(076) "Two *nwodo* lizards on one stump, look at them, one is more colourful than the other."

The *nwodo* is a kind of brightly-coloured lizard which bobs its head up and down in a dance which the tribesmen call "greeting the sun". At first glance all *nwodo* appear the same, but if two are closely compared their markings reveal that they differ slightly between males and females. The males are a little more colourful. The message of this proverb is a subtle combination of "Even similar things can be individually different" and "Individuals are equal, but some are more equal than others".

Another plant related term, *nja'a* meaning "broken or chopped kindling wood" appears in the following proverb:

(077) "Why is it that you have no kindling wood at home, when the path is long, the tree is hard, the axe is not sharpened and the rain is coming?"

This proverb poses a paradoxical question in the form of an elaborately constructed scenario in which it is impossible to light a fire. It is paradoxical in the sense that even if the faraway tree is cut into firewood, the rain will render it useless before it can be transported home for the fire. This proverb's basic message is

A LEAF OF HONEY

"Success depends on being prepared" because, without preparation, personal effort can be made in vain. The analogy is "Going out to find kindling can sometimes be equal to staying at home." An English equivalent to this saying is "Being stuck between the devil and the deep blue sea." Or in the words of my grandfather, "Finding yourself stuck between a rock and a hard place".

The following proverb uses the term *mvok:* "logs":

(078) "*Ekuri* is dying of carrying logs."

Ekuri is a certain kind of trap on which heavy logs are piled. When an animal comes along and springs the trap, the logs fall and kill it. Outwardly this proverb says "The forest has no animals" because day after day the trapper finds the *ekuri* unsprung and still supporting the heavy logs. The underlying message here is "I am tired of waiting".

In the following the term *afan,* "virgin forest", is used:

(079) "It is bad to have the virgin forest in front of the worked one."

The Ntumu tribesmen use slash and burn methods of ground preparation. This proverb prescribes that land should be developed systematically in such a way that one doesn't have to cross an undeveloped stand of virgin forest to get to a cultivated area. The prescriptive analogy is that things should be done in the right order.

The land along the path between two villages has a specific name: *okan.* Most Ntumu tribesmen live in clan-based villages, but now and then you can come across a lone hut between villages in the *okan.* This situation is at the heart of the following proverb:

(080) "A house in the *okan,* there is something."

Such a dwelling, in separation from the rest of the clan, is built there for some special reason. Normally the tribe builds their huts together in groups. However sometimes a dispute will lead to the expulsion of an individual from the village, but this is rare and there has to be some weighty reason for such extreme action. The message here is "If someone is ostracized or isolated socially, it must be for some good reason".

Sincerely yours, Joseph

227

43

PRAYER AND AN IMAGE
OF THE SOUL

Although Anisa had fully recovered from her bout of malaria, I hadn't. I still had nightmares. I could not dislodge the images from my mind. The vision of her helpless and near-lifeless form plagued my dreams. These nightmares were always accompanied by that terrifying feeling of powerlessness. As a result, I would sometimes wake up in the middle of the night feeling so anxious that I would have to check to see if she was all right. In the low orange light of the kerosene lamp I would watch Anisa sleep in her hammock. I often would be unable to doze off afterwards.

Her illness and recovery profoundly affected me and intensified the realization of my own feebleness and the might of God. It also reminded me to pray more often. For me prayer wasn't habitual and consistent; it was so easy to forget to pray. There were so many distractions and priorities to attend to. Living in a one-roomed hut didn't help at all. It was sometimes impossible to find the privacy to pray. For Fanny this didn't seem to matter, but for me an audience and the consequent self-consciousness inhibits the kind of introspection and personal communication which prayer is about. Prayer was often approached as a duty rather than a need but, after Anisa's recovery, prayer took on a more sincere aspect. I felt truly thankful and this was reflected in my prayers. No matter how hard it was to get started, I always felt refreshed and clear-minded afterwards.

However there was a niggling feeling of guilt that I had somehow been negligent in properly looking after Anisa's health. This thought affected my studies and I wasn't able to concentrate on my work. I felt that there must be something wrong with me not to put the health of my daughter first. After many sleepless nights of self-recrimination I dreamt the old dream again. I had almost forgotten about it. It had been years.

Everyone has a memory which is their earliest remembered image. Usually it is some event which lodged itself in the mind and was recalled often enough to make it stick. Mine is the memory of a recurring dream. One of the first things I can remember as a child is waking up with the vision of something glowing in my mind. I didn't know what is was, but I knew that it was special. It wasn't exactly a dream, more of a combination of a dream and a subconscious thought. Visually it appeared static, just an object without movement or motion. It had an amorphous shape and yet didn't. It was sort of spherical but wasn't. There was no way of determining its relative size because there was never anything else in the scene with which to compare it. It was like some unfamiliar object viewed through a telescope or a microscope, no perspective. It was neither suspended nor rested on a surface but glowed softly on its own in a hazy aura like a ball of round luminous fabric.

I recall that it would appear from time to time when I was young and I would gaze at it for a while and then it would go away. Sometimes it would look a little different, sullied and stained in places and at other times it would be bright and featureless again. I always had a pleasant feeling when I saw it and a lingering sense of warm contentment and security. I didn't see it very often. I wanted to see it more, but whenever I sought it, it would not appear. I could never conjure up the image of it willfully. It just appeared now and again. Whenever it did come, I relished the moment.

I felt that I was looking at something inside of me. As time went along, my mind needed to call this enigmatic "thing" something. I felt that it reflected something of my absolute and non-temporal being. It had a spiritual aspect to it. I decided that for want of a better name, this was a visual representation of my own soul.

It seemed to have an existence of its own. It didn't usually come to me in times of a crisis or anguish and reassure me as one might expect from some Freudian subconscious mental device to maintain homeostasis. It was more like a self-monitoring device. It allowed me to look at myself appraisingly. Although it followed many types of emotional states, I would usually see it during times of calm and after moments of introspection. It would appear during that mental twilight between sleeping and waking, and it never felt like the leftover symbolic residue of a dream.

The tribesmen paid attention to their dreams and had a saying about the memory of them:

"Do you forget your dreams because the night is long?"

The Ntumu word for dream was *biyeyem*, "that which we shall know". To the tribesmen, the soul saw the contents of dreams as meaningful and important as the events experienced during the waking hours of the day. The soul was the sentient part of man, the part that felt and perceived things. During the days it abided and animated the body and mind. At night it continued to be active and travelled to mysterious places and continued to learn. For the Ntumu, dreams seemed to have one foot in the present and the other in the future.

To come back to the subject, in the religious life of the community, prayer had both private and communal niches. The glorification and adoration of *Zamba* was celebrated in song and dance both within the liturgy of Sunday church-goers and in the social rituals which invited the entire membership of the village. Worship was a church affair complete with many of the trappings of services elsewhere. Divine supplication, on the other hand, was seen as personal and did not usually form part of communal religious activities. In the course of work I often heard individuals entreating *Zamba* for assistance and help. Speaking in low tones, they spoke as much to themselves as to God; a dialogue of roles spoken by the same person. Most often this kind of prayer was more of a meditative and contemplative process of quietly trying to understand and unravel some of the complexities of life.

In contrast to other peoples I had lived with, the Ntumu didn't resort to limiting the nature or power of God in order to explain Him. They accepted that God was greater than themselves. Even the adopted forms of Christianity some of the villages practised seemed surprisingly devoid of the simplistic rhetoric and dogma preached by the missionaries. *Zamba* was the creator of all things but not in the direct sense which a creationist might maintain. *Zamba* generated a universe in which the process of creation never ceased. As the elders of the tribe explained, *Zamba* was everywhere and enjoyed His creation. It was part of Him. He made Himself manifest in nature.

230

A LEAF OF HONEY

I had observed the religious practices of many native peoples, and compared to the inhabitants of the highlands of Guatemala, the Ntumu tribesmen of the jungle had a very different belief in God. In the Guatemalan town of Chichicastenango I lived for several months with some Quiche Maya Indians who believed that although God was very powerful, He was not quite omnipresent. He was a very busy Being with a little too much on His agenda. The problem was that God had more creatures than He could handle and subsequently He was assailed by prayers and requests from all sides. There just weren't enough hours in the day to make the rounds and to hear them all. The Quiche Mayans believed that the only way to assure that God would hear the prayers of a particular group of supplicants was first to get His attention. The Indians had a very novel way of doing this. It was the function of one member of the tribe to provide the town with the necessary equipment for a successful invocation. This man was a specialist. He punched holes in the sky so the prayers could get out. This was dangerous work. And because specialists were not always successful in doing special things, his hut was safely removed away from the rest of the town on a hillside by itself. It was there for a very good reason. This man made gunpowder.

This man's special equipment included a primitive aerial bombshell. This was made by filling a small cardboard box with black blasting powder and sticking a wooden spike into it. Around this was wound fibrous oakum dipped in hot sticky resin. When the bombshell was about the size of a baseball and the resin hardened, the spike was removed and a long fuse inserted. The now compact mortar shell was placed in a paper bag with a handful of loose gunpowder. The end of the fuse come out of the top of the bag. As both an airborne votive offering and a divine attention-getter it was very effective.

During certain religious festivals a procession of Mayan holy men would parade along the cobblestone streets of the town beating a very large and very loud drum. This was to call the town's people to prayer. The drum was apparently loud enough to call humans but not loud enough for God. Every so often the procession would stop and clear a circle for the specialist to set up his homemade pipe-barrelled mortar. At arm's length he would light the fuse and drop the paper bag with the shell inside down the pipe and then step back among the spectators. Being wary that it might fall over, all eyes would be fixed on the vertical barrel until

231

the fuse burned down to the powder and it fired. Then everyone would throw their heads back and watch as the shell was hurled high over the town. Several hundred feet up, and that much nearer to God, the shell itself would explode with a loud boom. Now they had God's attention! Murmuring aloud, the Indians would then quickly say their prayers with the assurance that God was listening.

44

FROGS DO NOT BURN
WITH THE RAFFIA

Dear Dr Kilngott,

As I wrote last week, the majority of Ntumu proverbs featuring plant personae do so in specific terms. This is because the tribesmen are surrounded by a jungle environment and because the Ntumu are species conscious. They have many words for plants and trees and I estimate that they are able to identify possibly thousands of species. This is to be expected. This is the same cultural isolation and environmental influences which have caused the winter-bound Eskimo to develop a multiplicity of words for snow and have facilitated the dwellers of the cloudless Guajiran desert to enlarge their word-stock of star names.

On several occasions, in walking through the jungle with the tribesmen, I have tested this tree-naming ability. I have found that most Ntumu adults can identify more than two hundred distinct species of trees and can explain the principal uses of their wood, roots, bark and fruit.

One of the most exploited and useful plants in the Ntumu region is the *zam*, raffia. Every part of this versatile palm is used in some way or another by the tribesmen. Nothing is wasted. The quaquaversal palm boughs are cleaned and used as poles in several types of dwellings as joists. Rattan-like splints from these boughs go into the making of numerous types of wickerwork baskets and fish drying trays. I have drawn a picture of one such storage basket, *angun*, which is made of the *eshishizam*, raffia pith. I have also enclosed a sketch of a woman's fishing basket used to hold shrimp and small fish. The long-bladed leaves are folded and pinned together around a long splint to form rain-tight roofing mats. The slender and curved tips of the boughs are used as fishing poles. The bitter red fruit of the raffia is cooked and eaten, and even the large parasitical grubs which bore into the base of the boughs and live in the pithy centre are extracted as a much-relished food source. The following two proverbs feature the *zam:*

(081) "Frogs do not burn with the raffia."

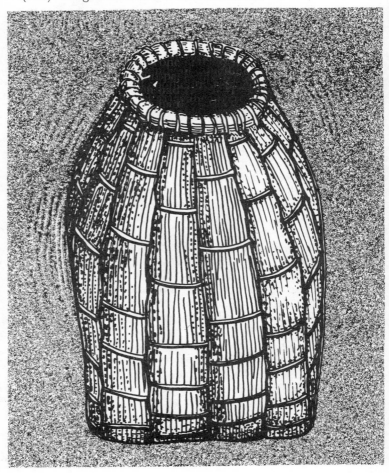

A LEAF OF HONEY

Like other proverbs, this saying conveys the cultural feature of forgiveness. As has been presented in other letters to you, conflict is something that is usually completely resolvable among the tribesmen. Resentment is not the normal postscript to conflict in Ntumu society. Here the proverb analogizes "There is always something left to draw people together after something has come between them." The analogy is that when a clump of raffia is burnt, the frogs escape and return after the disturbance is finished.

I don't know what there is in Ntumu culture which accounts for this natural subsidence of aggression. Other cultures I have lived with have not been so fortunate. The Guajiro Indians in Colombia developed a social device to contain arguments between two antagonists before it escalated into warfare. The Guajiro chiefs employed a kind of duelling ceremony which diminished aggression and conflict by replacing anger with pain. Two young men who had a grievance were told to stand some twenty paces

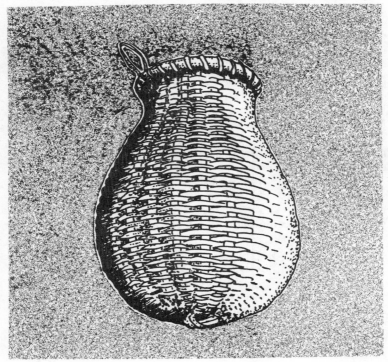

from one another and a circle was drawn in the sand around each man. The duel was basically a contest of inflicting and sustaining non-lethal injuries. Before the duel began each contender would cut about fifty slabs of a particular tall cactus and stack these slabs next to each circle in piles. The rules of the confrontation were simple. Each man had to stand in his circle and heave cactus slabs at the other. He could dodge but he could not step out of the circle. Under close supervision each man would take turns with an aim of hitting the other. Being hit by one of these was very painful and of course the spines would stick in the skin. They would continue like this, first one and then the other until one of them would declare that he no longer had a grievance with the other man.

The next proverb treats the subject of tenacity and self-determination:

(082) "One either makes his bag out of raffia or leather."

The fruitfulness of one's life is determined by one's own actions and self-direction. To the Ntumu, fate is not something controlled by chance. Destiny is the end of the path one has chosen to tread. There are many paths. To the tribesmen, certain things are inevitable and predictable like death and a river flowing downstream. But dying at a particular point in time can be avoided by learning how to swim in advance of falling in the river. The Ntumu believe that people can have control over things which are small and near enough to them to interact with, but not those processes which are either distant or large like the sun rising in the east.

I asked one of the children to make me a "raffia bag" so I could see what one looked like. She took a leaf and folded it into a purse-like carrying bag. I have enclosed a drawing of it. In the following proverb three specific plant terms are mentioned:

(083) "*Etutam* is one thing, *te'embolo* is another and *mbolonyiamendeng* is yet another."

The first term is "okra pod" and the other two are the edible fruits of plants with similar oblong green pods with a slimy liquid inside. All three are related by this slimy attribute but as the proverb points out, they are all different. They look similar, but taste different. The message is that individuality can exist in

236

commonage. Diversity does not exclude the acknowledgement of common attributes. In social terms, diversity does not mean division.

The last of this week's selection features a large "bush fruit" called *mfenek* and addresses the issue of knowing one's own capacity:

(084) "A small elephant swallows a *mfenek* being (over) confident in the size of its throat."

The *mfenek* is a jungle fruit which is not sought out by the tribesmen as a food source and is of such an enormous size as to be a challenge for even an adult elephant to attempt to swallow. One fruit can

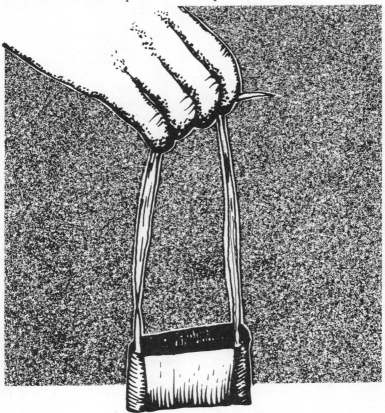

weigh as much as a large watermelon. The humorous message here is: "Each one should know his own limitations and capacity and never eat anything bigger than his own head". This is the Ntumu equivalent of the saying "Biting off more than you can chew".

Sincerely yours, Joseph

45

THE EXISTENCE OF THE PAST

By now we had become accustomed to living in Ma'an and, among
the tribesmen, the novelty of our presence had worn off. Everyone
knew us and we had stopped being the centre of attention. Every
day was similar now, less adventure and more familiarity. The
daily round of activities wasn't monotonous, just familiar. When I
woke up in the morning I knew that I would work hard and go to
bed tired that night. It was a good feeling. The rewards of living
among good people were physical work and good company. Unlike
my expectations before I left America, tribal life wasn't at all
simple or predictable. It was rich in the quality of life and more
socially satisfying than the hectic chaos of California.

I still spent time collecting and transcribing new proverbs but I
had reached that stage in my research when verification was more
important than new discoveries. Now was the time to understand
the social background and natural context of proverb use in speech.
In the course of doing this the men of the village had become more
than sources of anthropological data: they had become social
acquaintances, and then workmates and finally friends. I was
interested in their lives and the events which affected them as
individuals. Our conversations were more relaxed now that I
wasn't always struggling with meaning and nuance. Most of the
time now we chatted about normal events and the feelings people
have.

I could see a change in my family. Living in a tribal setting had
affected us. All three of us had become socialized, we had learned to
behave in ways which were acceptable to the tribesmen around us.
Among the men I maintained a good-natured and joking

relationship with my age-mates, but I showed a special respect and
deference to those older than myself. We appreciated each other's
talents. The tribesmen were far better at throwing a spear and
tracking game, but I could hold my own with an axe when the time
came to fell a tree and build a dugout canoe. Fanny was the
confidant and equal to her tribal sisters. She didn't act superior but
carried her weight in the activities of labour. Her ease of association
won her the privilege of being invited to participate in the rituals
from which men of the village, including anthropologists, were
excluded. Anisa was everyone's daughter and, like the rest of the
children, flourished in the love that was showered on her. She grew
to acquire a very Ntumu and respectful demeanour other
American parents would have envied. She wasn't treated specially
and her other mothers would send her out to fetch water with their
own children. She often joined her playmates in their household
chores. Anisa would regularly bring home some of her playmates
and ask me to fix their feet. I would stop working and get out the
first aid kit. I had become very adept at treating cuts and removing
jigger or sandflea eggs and larva from under the skin. I had lots of
practise on my own toes.

We felt at home. The tribal behaviour around us was
understandable now. It was based on beliefs we knew something
about. We had learned to respect that there were certain things
which were unseemly and taboo. It was not that our belief patterns
had changed. It was just that we respected their values. We always
remembered that we were strangers in *their* land. There were
certain things that you just didn't do among the Ntumu, things like
throwing the chewed pulp of sugarcane, seeds or anything which
had been rejected by the mouth, in the fire. Human hair or
fingernail parings were also banned from the fire.

I was learning more about their beliefs, especially magic. They
had many stories about magic. The word "magic" has undertones
in English and carries the pejorative stigma of "trickery". Not so in
Ntumu. Magic was the cover word for all phenomena which could
not be understood or explained well; it wasn't particularly
mysterious. It was like trying to explain a mobius strip and using
the word "scientific" or "technical" to keep from showing your
ignorance of physics.

One night around the fire in my efforts to better understand the
Ntumu concept of the word "magic", I hit upon an idea. What I
needed was an example beyond their experience which I could give

them and then ask if it were "magic" or not. A verbal description wouldn't work. What I needed was an example of magic they could see. Magic, however, is difficult to conjure up on the spur of the moment. But I was lucky. I remembered I still had an orange I had been given in my bag. I took it out and peeled it carefully trying not to bend the peeling too much. For once I used my pocketknife and not my teeth because what I was about to do with it might be seen as breaking a taboo if it had been in my mouth. I divided the orange and shared the sections of the fruit around the fire so that everyone could see it was a normal orange. I took a long stick and placed it in the fire. When the end of it was burning I asked one of the men to hold it. I took a large piece of orange peeling and squeezed it near the flame. The tiny liquid-filled vacuole-like sacks just under the skin ruptured emitting a fine spray of oil toward the flame. When the spray mixed with the oxygen in the air to the right proportions it naturally exploded, producing a fireball about a foot across. Although harmless and short-lived, in the dark it was very impressive. The tribesmen were startled but not frightened. I don't think there was anything I could do which would frightened them.

"Was that magic?" I asked the man holding the stick.

"Yes," he replied. The rest of the men clicked their throats in agreement.

Then I explained how it worked. The oil in the skin simply burned like the kerosene in a lamp. To show them that the oil really existed, I asked one of them to lick a fresh peel and then lick the one I had used to produce the fireball. He said he could taste the oil in the second one. I gave each of the men a piece of peeling so they could try themselves. One by one they passed the burning stick around and made the flame explode. They all laughed when Papa Akong's effort only produced a little puff of smoke. After they all had their turn, I asked them if it was still magic now that they knew how to do it and could explain why the flame exploded.

"Of course it is still magic," said the first man. "It is still magic because it still makes the fire jump, every time you do it." He paused and nodded towards Papa Akong and added with a grin, "Well, almost every time. If it had been done once and then no one could do it again, then it wouldn't be magic anymore. The magic would have gone."

There were other things which they did not call magic but which were mysterious. They talked about an old woman who came in the night with a lantern. No one ever saw her in the daytime and they weren't sure where she lived. I was told that she might live in the *okan*, the unoccupied jungle land between the villages. About once a week she would emerge from the jungle and walk down the main road through the village. She never said a word to anyone but talked to herself aloud. I knew who they were talking about. Lately this woman had begun to wander around in the jungle behind our hut. Occasionally I would see her light appearing and disappearing among the trees. Every so often she would put her lantern down and pat the ground. In the dim lamplight you could see that she was naked. It was eerie. She would spend hours talking to the ground, patting here and there and then listening with her head close to the ground. It was as if she had lost something and it was calling to her. The villagers were afraid of her. A neighbour told me that someone in the next village had seen her leading two or three men by a rope, tied around their waists in the middle of the night. The men had baskets of food and firewood on their backs. The person who had seen this recognized the men. The next day when he asked them where they were going the men couldn't remember leaving their huts. The villagers believed that she somehow had the power to make people work in her fields at night. Because of this and other stories, whenever some of the men woke up tired and stiff in the morning, they wondered if she had come in the night and got them. I must admit that these stories affected me too and I wondered what she was after behind our hut.

One morning after one of her night visits I went out into the woods and looked around. I found the place where she had been. The ground had been disturbed in a strange way. The vegetation had been uprooted in places leaving bare patches of ground. Hundreds of overlapping hand prints could be seen in the red soil.

Occasionally the subject matter of our nightly fireside discussions centred on the past: the history of the tribe and the adventures of their forbears. One night Papa Akong, who was a very old member of the tribe, talked about whitemen with such open frankness, I felt invisible. He spoke as if I were not there. I listened silently as he painted a picture of the times before and after the coming of the missionaries and the European administrators. He talked about the cultural iconoclasm the colonialists and missionaries had brought. He was very old and had seen much of it with his own eyes. What he described was the systematic destruction of the past. The whitemen had tried to make the tribesmen believe that the past didn't exist, that there was no time or past before the whitemen came. The elder said that this was a strange idea. The whitemen had a past, a history, but they didn't believe the tribesmen had. The whitemen were very powerful and in only a few generations they had overthrown tribal customs and beliefs which had endured ages before they came. Soon the younger generations of tribesmen were more *keke* than *ntumu*. They were empty. Their past had not just been forgotten, it had been removed.

The elder then said that it was late and everyone knew it was time to go to bed. Before he got up he said that he had told them all the stories he knew and that they shouldn't forget. They shouldn't become empty. He suffered from arthritis, and as he helped himself up with his walking stick, he joked: "Old men do not live forever, words do."

In listening to the tribesmen storytelling around the fire I could see that the colonists had not completely succeeded in eradicating the past. The past had simply gone underground. Parts of the past were still remembered. The heroes and wise men who once sat around fires like this one still lived, pieces of them were woven into the Ntumu stories and sayings. Many of the events of their lives may have been forgotten, but what remained was their wisdom. The proverbs were their relics.

Papa Akong was my neighbour and I walked with him as far as his hut and said goodnight. He said he was tired. I watched him enter his hut and close the door behind him. I promised myself that someday I would publish the proverbs I had collected here, as an effort to right the past, to replace some of the emptiness. I would make sure this generation and this man's wisdom would not be forgotten.

46

STRANGERS GREET PHANTOMS

Dear Dr Kilngott,

Recently I have recorded the tattoos which some of the very old in the surrounding villages have. Tattooing has long since ceased to be practised among the Ntumu and only the very old have them. These individuals explained that tattooing was a process performed by special men called *elumbikut*, "tattooers". The process began by drawing the design on the skin with some ash. The design was then pricked extensively with a fine porcupine quill. The sap of the *abe'e*, "cola nut tree", was then rubbed into the bleeding area and left for some time. The sap of the *abe'e* is dark blue and used as the ink. To insure that the wound would not become infected, young leaves of *ondondo*, "chili pepper plant", was mixed with *mbonemibong* "palmoil", and also rubbed onto the skin. I have enclosed several drawings of these tattoos. With the exception of the first design on the back of a man born in 1900, all the rest are facial markings on women born at about the same time. The man told me that he was tattooed at the age of 28 and the women said that they acquired their markings at between the ages of 5 and 14. I have collected two relevant proverbs:

(087) "The tattoo-maker's body is rarely tattooed."

This adage describes how one often neglects the advantages of skills one sells to others. It is like the man who bakes cakes for a living but hardly ever enjoys his own wares. The other proverb warns against requesting advice from someone who shows signs of ignorance on the subject.

> (088) "You get a tattoo from someone whose own tattoos are beautiful."

This week I will finish describing the various kinds of personae in Ntumu proverbs. Only two types of supernatural characters appear in the Ntumu proverbs collected so far: God and phantoms. I have already sent you one which mentions God.

SUPERNATURAL PERSONAE:

Phantoms, for the Ntumu, are the ghosts of the departed who are believed to wander about engaged in activities much as they would be doing if they were living: farming, hunting and carrying firewood. The Ntumu believe that such departed souls occasionally appear in their own bodies and can be recognized by those who knew them. The following two proverbs use phantoms to convey different messages:

> (089) "The strangers greet phantoms."

When a stranger first enters a village everyone he meets is a new acquaintance. He does not know the reputations or characters of the villagers he meets. He greets both chief and thief with the same respect. This social naivete is expressed in the above proverb. The

analogous message here is that the stranger does not know even who is dead and who is alive and could meet a phantom and not know the difference.

In the following, phantoms are employed to convey that equals cannot fool one another:

(090) "Phantoms don't play hide and seek with each other."

A LEAF OF HONEY

Shrewdness and cunning can only be truly recognized by someone who has these same qualities. When the council of elders meets, it is a battle of wits and the sagacious participants come well armed. The above proverb is sometimes used to inform a council member that fellow elders are too old to be hoodwinked.

Sincerely yours, Joseph

47

DOWNSTREAM IS THE FUTURE PASSED BY

The next morning I overslept. I had awakened in the middle of the night with my mind full of thoughts and couldn't get back to sleep for a long time. Another birthday was approaching. Lying there in the dark, at twenty-eight, I felt old. Birthdays always seemed to arrive at the wrong place and at the wrong time for celebrating. I had missed my twenty-first birthday altogether. I had left Colon on the Atlantic side of the Panama Canal a few days before my birthday on a small fishing boat headed for San Andreas Island. The sea was terrible and I became so violently seasick that when I woke up it was the day after my birthday. I wondered what would happen this year. In a few weeks it would also be the anniversary of the day on which I had become a Baha'i. It seemed so far in the past. I remembered what it was like thirteen years ago. It was at the dedication of the House of Worship in Frankfurt, Germany. I had turned fifteen two weeks before and now I was old enough to choose my own religion. I had decided to be a Baha'i. For me the day was full of special events, each thing that happened seemed significant. Thousands of people were there. Around the House of Worship, there were row upon row of cars parked in the meadows. Their licence plates showed that they had come from many countries in Europe and Asia. There hadn't been enough room in the hall for everyone to sit and my mother and I had been among those who had arrived late and had to stand outside. We now waited to take our turn to go in and see the beautiful round modernistic building. My mother was very proud of me that day, and she told everyone we met that I had just become a Baha'i.

A LEAF OF HONEY

In the jostle of the crowd, I turned around and accidentally bumped into a white haired old lady, who reached out and grabbed hold of me to steady herself. She had a radiant face full of wrinkles and laugh lines. Her eyes were bluish-white and opaque. She was obviously blind. She held my arm the way blind people sometimes do, and began to ask me my name and if I had come far to the dedication. My mother came forward and said that this was a very special day for her son.

"Today is his spiritual birthday. He has just become a Baha'i," said my mother. I was a little embarrassed by the attention, but the woman couldn't see it. The woman was accompanied by a tall lady who might have been her grownup daughter. The old woman maintained a firm hold on my elbow and asked me in a very pleasant, grandmotherish sort of way, if it truly was my "spiritual birthday". I said it was, embarrassed again.

"Well then, I am going to show you something that is the most important thing in my life," said the blind woman. "I am an old woman, and this is the thing that is keeping me going. It is my most prized possession." While the old woman was saying this, her guide silently raised her hand to get my attention. She shook her head from side to side, held a finger up to her lips and gestured that I should not say anything. The blind woman opened her coat with old arthritic hands and brought out a gold doughnut shaped locket on a sturdy chain. She held it tight, close to her chest, and described it to me in detail from memory, as if I were also blind. I wondered how long she had been sightless.

"This is the most precious thing in my life," she whispered again. "Because this day is especially important to you, I would like to show it to you. I want you to remember this day." She cupped her hands around it as if it were a candle that might go out in the wind. Very carefully and meticulously she undid the latch on the side of the locket.

"Now bend near and look what I have," she said as she opened it up. I bent near to see. "A hair from the head of Baha'u'llah," she whispered reverently. I looked inside the locket for a moment and then looked up at her. The lady's guide put her finger up to her lips and shook her head again.

"It is truly wonderful." I didn't know what else to say. The old blind woman sighed and looked past me and saw a scene painted in her memory, a scene I could not see. She closed up the locket, kissed it and put it back in her bosom next to her heart.

A LEAF OF HONEY

"Imagine me having a hair from His head," she said humbly. I looked into the faraway stare of her eyes. She didn't know. There was nothing in the locket. I assumed that there had once been something there and I wanted to ask her how she came to have it, but I didn't dare. Her guide also sighed and nodded her head in a way that said thank you. The old woman kissed me on the cheek and said goodbye. They then moved off and were lost in the crowd.

I wondered if after all these years she was still alive. I didn't know how old she was then, everyone looks old when you're fifteen. But she might have been old enough then to have been alive during the last years of Baha'u'llah's life. Perhaps there had been a hair in the locket at one time. But it really didn't matter. Her reverence for the relic was secondary to her reverence to the Man it came from. That was what mattered. One thing she was right about: I had never forgotten that day.

From what I had learned the night before, it seemed that my religion was similar to Ntumu beliefs in its reverence to knowledge and wisdom. Like the tribesmen, the old woman revered the past and the objects associated with it. The locket was like the old wooden Ntumu statues which still existed, tangible pieces of the past. A physical reminder of something holy, something now treasured in the memory.

It was almost dawn outside as I lay awake in the hammock thinking. Fanny and Anisa were still asleep. I smiled to myself. I could hear my wife gently snoring that snore she assured me she didn't have. I decided I would go see Papa Atanga in Meyo-Ntem. It had been a while since I had seem him. Listening to Papa Akong last night had reminded me of him. These two had something in common. Each was the eldest male of their village.

I remembered the last time I talked to Papa Atanga. I had gotten up enough nerve to ask him about the day of my initiation when he sent me up the river alone in the dugout. He knew that I had almost died and it was for that reason I had never mentioned it before. But now he seemed to like me more than then and I wanted to ask him something that had bothered me since that day. I reminded him that the chief had asked me if I would like to see "something in the river". I had a feeling that these were Papa Atanga's words spoken by the chief. I had gone several times with Sylvain far up river and I had not seen anything unusual.

"What was in the river up around the bend?" I asked.

"Up river is the future." he said simply. I hadn't expected this kind of answer, but it sounded compatible with what other elders had said. The Ntumu view of the future was a string of events which had not come to you yet.

"And down river?" I asked carefully, intimating about the waterfall and the death it held for me.

"Downstream is the future passed by," he said. It was as if I had witnessed the birth of a proverb. I accepted his answer and I decided I would never bring up the subject again.

When I awoke, Fanny was already up and she and Anisa had the fire going. It wasn't late but it was well after sunrise. I had just put my clothes on when the women next door began to wail. Papa Akong had died in his sleep.

48

THE ORAL PALIMPSEST

Dear Dr Kilngott,

Although notions of style and examples of personae may be useful in isolating and examining proverbs, understanding the content of meaning within them is the real worth of my cultural research. I have tried to communicate in these letters as much of the meaning and purpose of the individual proverbs I have collected and to provide drawings which illustrate and contextualize the material environment. Above all, I have tried to reveal that Ntumu proverbs are not just short sayings embodying commonplace facts. They allow me an access to a world of beliefs and values which otherwise would be inaccessible. Ntumu proverbs are oral palimpsests. They are oral parchments with meanings super-imposed upon meanings.

COMMUNICATING CONTENT:

I hope I am conveying to you the meaning and relevance of this body of oral tradition with enough supporting information so that you can sense the cultural flavour. The tribesmen manifest an eloquence of speech which is difficult for me to describe adequately. I have tried to group proverbs in this section according to their similarities in underlying meanings. Often Ntumu proverbs which convey the same message will differ in the personae and situations. By grouping the following proverbs according to latent content, these differences in style and personae can more easily be seen.

252

A LEAF OF HONEY

Presented here are messages and concepts frequently conveyed by different folkloric means in everyday Ntumu conversation. Also included here are those proverbs which appear to be borrowed from other cultures which have been in contact with the Ntumu. In weeks to come I will send you groups of those which seem equivalent to some European proverbs.

The following group of proverbs deals with the giving and taking of advice. Among the Ntumu, a person who does not take advice is said to be *etam*, "alone", that is to say, without the companionship of good counsel. Hence, the following:

(091) "The river is crooked because it goes alone."

When advice is first solicited and then subsequently rejected, it is said:

(092) "Choice is not like a recommendation."

And similarly to convey the idea that advice, founded upon experience, is being given, it is said:

(093) "One doesn't move his mouth without any cassava in it."

Restated, this says, "When an elder speaks, it is because he has something worthwhile to advise".

An elder of the tribe passed away in his sleep the other night. He lived next door and had provided me with this last proverb. As he

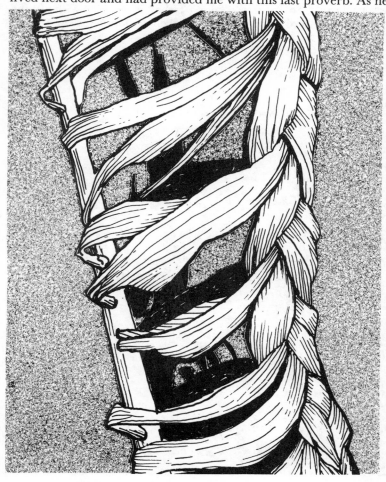

was buried in the backyard of his hut, I was able to attend and record the event. He was a pleasant old man who knew he was going to die.

As several of the proverbs I have already sent you deal specifically with funerals, I thought it would be appropriate to provide you with a couple of sketches. Particularly interesting is the use of raffia in constructing the ornaments of this grave. At the four corners of the grave-mound a canopy of plaited palm fronds was placed and attached such that they met in the middle. Flowers were inserted into the plaits to add colour to the decorations. The second drawing is a close-up of the palm frond plaiting technique.

Sincerely yours, Joseph

49

THE COLD OF DYING TWICE

In many societies, death, and the human activities surrounding the disposal of the body, is a time of heart-rending grief and mutual consolation on the part of the survivors. This is true for the tribesmen of the rainforest. Whatever death may mean for the one departed, it was the loss of a valued member of the tribe for the survivors. The news of the death of Papa Akong travelled by word of mouth and drum with that same mysterious rapidity which maintained an almost instantaneous knowledge of events throughout Ntumuland.

I had heard the drum before but this was the first time I had actually seen it played. It was called *nku* and was reserved for special occasions. It differed from the "music" drums which were made from *olong, ebang* or *esi* trees and had skin stretched over on end. The *nku* was the talking drum. It was a large hollowed log of resonant *bibinga* hardwood laid on its side. It had a slit along the top and a raised striking surface. The drum had a very loud and deep voice which carried well through the jungle. The *nku* made three distinct notes depending on where it was struck. These three notes corresponded to the three tone levels of the vowels in the Ntumu language. One of the younger men started to play. With his two drumsticks he accentuated the syllables and paused between the words. The result was a beat which could be matched against the natural beat of the language. I understood how it worked but it required a special knowledge of the language I had not achieved yet. The drum provided a tonemic template onto which the mind had to find words to fit. I listened hard but I couldn't find all the words. Once someone repeated the words the drummer struck, I could hear them plainly.

b'bom-bim-bim   b'bom-bim   bom-bom   b'bum   b'bim-bom   b'bom
e   kom   bi   te   a   ku   lu   pa   pa   akong   a   wu   ya   ma   an

Village of Ekombite, Come, Papa Akong has died in Ma'an.

The young man played and the *nku* spoke the same message over and over again. Each time it called a different village. In their fields and huts the tribesmen of Ekumujum, Oveng, Vankpwa Evele, Konumekak, Okong, Mebem, Njezeng, Nkoondoo, Aloum, Mokok, Ndemdem, Biyan, Mingkan, Tya'assono and others heard their village called.

When the news of death arrived everyone seemed to know what to do. It was like a well rehearsed fire drill in school. So well known were the individual responsibilities to kinship and community that very little was discussed. Immediately people put together the necessary items and set out for the site of the burial preparations. Before ten o'clock, fifty women and nearly as many men had converged on the hut next door. The *nda mininga* of the deceased's senior wife was soon filled with female mourners, many of them widows themselves. Inside the hut, the walls were lined with a sisterhood of black dresses. With each new arrival the wailing would increase and then subside as each woman joined in the sorrow.

The cold and gaunt body that was Papa Akong was laid in the centre of the room on one of the low raffia beds. It was probably the bed he died in. He had been stripped naked except for the towel placed across his loins. His head was raised on the wooden cross-plank which formed the pillow of these bare and mattressless beds.

By eleven o'clock the number of people had doubled. Many had heard the news while they were far into the jungle hunting or tending their fields and it had taken them awhile to arrive. More would come. Sylvain and his wife Jacqueline arrived along with all of the villagers of Meyo-Ntem. Papa Atanga and the chief of Meyo-Ntem were among them. By now much of the preparation for the burial had begun.

The body was washed of the smell of death and dressed in new clothes. Papa Akong looked quite different now from anytime I had seen him. He usually wore a cloth wrapped around him and tied behind the neck. The old man was probably dressed better now

257

in death than he had been in life. His wives wanted him to look good. He was going to be dead for a long time. Someone had brought a brand new shirt and someone else trousers. The factory packed creases of the yellow shirt and stiff collar detracted from the wrinkles of lifelessness in the man's slung jaw and slightly parted lips. The new dark trousers were a little too short for him and his bare feet lent a sense of humble dignity to the form. The deceased's ablution had been completed and the body dressed ready for burial a mere six hours since his wife had tried to wake him. It was almost noon and time for the funeral. Bodies decompose quickly in the heat of the jungle.

While the women were preparing the body, the men had been digging the grave. Papa Akong would be buried in the cleared area beside his hut, not in the jungle. The tribesmen spent a good portion of their lives trying to keep the jungle from reclaiming the clearing they lived in. It would not be right to surrender one of their elders so easily to it now. He was to be buried so that people would continue to clear the vegetation above him. An itinerant carpenter from a nearby village had been called and was busy fashioning a rough wooden box for a casket. Papa Akong was not going into the ground just wrapped in his cloth. The children were sent out to find flowers and some of the younger men climbed the *alen* trees to collect palm fronds for the canopy.

Although I only knew him for a few months, I wanted to help with the preparations. At the gravesite, I asked if I could help with the digging, remembering the proverb,

> "The hole goes deeper with one digging
> and the other removing the dirt".

"One hand never pulls anything," I said to the man loosening the ground with a digging hoe. "Let me help remove the dirt."

"Helping never breaks the handle of the hoe," I was told. I lowered myself into the hole and used a bucket to lift the dirt out. All of Papa Akong's neighbours took turns helping to dig and remove the dirt.

When the hole was deeper than the height of a man standing in it, it was finished. It was time to bring the body. The carpenter had completed the casket and had placed it on the mound of red earth beside the grave. The casket was basically five planks of hand-hewn wood nailed together and a lid. Several young men went into the hut and lifted Papa Akong gently from his bed and brought

258

him outside. The wailing of the women increased as he was placed in the casket.

The tribe gathered round the grave and the lid was nailed down over Papa Akong. The casket was placed in the ground and everyone with a shovel or hoe began to fill in the hole. When it was about half full some of the men jumped into the hole and tamped down the red earth until the soil was compacted around the casket. The women brought armfuls of the square green bottles and passed them around. Amidst the loud cries of lament, one by one each of those present broke a bottle and let the pieces fall into the grave. The displacement of the casket would produce a mound, but this would only be temporary. The loose dirt which remained above ground would soon be eroded away by the rain and there would be no way to tell where the grave had been. The layer of broken glass would protect it from animals burrowing and from fellow tribesmen digging post holes for a new hut in the future. Whenever people dug down and found a layer of glass they would know that someone was buried underneath. The rest of the dirt was then filled in.

I asked Sylvain and was relieved to know that there would be no *akus*, there would be no "squaring of debts". Papa Akong had outlived his brothers and sisters and there would be no argument as to inheritance. What little he owned in life now belonged to his wives and children. Widows were sometimes made to accept verbal abuses and accusations of negligence at the funeral of their husband. They were sometimes accused of causing the death of their husband. This was not the case here. Papa Akong's old wives had been faithful to their pledge to look after the health of their husband. He had lived a long time and no one would accuse them of negligence.

A canopy of plaited palm fronds was constructed over the grave mound. The children placed flowers in the plaits to add a bit of colour. The canopy would remain until it withered and fell apart. After that, nothing. The Ntumu do not permanently mark their graves.

During the next few days the village was quieter than usual. Papa Akong had always been there and people were used to having him around. It was strange without him. No one wanted to talk much in the *aba* at night. The men carved their bits of raffia wood and smoked. Papa Akong's stool was empty. His short pipe and cache of tobacco leaves were still wedged in the thatch above his place by the fire. It would be many days before I heard a proverb again here.

I went to Meyo-Ntem to see Papa Atanga. I wanted to play a few games of *songo* and ask him about a proverb I had collected some months before:

"Dying twice makes the cadaver cold."

I had not sent it to Dr Kilngott yet. I had kept it aside for future explanation and I felt it was now time to ask its meaning. When I arrived the village was deserted. I knew most of the places where Papa Atanga hung out and I started to make the rounds. There were only a few places to look. He wasn't at his manioc clearing or at the corn-mash still he and others maintained in a secret place by the stream. The fire under the still was cold and the place looked like no one had been there for days. In fact, I hadn't seen any of the tribesmen yet. If they were all together, there was only one place they could be. I found everyone at the canoe-building site.

Papa Atanga was sitting on the stump of the tree which had been felled some weeks before, giving instructions. The huge tree which had laid there for months drying out was now hewn into the recognizable outline of an Ntumu dugout. The axe work was done and now it was time for the adze to hollow out the interior. The dugout lay on a thick bed of wood chips. The tribesmen had several fires burning to drive away the mosquitos with the smoke. Papa Atanga was making himself a new pipe. The tree they had felled had many large hollow horn-like spines around the trunk. He had sliced off one with a machete and was boring a hole at the point with a red hot piece of stout wire.

Sylvain was there and said that they would have to put more chips and leaves on the fire now that "Mr Fresh Meat" had arrived, because this little smoke would never keep the flies away. I was glad to be back working among men who were at ease with my presence. I wished I still lived among them in Meyo-Ntem.

In the afternoon we all went back to the village to eat. This would be the right time to ask Papa Atanga about the proverb. Life was much better now that he seemed to like me. I knew that if I came to him with a proverb, I would leave with two. He wasn't about to be outdone by some other *nyamboro* from another village who had supplied me with the first proverb. We sat with the other men in the *aba* and ate our meal of yams and sauce. After we finished, Papa Atanga and I played *songo*. The mathematics of the game required you to think in base fourteen. I couldn't, so he always won.

"I have a question," I said to Papa Atanga to introduce the subject.

"Why does he always say 'I have a question' instead of just asking?" asked Papa Atanga with a friendly grin.

"I have heard the saying 'Dying twice makes the cadaver cold', but I don't know what it means."

"Do you think you are old enough to know," he said.

"Living with you has made me old," I said.

"Alright then I will tell you. When life is finished, a man's body no longer moves. It is like he is asleep. The man has died once. The man's spirit is still there but if you call the man's name he will not answer. After a while the spirit leaves and goes elsewhere. When his spirit leaves, the body goes cold. This is dying twice. Sometimes a man will die only once and his spirit will not leave. It will wait. If you call his name, the man will wake up and answer." Papa Atanga got out his new pipe and loaded it with tobacco. "As long as the body is warm, his spirit is still there deciding to answer or not."

"But Papa Akong seemed to know he was going to die," I said. I told them what he had said the night before his death.

"Everyone knows he is going to die," he said. "Death is part of life."

"No, I mean Papa Akong seemed to know he was going to die soon," I said.

"If a young man says he is going to die soon, he is right, but if an old man says he is going to die soon, he is more right. There is a proverb which says

'If they say you will die tomorrow, it is not so far off'."

I thought about his words for a moment but before I could ask him to continue, something happened.

There was a loud creaking sound across the way and we all looked up just in time to see Papa Atanga's hut cave in. Three of the four walls leaned to one side and collapsed. The roof came down with them. The remaining wall with his door in it teetered for a moment as if deciding to join the rest and fell on top of the heap like the last one in a house of cards. We all just sat there stunned in silence staring at the dusty mound of rubble which a moment before had been his hut. The termites had finally won. They had eaten through the four corner posts. Then, all of a sudden, someone

261

burst out laughing. Thank God it wasn't me to start it off. He had a long memory. After the mirth was over Papa Atanga would remember who it was. But instantly everyone was leaning back and laughing without any control. Even though he was the last to join in, Papa Atanga finally saw the humour in it.

"That old hut died for the first time ages ago. I think the body is now cold," he said.

50

THE DEPTHS OF SUPERFICIALITY

Dear Dr Kilngott,

It is difficult for me not to compare what I perceive of Ntumu culture with my understanding of American culture. Perhaps this is natural. Everyone has a social point of reference; America is mine. Barthian transactional analysis of political relations is not my *forte*, but compared to the aggressive, informal and loud social standards of California, the Ntumu tribesmen are somewhat calm, ceremonial and laconic. They seem to have developed an unruffled temperament and pace which somehow allows them time to perceive and enjoy life and the world around them. More importantly, they have time to think about things below the surface. Patient speech patterns and profound observations are the cultural characteristics of this serene and quiet-minded people who do not appear to suffer the mental cacophony of my own urban technological society. Typically, the elders of the tribe are terse in speech and tend to avoid the kind of banal conversation which simply states the obvious. This is important in this verbal society, where the wielders of proverbs and wisdom try to set a standard of communication which dives deep into the "connectedness" of meanings, relationships and significances.

Overall, the Ntumu elders' use of proverbs and the quality of their collective consultations reveal the profound responsibility they have accepted for the moral and social well-being of the tribe. These demonstrate that homeostasis and continuity are important to the Ntumu. Social equilibrium can only be maintained through the realization that the talent and participation of every individual is vital. It is where culture and personality overlap in a very special way which, no doubt, Gregory Bateson would have enjoyed. In the tribe no one is socially expendable. This is more than just an idealistic or philosophical statement. I feel that it is especially valid for tribes like the Ntumu where the population is so small. It is here that I find that I cannot help but compare cultures. America has attained a large enough critical mass of population to view social expendability as acceptable within the safety margins of individuals they might term "non-vital members". Perhaps the lack of a community identity allows this to happen.

An example of this realization was demonstrated in a council meeting I attended recently as an observer, where I was allowed to sit outside the circle of elders while they consulted together concerning a theft. Surprisingly, the items stolen, the thief involved and the details of the crime were never mentioned. Everyone seemed to be sufficiently informed of the details of the crime before they arrived at the meeting. The purpose of the meeting was to examine more important issues. The elders concentrated their attention on the implications of the crime, the social effect it would have on the entire tribe. An equivalent assemblage of social elders in America would have been called judges, but the function of these Ntumu elders had gone a step beyond adjudication and the final conviction or acquittal of the accused. Their consultation seemed to begin at the point which American judges would have seen as the end of their responsibility. In American society the goal of a trial would simply be to determine the guilt or innocence of the individual and prescribe the appropriate punishment or retribution. At the tribal council meeting, however, the issues of guilt and punishment were not as paramount as the social consequences and cultural ramifications of the crime. Social survival took precedence here. The elders did not dwell on unproductive accusations and recriminations by discussing what everyone already knew.

They approached the matter quite differently. Justice was married to continuity. Adjudication included the process of re-establishing tribal unity and cooperation. The thief was not seen as an automatic outcast but rather as a needed member of the social workings of the tribe who was morally disabled and needed rehabilitation. This rehabilitation included discovering the hidden root causes of the crime and understanding the probable effects on the fabric of the community. It was understood that the theft may have been the fault of the individual concerned, but the responsibility of the crime rested on the shoulders of the elders, whose job it was to oversee the social and moral well-being of the tribe.

Included below are some of the proverbs which the elders used to remind each other to look deeper than just the apparent, conspicuous and self-evident things in life. The multi-layered construction and compounded dualism of meanings in all Ntumu proverbs reveal that the tribe has acquired a great depth of perception about human existence and human potential. This group of proverbs communicate obviousness. They are all quite different in the way that they do this, but the function that they serve in conversation is fairly similar.

(094) "The contusion on the face is seen by everyone."

When someone comes home from the fields and has a bruise or a scratch on his forehead, no one comments that he has a bump on the head. They ask him, rather, if he is hurt in other places which cannot be seen. The proverb analogizes the fact that everyone has the ability to see the obvious and that people should look deeper at the things they cannot readily see.

In the same way, the following interrogative riddle uses a play on words:

(095) "Do you look for a chicken's horns on his head?"

The tacit portion of this question needs to be explained. The full question should read: "Do you look for a chicken's horns on his head, when they are on his legs?" This is a conundrum. The Ntumu term *tang:* "horn" is most often used in conjunction with specific animal terms to identify what kind of horn it is. For example, *tangnyat:* "cape buffalo horn" and *tangzo'o:* "antelope horn or antler". In these and most other cases, "horns" are found on the head of the animal. However, *tangkup:* "chicken horn" mentioned in the proverb translates as "rooster's spur" which of course is not found on the head but on the rooster's leg. This provides a clever play on words. This question is the cultural equivalent of telling someone he had a firm grasp of the obvious.

The following chiding proverb compares the person who does not see the obviousness with a fool:

(096) "The fool already knows the lie."

A LEAF OF HONEY

The word "fool" in Ntumu carries with it a rather strong implication of imbecility, because it not only describes a person who lacks judgement, but also the village idiot. Another example:

(097) "One never asks if the *zong* will be put in the cassava leaves."

Zong is an edible leaf which is always pounded with cassava leaves and then cooked. It is never served without cassava leaves and is an obvious ingredient to one of the tribesmen's favourite dishes. The following share the same content:

(048) "If the hoop is too big for the elephant, what animal will it fit?"

(099) "The hoop is bigger than the elephant but the antelope wants to try it."

The antelope mentioned here is the *okbweng*. It is cat-sized and the smallest of all the antelopes in the Ntumu region. By analogy, it is opposite in size to that of the elephant. These two proverbs deal with mental capacity and the appropriateness of the elders to handle larger issues in the administration of the tribe. They convey the message "It is obvious that you lack the capacity to deal with this matter". All of the above proverbs express a sense of obviousness by presenting examples and situations common in the everyday life of the Ntumu, or clear exaggerations.

In my conversations with the elders, I have discovered that evaluation of cultural practices goes both ways. The Ntumu have some acute observations about *ntangan*, "whitemen". The tribesmen sometimes admit that they find whitemen rather shallow: all style and no content. This belief, they say, is substantiated by the apparent habit whitemen have of talking about obvious things as if they were novel or new. The most ludicrous example one elder cited was meeting a missionary in a torrential downpour and hearing him say, "My goodness, it's really raining hard today". What makes it even more incomprehensible is that whitemen make this kind of statement knowing full well that the listener knows it is obvious too. The Ntumu do not see this as rhetorical but rather as a cultural sickness or handicap. They say that whitemen seem to use speech to avoid thinking. Even some of the tribes the *ntangan* have influenced are beginning to fill their conversations with meaningless comment which merely states the obvious. The neighbouring Bulu tribesmen have adopted the superficial greeting *mbung kiri*, "good morning", which is meaningless to the ear and an American missionary invention.

The Ntumu find this somewhat repugnant. It is also difficult for a tribesmen to understand the function in whitemen's society of asking a question to which the speaker already knows the answer. Talking is not a pastime. Simplistic comments in America about human existence, like:

"Life is hard . . . and then you die",

may be funny in English, but translated, humour of this nature would only lend credence to the Ntumu belief that, as a people, whitemen have not yet fathomed the depths of their superficiality.

All of these are aspects of *ntangan* culture which the Ntumu elders can clearly do without. Perhaps this is why there was such opposition to my initial application to stay in the village. One elder has pointed out that if the eyes only see the superficial part of reality and the ears only hear the noise in life, then together they will teach the mind to become dull and lazy. The result will eventually be a tongue which only describes the obvious and a soul which speaks primarily to hear itself talk.

It was devastating to listen to such an insightful evaluation of my race. In defence of my culture I decided that sometimes the wisest thing to say is nothing.

I have included a composite drawing of four ancestral statues I have seen. There are not many of these left. No one seems to make them anymore. They are representational of a mental and physical world far removed from the present.

Living with the tribesmen, learning their language and studying their proverbs, literally at the feet of their elders, have together permitted me a glimpse of a new world-view, a different reality. This has not been quite the mystical experience Carlos Castaneda has described, but I have learned a great deal about the world and my fellow man and have come to realize that their world-view is not a separate reality but rather a hidden portion of all reality. All cultures seem to have a piece. With tolerance, loving-kindness and careful guidance, they have shown me where to look to find the other world among the leaves.

Sincerely yours, Joseph

51

HUMILITY AND CULTURAL ARROGANCE

Papa Atanga rummaged through the rubble of his hut and salvaged the items he wanted to keep. We spent the rest of the day collecting fresh material from the jungle for a new hut. He chose a spot across the common area from the old hut for the site of his new one. He didn't want to clean up the rubble and build again on the same site. So he just left it there. He said that the termites needed something to eat. Better that they should finish eating his old hut before they started on the new one. By the end of the next day he had a new hut. We spent the morning digging post holes for the uprights and the afternoon tying the horizontal slats in place and putting the roof on. He said he would wait until the next heavy rain to mud-daub his walls.

Working shoulder to shoulder with my friends felt good. Living among the Ntumu afforded me the opportunity of experiencing again the fundamental cooperation and unity that can exist between different cultures and races. My year among the tribesmen would be over all too soon and this saddened me. I owed them more than they knew. They had provided me with experiences that had dug deep into my own psyche and rooted out layers of ignorance and prejudice I would have otherwise been unconscious of having or perhaps unwilling to admit to possessing. In the presence of these men I had learned more than they taught me: I had learned something about myself. Perhaps this is why Papa Atanga's attitude towards me had changed some months back. Perhaps I was now worth knowing after I had realized that just below the surface there still lurked the traces of racial

269

preconceptions which I had probably carried since childhood, things I had probably acquired from schoolmates and television. I knew I now had a more realistic appraisal of race and culture. Perhaps Papa Atanga's attitude had changed because mine had.

Mental self-awareness is an ongoing and sometimes painful process. The tribesmen continued a process of mental and cultural education which had begun in Latin America. It was there I learned the first big lesson: what cultural arrogance is.

I had just began to work for the *Instituto Baha'i* in Riohacha, Colombia as a religious teacher among the Guajiros, a nomadic people who owned few personal possessions, usually no more than what they could carry. The women wore colourful dresses that covered them from head to toe and the menfolks went about semi-naked. They were herdsmen who rarely built permanent huts and who spent most of their time out of doors because it hardly ever rained in the Guajiran desert.

Although I never consciously thought that they were simple-minded, I had come to the tacit supposition that they had a limited vocabulary. There naturally seemed to be a one-to-one correlation between "primitiveness" and lack of "knowledge". First of all, it was hard to take men seriously who went around in multi-coloured loincloths and wore little pom-poms on their sandals. It was like being in the company of clowns dressed only in their underpants. It was not what you would expect from verbose and erudite sophisticates. I felt I had my work cut out for me in bringing religious enlightenment to this primitive tribe.

One night I was sitting around a campfire in a village near Uribia and I thought it might be a good time to begin to try and translate a simple children's prayer which began:

"O God, guide me, protect me,
illumine the lamp of my heart
and make me a brilliant star . . ."

It was a straight-forward sentence full of uncomplicated concepts, presented in images which would be easy to translate. The verbs seemed to be sufficiently unambiguous. I asked the group of men present if they would teach me some Guajiro words. I would say a word or phrase in Spanish and the Indians would give me their equivalent term. It was lucky for me that all of the men were bilingual. The men had no trouble with the first few words but when I got to the word "illumine" I ran into a conceptional snag.

A LEAF OF HONEY

"What does 'illumine' mean?" asked one of the men. It seemed reasonable that they didn't understand the word. It was a little more complex a concept than "to guide" or "to protect".

"Illumine means 'to give or receive light'," I said simply.

"What kind of light?"

"Well, how many kinds of light can there be?" I said with an air of patronizing superiority.

"Well we have more than one word for this," he said as he proceeded to tick off on the fingers of one hand several words in Guajiro. The other men supplemented this list until all ten fingers were extended. I didn't speak any of their language so I asked him what all these words meant.

"Well, we have different kinds of light and we don't know which kind you want." he said.

"Give me some examples." I said.

"To begin with, we have 'primary' and 'secondary' and 'tertiary' light," he said counting on his fingers again.

"I don't understand," I admitted. The man pointed at the fire.

"Well, look at the campfire, you can see those flames because of primary light." The other men nodded in agreement. "And secondary light . . . " He paused as he pointed at me. "I can see you because of the campfire, that's secondary light." One of the older men whose command of Spanish was greater interrupted vying with the others to give the next word.

" 'Tertiary' light is when you're walking at night in the full moon. Sometimes it is as bright as day so you can actually see without a lantern: that's tertiary light. The light comes from the sun to the moon to the ground." The man repeated the words in Guajiro and then translated. "Primary, secondary and tertiary light, and we have a word for each of these different kinds of light". Out of the darkness and away from the campfire someone called out a word. The Indians beside the fire talked with the unseen voice for a moment and soon a very old man joined us in the circle. He didn't speak Spanish so the younger man translated.

"There's another word we forgot about," he informed me.

"What is this other word?" I asked.

"Well, roughly it's 'quaternary light'. Our grandfather here explained that if, on the same moonlit night, you hold out your hand like this, above the ground and bend down and look up at it, on the underside, you can actually see your palm in the shadow of the moonlight. You can see it because the 'tertiary light' bouncing off the ground is coming up and hitting your hand, so we have this word 'quaternary light' for that too." If it wasn't enough that from the words he used like "bounce" and "hit" that these Indians knew the highly sophisticated fact that light "travelled", the man then went on to describe the Guajiro words for reflection, refraction, diffused, direct, incessant, coloured, non-coloured, and something they called "double-light". Each of these concepts had a distinct word. This didn't appear to be a specialist knowledge; everyone seemed fluent and conversant on the subject.

"What is 'double-light'?" I knew that if I didn't ask, the word would haunt me forever.

"Sometimes the moon passes in front of the sun and the edge of sun shines around it. When this happens, everything has two shadows on the ground." With his description of the effect of a partial solar-eclipse, I began to re-evaluate my expectations as to the size of their vocabulary. I finally chose "primary light" as the appropriate word to use in the translation of the prayer. Things went along smoothly until I got to the part that read: "a brilliant star".

"Brilliant star?" one of them blurted. The rest burst out laughing. It was contagious. I joined in with that nervous and irrational laugh of someone who is left out and doesn't understand what's so funny but laughs anyway.

"What are you laughing at?" I finally inquired.

"Which star?" he asked cheerfully, wiping his eye. He took his hand and swept it across the vault of the sky and said, "All the brilliant ones have names; only the faint ones are nameless and called just 'stars'. You can't say 'brilliant star' in Guajiro. Its like not knowing your mother's name, and referring to her as 'beautiful *thing*.'"

Over the course of the next few hours I learned the Guajiro names for Procyon, Sirius, Betelgeuse, Rigel, Aldebaran, Capella and many more. All of them as familiar as their mothers' names. I discovered that their mental catalogue of stellar names wasn't their only cultural *forte*. Their starlore included legends about gods and constellations which differed from the Greco-Roman ones I knew. The pearl-like Pleiades were called the "wanton-women" and the belt of Orion was called:

"three-men-standing-abreast-at-arms-length",

all in one word. We eventually chose the pole star Polaris as the most appropriate celestial body for the translation of "a brilliant star" because it carried the sense of "guide-star" and agreed nicely with the verb at the beginning of the prayer.

During the day, they were nomadic herdsmen, but at night they were superb astronomers and could distinguish planets from stars by keeping mental track of their movements. The youngest among them knew more about the heavens than I did. I will always remember that night. That was the night I discovered how culturally presumptuous I had been. From then on I felt befittingly humbled in their presence and stopped acting and thinking like a culturally arrogant missionary.

52

TEMPTATION, FRIENDSHIP AND SHARING

Dear Dr Kilngott,

The concept of temptation does not occur in many proverbs I have collected but it is an interesting abstraction in that the tribesmen seem to lack those behavioural rationalizations which give rise to statements in English like "the devil made me do it" or "I couldn't help myself". From conversations on the subject and their explanations of motives and conduct, I have come to the conclusion that the Ntumu believe that temptation is self-induced and not caused by external forces. I know that this is a subtle conceptional distinction but the absence of an extraneous impulse helps to explain the tribesmen's tendency toward introspection and auto-accountability.

Naturally there are situations which are considered to be more conducive to succumbing to temptation than others. The following two proverbs demonstrate that repeated exposure is one such situation:

(100) "*Zuing* ate the millepede because it saw it frequently."

Zuing is a small canine and perhaps related to the hyena.

(101) "The young man killed the viper because he saw it very often."

Neither the millepede nor the viper are sought by the *zuing* or the Ntumu as particularly tasty food sources. The ease of capture, however, is attributed as the reason for choosing it over something more delicious but harder to find. In the second proverb, however, the lack of age of the "young man" implies that an older man would not have been tempted.

Friendship is important among the tribesmen and in analyzing the content of Ntumu proverbs I have found that through these adages certain aspects of friendship are defined. In the following group there are more examples of horns, which follows on from last week. All of these relate friendship to sharing, giving and receiving. The first is the Ntumu equivalent of the English saying "A friend in need is a friend indeed".

(102) "You think of me as you think of a spoon."

"When someone wants to eat he needs a spoon" is the message here. When someone is hungry he thinks of his friends. In the following, the expected benefits of friendship are shown to be defined differently by different people. It advises that friends shouldn't expect too much:

(103) "Pig missed getting horns though they were distributed by his uncle."

Here pig's uncle doesn't refer to any real or attributed animal relative but symbolizes close friendship. *Ndomo,* "mothers' brother" in the Ntumu society is seen as an amicable kin — not a substitute father figure but rather a caring relative whose role or function it is to give guidance and support to his nieces and nephews. The situation in this proverb is created to parallel by analogy a real-life situation in which a friend misses receiving a share of something his friend is passing out because he was sure his friend would save him a share. Instead of coming forward with the rest to take a share, he is left out. In a sense, solicited nepotism. The above is sometimes used in response to the following proverb in which a friend is admonished for not being more generous:

(104) "My friend, share again because man doesn't know what the last share will be."

The word *mbot* here is the singular of "a man" and is not necessarily collective nor does the syntax of the proverb imply a divine recompense.

Sincerely yours, Joseph

53

ONE ARROW IS NOT SAFE

Just after dawn one morning as I rode through the Ma'an on my way to a nearby village, I saw the *Secretaire du Commissaire* standing in the middle of the road with his hands on his hips. He put out his hand and indicated that I should stop. He told me to get off my bike and follow him to his mud hut office. He was usually unpleasant and curt, but it was plain to see that this morning he was in an especially foul mood. I got off the Yamaha and pushed it along behind the *Secretaire.* I wondered what this was all about. I knew that the *Commissaire* was away on business, so this summons was his idea. He unlocked the door of his office-hut and went in. The hut consisted of three rooms: an anteroom and two offices. He unlocked a second door and told me to go in. This room must be his office. It was just big enough for a wooden desk and chair. He followed me in and sat down behind the desk. I noticed that there wasn't another chair.

"Where were you going just now?" he asked me in French.

"I was going to Bitoto," I replied.

"What were you going to do there?"

"I wanted to do some research, I wanted to collect some proverbs from a man there," I said struggling with the French. I always had trouble with verb tenses other than the present. He continued to ask questions about the past which were more and more difficult to answer with my limited knowledge of French. Every time I fumbled through an answer, he grimaced. He would wrinkle up his nose in disgust as if I had just produced an unpleasant odour. Finally he had enough.

A LEAF OF HONEY

"Why don't you speak French properly?" he shouted. "You are trying to make believe that you don't speak French. What are you trying to hide?" He continued to shout and ranted on about foreigners and whitemen. He was getting himself really worked up. I just stood there listening and wondering what this was all about until I heard the word *"terroriste"* in French. All of a sudden he banged his fist on the desk and demanded that I empty out my pockets and show him what I had in the leather bag over my shoulder. I wasn't about to refuse. I tried to tell him that I respected the laws of the land in which I resided and I respected his authority to search me. I had nothing to hide. I placed everything on his desk: a few coins, my passport, a copy of my research permit, a bound notebook, a few pencils and a camera. He examined these for a moment and looked dissatisfied. As I stood there with an empty bag at my side and my turned out pockets hanging like ears at my hips he demanded that I remove my wristwatch and wedding ring. I silently complied and I added these to the pile.

He opened his drawer and took out a piece of paper. He looked at it for a moment and showed it to me. It was an Interpol wanted poster. It had two photographs of some terrorist simply called "Carlos", no last name, who was apparently wanted for several political assassinations in France. The *Secretaire* must have just received it and this was the reason for all these questions. He held the mug shots up beside my face and told me to stand so that he could compare the profiles. He said he could see some resemblance. It was not difficult to see that he was lying and disappointed in not making the biggest arrest of his career. Not only was it unlikely that an urban guerrilla like Carlos would be posing as an American anthropologist with a wife and family, and roughing it in the jungles of southern Cameroon, the only physical characteristics the man in the photograph and I had in common was the fact that we were both featherless bipeds.

The *Secretaire*, however, had gone this far and wasn't about to back down and say that he was mistaken. Apologising wasn't in his character. He was the kind of man who was taller and stronger than those around him and who had grown accustomed to the rewards intimidation and violence could bring. His position made him the second most powerful man in the district and with his boss away he was temporarilly *Numero Uno*.

He asked me what I was really doing in the District of Ma'an. I told him that, as he could see from my passport and research permit, I was an American anthropologist studying Ntumu language and culture. At this point he decided to test me. He now insisted on addressing me in Ntumu rather than French. Being a stranger here like myself, Ntumu was not his native tongue either, but during his long stay in Ma'an he had acquired much more of the tribesmen's language than I had. The questioning continued. He began to bombard me with questions in Ntumu and didn't wait for any response. He really wasn't interested in hearing the answers. This was becoming the setting of some kind of interrogation.

"To what end?" I asked myself. The *Secretaire* was just using the wanted poster as an excuse to question me. But what did he really want? His questions were latent with all kinds of accusations. Did he want to have me confess to something for which he could then arrest me for?

Hanging on the wall next to his desk in plain sight were two long rubber truncheons. I knew what they were for. I had heard about them from the whisperings of the villagers. They were used when people couldn't pay their taxes or didn't act with sufficient respect. They were also used to extract confessions. He reached over and took one down and slipped his hand through the cord at the base. This was not a good sign. He began to gently slap it against his palm. He increased the force and frequency as he continued asking me questions. It made a sickening thump. Although it must have been painful to him, he was obviously enjoying the feel of it and watching me squirm. I knew that if he succeeded in intimidating me, my research here would be finished. Being an expatriate provided me with a very thin immunity. That seemed not to matter to him as he continued tacitly to threaten physical violence. Striking me would change my status forever and begin a process of bullying which would soon affect my wife and child. Ma'an was very remote and local officials weren't as interested in the national reputation of the country as they were in the larger towns and cities.

If I was going to be forced to respond to accusations in Ntumu, then the only thing left was to show a bit of class. I would have to resort to using some of the phrases which I had learned from my study of Ntumu proverbs. I had to begin to direct the situation away from its course towards physical violence. The *Secretaire* seemed like the kind of person who only thinks in terms of winning or losing. If he hit me he would win; if he didn't he would lose. I had to introduce a route which could end in a draw. The challenge of verbal confrontation seemed the best route. I had to think quickly. I had to move the challenge of verbal confrontation towards him before his plan of violence reached me. I hoped such a challenge would lure him to engage in a battle of wits instead of an act of violent intimidation. There was only one proverb that I could think of appropriate to the situation. I took a chance and called his bluff.

"If your machete is not cutting down trees, put it back in its sheath," I said pointing at the truncheon. "Unless you intend to use that thing you had better hang it back on the wall." He recognised this proverb for what it was and demonstrated that he had learned a few sayings himself during his long posting in Ma'an.

"The machete is doing the axe's work," he countered, referring to the fact that the *Commissaire* was away and that he was acting in his stead. This also intimated that his actions would be supported by his boss. He was now distracted by the word play, but I needed something really audacious for him to rise to the bait of the challenge.

"When you think the machete is getting sharper and sharper, it will soon break," I said snapping my fingers. I blew across my fingers to show that there was nothing left of the broken machete. The *Secretaire* sucked air audibly at the exaggerated bravado of this gesture. Although his fluency of the language was great, my repertoire of Ntumu proverbs and gestures was equal to it. A battle of wits would be on even footing. He leaned back in his chair and smiled. He unconsciously began to respond to the change in confrontation and had stopped slapping his hand with the truncheon. He was hooked.

"You think you are pretty smart don't you?" he asked. "I have your passport and your belongings. You can't go anywhere or do anything. We will see who will win the fight." To keep control over the direction of the conversation, the best thing I could do would be to answer exclusively in proverbs.

"One never counts how many times he falls while fighting," I replied. It is at the end of the fight when people count.

"A small puppy never frightens a big animal," he countered, swelling out his already large chest. He seemed to be enjoying this tit for tat. He put the truncheon down to free his hands for gestures.

279

"If I say I don't want to quarrel, it does not mean that I am weak. Two people who disagree is not a fight," I said, joining two proverbs together.

"You should treat me with more respect in front of the tribesmen. If you did, there would be no fight, we could be friends," he said. Although I was never discourteous to him, I never chose to socialize with him nor had I invited him to my hut for dinner.

"The mouth which ties friendship is the same one that kills it," I said.

"Do you know the proverb which says 'After having killed a person, you go to his funeral'?" he asked.

"Death is easily communicable," I said.

"You should watch your tongue. 'The crab's pincher has killed the crab itself'," The crab's pincher has killed the crab itself," he said.

"Crab couldn't dance because of his many feet," I said lamely. I couldn't think of another proverb with a crab in it.

" 'You speak like a broken drum.' You are stupid. You speak nonsense. This is not the place for you. You whitemen should go home to *chez vous*," he said pointing at me and lapsing into French."

"When you point your finger at someone, your elbow points at you," I said, reminding him that he wasn't Ntumu either.

"I am warning you, listen to my words and 'stand under the tree of wisdom'," he said. "I moved you off that island and I moved you out of Meyo-Ntem. Soon I will move you out of Ma'an and be rid of you. You have no right to be here. You are alone here. Go back to your country. 'One arrow is not safe.' "

"One spear doesn't make noise in a sheath," I answered, intimating that I was more than an arrow.

With a wave of his hand, he dismissed me. The game was over. I asked for my belongings back and the *Secretaire* saw this as an affront and ordered me to get out of his office. I beat a hasty retreat. For the moment I was satisfied that I had been able to divert his attention away from violence, but this was only temporary. He would try again and I knew I would not be successful a second time to distract him.

I rode my motorcycle back to the hut and told Fanny what had transpired. She was worried. Looking at the expression on her face I could see that this kind of harassment had to end. I needed to do something which would force the *Secretaire* to stop or at least long enough for me to finish my research and leave his jurisdiction. I didn't believe the *Commissaire* would help. There was only one person I could turn to. I decided to seek the help of the *Prefet*. I immediately sat down and wrote him a note:

His Excellency
Prefet du Ntem
Ebolowa

Dear Sir:

I have this day been interrogated by the Secretaire du Commissaire in Ma'an who confiscated a number of personal belongings including my passport, wedding ring, research permit, notebook, camera and wristwatch. When asked when they would be returned, he said that they were now his property and that he would keep them. I asked to speak to the Commissaire de District de Ma'an about this matter, but the Secretaire du Commissaire informs me that the only way I can speak to the Commissaire is through him and he assures me that he will never consent to this. So having no one else to turn to, I humbly request that you investigate this matter and have these stolen articles returned to me.

                    Respectfully yours,
                    Joseph Roy Sheppherd

carbon copy: His Excellency the American Ambassador
                    Commissaire du District de Ma'an
                    Secretaire du Commissaire

I kissed Fanny and asked her to find Anisa and for the two of them to stay in the hut until I returned. I told her that the *Secretaire* would probably be around to the hut to ask her where I went. She should tell him the truth that I had gone to see the Prefet in Ebolowa. I feared that if we all got on the bike and tried to leave we would be stopped and my wife and child would be directly involved. I hated to leave them but I knew they would not face any danger while I was away in Ebolowa to see the *Prefet*.

281

A LEAF OF HONEY

I filled up the Yamaha with gasoline and put two copies of the letter in a sealed envelope addressed to the *Commissaire*. I drove up to the office of the *Secretaire* and left the bike idling outside and went in. I knocked respectfully at his door and waited until he said "*Entrez*". He was still sitting behind his desk examining my things, obviously pleased with himself for having won the battle of wits. He was surprised to see me back so soon and grinned odiously and showed me how nicely my wristwatch looked on his arm. I smiled back at him and handed him the sealed envelope without a word. He was still turning the envelope over and deciding whether to open it, when I got on my bike and rode away. Although it was sealed and addressed to his boss, I knew full well that he would open the letter and either reseal it or replace the envelope. I counted on the fact that he couldn't read much English and that it would be some time before he could get it translated. By the time he surmised what it contained, I would be so many hours down the road that even the *Commissaire's* Land-Rover couldn't catch up with me.

54

MIND YOUR OWN BUSINESS

Dear Dr Kilngott,

Several Ntumu proverbs communicate the message of "Don't involve yourself with that which doesn't concern you". The ones presented here do this in quite different ways. The first is a complex situational analogy showing the social interrelationships of certain animals:

(105) "*Soso* warns of the presence of *ayan*, sparrow warns of the presence of hawk, But the maiden who stands with red eyes, what is her problem?"

Here, the *ayan* is a non-poisonous green snake and the small *soso* bird his potential dinner. *Soso* warns other *sosos* for this reason, just as the sparrow warns of hawk. The sparrow is also called "Jesus' stone". The myth from which this name comes is as follows:

"When Jesus was a child He played with other children. One day He entered into a child's contest of throwing stones. The other children threw first and their stones went far but when Jesus threw his stone, it went higher and farther than the rest. It went so high and far that it became *mveakuna,* the sparrow."

The origin of this myth is unknown to me. However, if I had to guess, I would say that it is an old myth from the neighbouring Bulu tribe which has been modified and propagated by missionaries.

In the proverb above, after two analogous relationships are established, the maiden is added as a literal example. This is a

283

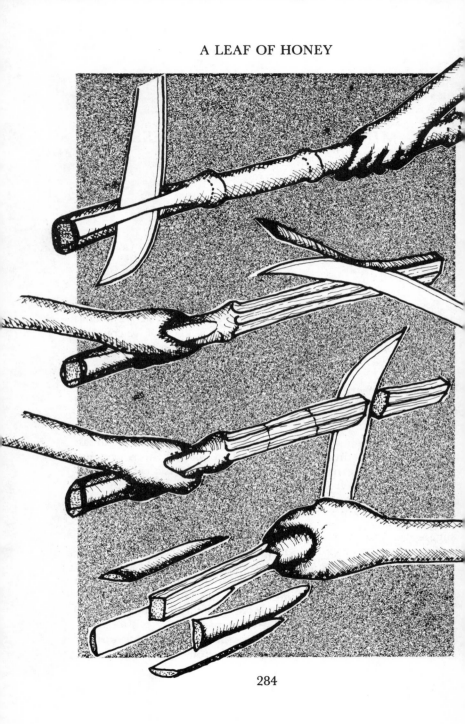

284

common format. But this addition is subtly and cleverly related to the analogous animal elements. The question "Why is she crying?" is asked, for neither *ayan* nor the hawk will attack her. She should therefore be unconcerned. The situation created here appears to be condensed in the following:

(106) "The people concerned with the problem are doing nothing but your eyes are red. Why?"

In a mocking short proverb in the first person, another situation is created to communicate "Mind your own business":

(107) "I am just helping and people are shouting."

And in humorous imagery, the following is another example of a situation created to show the futility of becoming involved in something in which a person has no role:

(108) "In a dance, where you have no girl friend, you come with a fat and long sugarcane on your shoulder."

During traditional dances in which public social interaction between unmarried males and females is acceptable, it is customary for a boy to bring the girl of his fancy a gift. Formerly this gift was some food stuff such as sugarcane. Now it is more likely to be money. The sugarcane also figures in a few other non-related proverbs such as:

(109) "The one who says 'give me' never eats the lower part of the sugarcane."

Giving is better than receiving. For the Ntumo the one who requests something never receives the best part of the gift. In short the one who is generous to others is rewarded himself. The tribesmen have a clever way of peeling and serving a stick of sugarcane. The best part is at the fat end, at the base of the cane. It is the last part to be given away and it is impossible to peel this last section without getting your hands sticky. The proper manner is first to loosen the bark at the fat end and then hold on to it while the rest is peeled and cut into segments. This custom is the basis for this proverb. It is hard to imagine without having seen it. I have included a drawing to illustrate.

Sincerely yours, Joseph

55

CULTURE AND WORLD-VIEW

I took my letter of protest directly to the office of the *Secretaire du Prefet* in Ebolowa. He wasn't there, nor was the *Prefet*. There was only one clerk in the building who said the *Secretaire* would be back in about a week. The *Prefet* and his entire staff were touring some of the towns and villages to the south, near Ambam and the Gabonese border. I couldn't wait a week. I handed the clerk my letter asking if it could be delivered to the *Prefet* at his earliest convenience. I turned the bike around and headed home. The fact that the letter was now in his office would have some effect on my adversary in Ma'an. Maybe it would be a restraining one. Perhaps delivering this letter would buy me enough time to finish my research. Perhaps the *Secretaire du Commissaire* would ease up while the *Prefet* reviewed the matter. In any case, knowing how slow the wheels of bureaucracy turned, it could be months before I even heard from the *Prefet*. In the meantime, I would concentrate on writing up my research and staying out of the way of the *Secretaire* in Ma'an. I was counting on the fact that I had carefully written the letter, not intimated that the *Commissaire* had any part in this matter, only his *Secretaire*. This would allow the *Commissaire* to put the entire blame on his underling if the *Prefet* began to ask questions. It would also allow me to seek the *Commissaire's* help in returning my possessions. In any case, the seized items would probably be returned as a gesture of correcting a "misunderstanding". There seemed to be an awful lot of maybes and probablys in this thinking but there wasn't much else I could do about it now. I hadn't started this confrontation and I would just have to ride it out.

A LEAF OF HONEY

The ground was dry and I had made good time that morning on the road alone on the bike and if I pushed it, I could be back in Ma'an just after nightfall. I wouldn't have time to see the Elakas on this trip, but I did stop off at the post office. There was a stack of letters waiting for us from Dr Kilngott, my mother, Fanny's family and others. One letter was from my brother Paul. I had wondered what had happened to him. He had promised to write me almost a year ago and this was the first letter I had received. I didn't stop to read any of the mail now and put it in my bag. When a load of mail came, Fanny and I liked to open one a day and savour each letter.

Sending letters to Africa was always a gamble and the odds were that many things would never get through. Some people were luckier than others. My mother's letters were always going astray. I suspected that somewhere in Cameroonian postal service there was a person who thought he was her son and collected the letters from my mother. My postal "brother" certainly got more letters than I did. Paul's letter must have been the luckiest letter I had ever seen. It was simply addressed as follows:

Joseph Sheppherd
Ebolowa
Africa

It lacked a post office box number and, worse yet, it had no country. Ebolowa was about the fifteenth largest town in Cameroon and there were some fifty countries in Africa. The probability of this letter ever reaching me was about a zillion to one. The envelope bore many rubber stamped messages which indicated that at some stage it had been returned to sender, not because of an incomplete address but for insufficient postage. Apparently, my brother had initially put only 17 cents worth of stamps on it. This wasn't enough of a wager to bet on its getting to Africa. When it was returned for insufficient postage, he had put another 14 cents on it and upped his ante to 31 cents: the minimum house stakes. This proved to be enough to speed it on its way via snail mail. 31 cents certainly wasn't enough money for the work someone had to do in looking up the name of the small town of Ebolowa in African atlases and gazetteers.

The villages I passed through were familiar to me now. I had been over this road so many times. I knew the names of all the villages and some of the villagers. They often waved at me as I passed by. In some villages, the children would hear me coming and run to the side of the road and jump up and down shouting either "*Ntangan! Ntangan!*" — "Whiteman! Whiteman!" or "*Yoser, Yoser, Yoser*". There weren't many motorcycles on the road and they knew it would be me. I waved back but didn't stop this time. I knew they would be disappointed. I always carried candy for the children and usually I would stop and give them each a piece. I wanted to get back to Fanny and Anisa as soon as possible. I tried to stop worrying about them and feel the relaxing wind in my face. I reminded myself that it was a beautiful clear day but my mind was still filled with troubled thoughts. I told myself that I was going as fast as I could and I would be home that evening. I would just have to wait. I was also worried that this trouble with the *Secretaire* would interfere with the last stages of my research.

It was almost time to submit my final summary of the fieldwork and I needed time to collect my thoughts. It was time to review the things I had learned and write them down coherently. I had sent Dr Kilngott a fairly complete phonetic and phonemic analysis of the Ntumu language and some notes on tribal technology, but it was now time to tackle the most difficult objective of my research, a description of Ntumu world-view based on a content analysis of their proverbs. Thinking about this problem helped me to forget about what might be waiting for me in Ma'an.

There are those things that you feel and believe and then there are those things you write down to be read by your supervisor. Basic ideals sometimes sound so trite when they are staring up at you from a sheet of paper. I valued the esteem of my supervisor and didn't want to write things which would lower it. The fear of ridicule is an effective inhibitor. How could I write in a profound way the simple or even simplistic notions I had? Dr Kilngott was used to supervising doctoral candidates. What would he think of the twaddle I was apt to write as an undergraduate? I didn't have the academic experience yet which would tell me what his expectations were.

To write about someone else's world-view is not easy. So many of the voiced beliefs people have are built upon tacit or unrealized basics which are difficult to articulate. This is especially difficult if your overall objective is to understand something about the commonalities which support all systems of self-preception. Culture and world-view are linked. You couldn't describe one without an understanding of the other. This was depressing. I was a student of culture and I still didn't understand what culture was.

A LEAF OF HONEY

I glanced down, checked the odometer and did the mental arithmetic which calculated the distance left, the capacity of the gas tank, the average fuel consumption at this speed, and the mileage reading at the last time I filled up the tank. I figured I would have plenty of fuel to reach home going this fast.

Basically, culture is man's creation. It doesn't exist without him. It is everything he knows and believes he knows, everything he does and wants to do. That wasn't particularly the way I would say it to my supervisor. What I probably would write as a definition of what I meant by "culture", something like: "an identifiable system of social and personal interactions, practices, rituals, traditions, beliefs, and knowledge which maintained a verbal and/or written folklore, history and literature, from which its members define wisdom, and prescribe and proscribe collective and individual behaviour". But even this doesn't quite say it all. Culture is much more complex than this. Culture is mankind's greatest creation. All of its material, intellectual, social and spiritual achievements are facets of this creation. Culture is complex because it reflects the complex structure of man's mind.

The ground was dry and the wheels threw up a trail of rust-coloured dust as I rode along. The leaves on either side of the road were covered with a thick layer of this red dust. It hadn't rained in days. Through the visor of my helmet, it was a world of basic colours. The speed and vibration of the bike blurred the image in front of me into three monochromatic bands: the red ground below, the blue sky above and the green vegetation between them. It was hypnotic. I had been riding all day and my eyes were tired. I stopped at the next village so I could close my eyes and rest a moment. Most villages looked the same, the huts were made of the same sorts of material. Bulu villages were laid out slightly differently from the ones in neighbouring Ntumuland. There was a recognizable pattern. A young man was standing in the shade of a nearby hut sharpening his machete in a "Y" shaped branch set in the ground. The original handle had been removed and the blade rehafted with a distinctive long-handle. Even though I knew that this village was still within Bululand, the style of machete told me that this was an Ntumu artefact.

"You are a child of the Ntumu. What is your clan?" I asked the man in Ntumu. He looked startled that I should be speaking to him in his language.

"I am of the *esamengon* clan," he replied.

A LEAF OF HONEY

"Then you and I are *avuzo'o*, our clans are tied in friendship. I am of the *eba* clan of Meyo-Ntem," I stated. The man throat-clicked his acknowledgement of this fact.

"Where are you coming from?" he asked.

"I come from Ebolowa," I answered.

"Where are you rolling to?" he asked.

"I roll to the hut of my wife in Ma'an," I said.

"Ma'an is of the clan *esambita*. Do you have a second wife in Meyo-Ntem?" he asked assuming my wife was Ntumu.

"No. My first wife said she would kill me," I joked. The man laughed and I said I had to go. The conversation was typical of the kinds of questions and answers which would pass between two Ntumu tribesmen who had never met before.

As I got back on the Yamaha, I realized that this kind of exchange was indicative of a particular culture. It was Ntumu. Aside from the language of the conversation, the structure and sequence of the questions about clan membership and inter-clan ties of historic friendship were distinctive elements of Ntumu culture. It was a communicative ritual which was always followed, as was the next stage, of asking where you were coming from and where you were going to.

There were many things like this among the tribesmen which could be pointed to and identified as being components of Ntumu culture. Most of them were conceptional. I suppose that it stands to reason that when a group of people live in the same environment and share the same sort of experiences over an extended period of time, over several generations, they would tend to develop a common vocabulary and language with which they could exchange ideas and recount to each other the events they remembered from the past and their perceptions about the present. The ability to articulate ideas would allow people to address problems of cause and effect. This would eventually expand beyond speculations about the past and present and would give rise to beliefs, beliefs about things which could not be seen directly, things which they might apprehend but not comprehend. As a result of this, private and communal belief-based values would develop which would provide stability in the interaction of the individuals in the group. As the group grew, it would accumulate a vast amount of collective knowledge about its beliefs, history, technology and environment. Eventually the appropriate use of this knowledge would become known as "wisdom".

290

A LEAF OF HONEY

I reached the junction village of Meyo-Centre and turned right. The road west led into the Ntem basin and Ntumuland. By now it was late afternoon and I had to fight the glare as I rode towards the sun.

The concept of "wisdom" was central to the functioning of the tribe, especially to its elders. Among them, wisdom was equated with the knowledge of proverbs. These were the embodiments of the beliefs and experiences of their ancestors. Proverbs were pivotal to Ntumu culture. Around them revolved the standards for advice-giving and jurisprudence. They lent stability to Ntumu society because they were a readily transferable form of wisdom. Proverbs outlived people. As a cultural element, wisdom must be inherited and cumulative if there is to be continuity and progress. Proverbs provided this continuity.

It was going to get dark soon and I would have to ride slower and watch out for goats sleeping in the road. The exposed red laterite soil absorbed more sunshine than the floor of the rainforest and the goats sought the warmth of the road after the sun went down and the air became chilly. The goats never got out of the way when they heard me coming or saw the headlight. This evening I would have to weave in and out of a sleeping herd of goats every time I passed a village. Someday I knew I would hit one. Somewhere out there, there was goat with my name on it.

I wondered if I had got it right. Knowledge and a sense of wisdom were things which were held in the mind and it was always difficult to understand what was going on inside other people's minds. It was especially difficult to weigh accurately the importance other people place on things. The world-view I was trying to discover depended upon understanding the importance of the proverbs to Ntumu society. On this subject, all I had to go on were the statements of a group of apparently sagacious old tribesmen. I hoped Dr Kilngott would be satisfied with the amount of verification and cross-checking I had done. Understanding approaches, but never encompasses, a subject. This was a fundamental limitation of knowledge. I felt confident of the role these proverbs had as indicators of the Ntumu world-view, but then I wasn't the one marking my work.

The sun finally set behind the vegetation and I didn't have to struggle with glare. In a matter of minutes the green forest became black silhouettes of towering trees against a fading grey-pink sky. I hated night-riding. I reached over and turned my headlight on. It was already night in the undergrowth beside the road; soon it would be dark ahead of the bike. It had been a long day on the back of the Yamaha and I was bone tired. The confrontation with the *Secretaire* didn't seem like an event of just this morning. I wished that I was already home in my hammock, but I still had about an hour's journey ahead of me. I would have to resort to mind games to stay alert. The headlight flashed into the dark rainforest with every turn in the road and illumined the trees for a few seconds. I started to try to identify the tree types I saw to stay awake: *assas*, good for firewood; *ewome*, used as roof supports; *etut*, machete handles; *akom*, boat building; *akondom*, pounding mortars; *meviniele*, ebony for sculpture; *akak*, firewood; *alen*, oilpalm; *olong*, bark is a headache medicine; *akoa*, pestles and paddles; *elolom*, too big to be used for anything.

I thought how societies naturally tended to develop vocabularies which reflected their reliance or interaction with things which surrounded them. The more important those things were, the more detailed would be the way in which they divided and subdivided them. Canadian Eskimos perceived many types of snow and weather. Californian surfers had names for many kinds of waves and surfboards. For the Ntumu tribesmen, there was an abundant vocabulary for trees and plants. This wasn't surprising, considering their environment. These plant and tree names were classified into taxonomic groups based on perceived similarities of size, structure, colour, texture, origin, use and worth. These were then arranged into hierarchies. The Ntumu weren't the only ones to do this. English has subtle hierarchies of relative size built into its vocabulary. I thought about the succession of related concepts which included tree, trunk, bough, branch, stem, twig, offshoot, leaf. Each was relatively larger than the next. Words are magic. Words imply the existence of other words. Words are concepts and concepts are the gateway to new discoveries. Language is an ever-expanding system of consciousness.

At last I rode into the village of Ma'an. It felt good to be home. All the huts had their lanterns on inside as people prepared for bed. It was now night-time and no one was out of doors, just the drowsy goats on the road. I rode past the office-hut of the *Secretaire du Commissaire*. It was closed up tight for the night. I would see what tomorrow would be like with him. Fanny and Anisa would be home waiting for me. Maybe there would be something to eat before I went to bed.

When I got to our hut the *Commissaire* was inside waiting for me.

56

EUROPEAN BORROWINGS AND EQUIVALENTS

Dear Dr Kilngott,

Many Ntumu proverbs collected here appear to be borrowed from either French or English adages. They translate almost word for word from the originals. The following are the more blatant examples of these:

(110) "Many cooks spoiled the sauce."

(111) "The earliest bird in the trees is the one that eats the most."

(112) "Iron is good to form when it is still hot."

(113) "If you want to know what your wife will look like when she gets old, look at your mother-in-law."

Some others are far more Ntumu in flavour but, nevertheless, still appear to be similar in meaning to certain European proverbs. I would say that these have arisen without exposure to the equivalent proverbs presented below and were not borrowed.

"La goutte d'eau qui fait deborder le vase":

(114) "Supporting many times cut his vein."

"The squeaky wheel gets the grease":

(115) "Food gets cooked by frequently stoking the fire."

A LEAF OF HONEY

"You can't teach an old dog new tricks":

(116) "Born with scar, old with scars."

"Too many cooks spoiled the broth":

(117) "Crab could not dance because of his many feet."

"If wishes were horses, beggars would ride":

(118) "If it were as it should be, chameleon would have hunted with a *mfan* and crab would have played the drums."

"Cross that bridge when you come to it":

(119) "Ghosts don't speak without rain."

"Don't count your chickens before they're hatched":

(120) "One never measures (the size of) the kidney before it is cooked."

"Where there is smoke, there is fire":

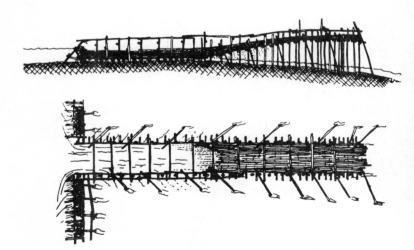

(121) "The elephant goes and leaves the blood."

"There are many fish in the sea":

(122) "You never struggle for a lizard's tail."

Not only is this week's letter short, there is only one drawing. I have finally completed a drawing of the *olam kwas* fish trap I described a few months ago. It was washed away in the flooding recently. The deadline for submission of my dissertation is fast approaching and I am trying to prepare a complete summary of the research.

Sincerely yours, Joseph

57

THE BEAUTY OF DIPLOMACY

I felt uneasy to find the *Commissaire* sitting at our table. It was the last thing I expected. This could mean trouble: he had never been to our hut before. However, he and my wife were talking pleasantly as I opened the door. I looked around the room to see if the *Secretaire* was with him. He wasn't. Anisa was asleep in my hammock near the table. The *Commissaire* had a cup of coffee at his elbow and on the table were the items the Secretaire had seized that morning. That looked promising. I came in and greeted the *Commissaire* and then gave my wife a hug in front of him, unashamedly.

"Is everything all right?" I asked her in Spanish.

"Why yes," she answered in French so our guest could understand. "The *Commissaire* just returned this morning from his trip and this evening he dropped by to see how we were. I just made him some coffee. Would you like some?" Fanny's relaxed air eased the situation.

The *Commissaire* sat silently and listened to this exchange. We sipped our coffee and engaged in agreeable and meaningless talk until he brought the conversation around to the subject everyone was avoiding.

"I understand from speaking to your wife here that you went to see my Secretary this morning. She told me that you gave him a letter and then went to Ebolowa."

"I went to Ebolowa to deliver a letter to the *Prefet*." I didn't mention what the letter said or that I hadn't seen him because he was away on tour.

"My Secretary said that there was some kind of misunderstanding this morning. When he received the letter, he was very sorry. He claims that it was all a big misunderstanding and that you left in such a hurry this morning that you forgot your things." He pointed at the items on the table. "I have brought them for you. I think it was all a problem of language. You see, you couldn't understand his French and he couldn't understand your English. But there is no problem now. This was merely a misunderstanding that should never have happened." The *Commissaire* spoke in an overly calm and conciliatory voice through a very polished diplomatic smile. Although it was loaded with inaccuracies, I was relieved at what I heard.

"That must be it," I responded carefully. He was obviously constructing a scenario of the events which minimized the conflict. It was also obvious that he didn't believe a word he said. That is the beauty of diplomacy: everyone knows everyone is lying. However he chose to describe the events, I was sure that he knew more or less what had actually happened. It would be detrimental to try to correct him at this point. It would be better to let him continue and see what he would offer as a solution.

"I am your friend. If you had a problem, why didn't you come to see me?" he asked.

"Because I believe in respecting authority," I said enigmatically.

"Authority?" he asked.

"I am a foreigner here and it is my duty to obey the laws of Cameroon and respect the authority of its officials. Well, when I asked him if I could speak to you about our 'misunderstanding' he said that he was the *Secretaire du Commissaire* and he had the authority here in Ma'an. He said it was for him to decide who saw the *Commissaire* and that he would never let me see you. What else could I do? I was obliged to respect his authority." I explained using the same air of simplistic innocence the *Commissaire* was feigning.

"But why did you then go to see the *Prefet?*"

"I had no one else I could ask to help me. And besides the *Prefet* speaks English." The *Commissaire* thought about the implications of this for a moment.

"Whenever you need help, please come and see me. I give you permission to see me directly. I am the authority here in Ma'an, not my Secretary," he said.

297

"Thank you. Now, let me ask you how we can avoid having 'misunderstandings' with your Secretary in the future. What should I say to him when I see him tomorrow?" I asked.

"I am very sorry but my Secretary had to go to Nyabessan this afternoon to check on the condition of the road. The *Prefet* will be touring the villages around there next month and the road needs to be repaired. My Secretary will be gone for a few weeks. I suspect that there are many pot holes to fill." With that the *Commissaire* said goodnight and left.

It seemed that the confrontation with the *Secretaire* was resolved for the moment. A few weeks would give me enough time to finish writing my summary. My wife and I chatted for awhile about what had happened and then we got ready for bed. Nyabessan was a long way from Ma'an and I could see him having to organize the repair of that long stretch of road. I couldn't help but chuckle. There is justice in the world. Just in case it rained in the night, Fanny went outside to bring in some of the clothes left on the line out back. When she came back in she said she saw a lantern in the woods behind our hut.

"I think the old naked woman is back," she said. I went to the little square hole in our mud hut and looked out. It was her again. I could hear her talking to herself. I wished I could understand what she was saying and who she was talking to. I reached out and pulled the wooden shutter closed. I would probably never know what she was doing out there. Fanny checked Anisa's net and turned the kerosene lamp down. We got into bed and she tucked our mosquito net around us. I was asleep before I could close my eyes.

I always seemed to have the strangest dreams when I was really tired. Lately I had begun to dream more and more in Ntumu. I saw myself sitting in a familiar setting, in a ring of tribesmen around the fire in the *aba*. The *aba*, however, was in the middle of the jungle instead of in the village. Tall *dum* trees formed the walls. One person wearing a long wooden mask with a fringe of white feathers around the edge stood to one side. The mask was so big it covered the person's entire body – only his legs could be seen. The mask was telling a story about a far off people who lived beyond the rainforest. He never called them by a name but somehow I knew the mask was talking about my people.

"These people have strange beliefs," said the mask. "They believe in a bird that does not fly. A bird as tall as a man with a neck as long an arm." The storyteller made a fist and raised his arm up from behind the mask to imitate the bird's head. "These birds do not live among these people but still they know about them. They have seen them in *bekalata*, in books. What do the *bekalata* say about the birds? They say that the birds run very fast." The mask ran in place until a dust rose around his feet. The tribesmen laughed. "They say that the bird lays an egg the size of a water gourd." Out from under the mask a gourd appeared between his legs and fell to the ground. The tribesmen laughed louder. "They say that these birds bury their heads in the dirt." The arm overhead disappeared behind the mask and reappeared beside the storyteller on the ground. The man bent his hand back so that the wrist rested on the dirt to make the "head" look like it was underground. The tribesmen now howled with laughter.

When the tribesmen were quiet again, the mask continued. "How can these people believe these things? They believe whatever the *bekalata* says. They even have a proverb about this:

'A man should not bury his head in the dirt'."

Everyone began to laugh again. "The *bekalata* is not always right." The man drew his arm back in behind the mask and then turned it so that it looked at me. The laughter stopped suddenly. "The fact of the matter is that this bird does not bury its head at all. It merely places its ear on the ground to listen for the approach of its enemies." The mask fell away and revealed that the storyteller was really the naked old woman who sometimes came in the night. She bent down and patted the earth and grinned a toothless grin at me and then demonstrated how to listen to the ground.

I awoke with a start. The lamp had gone out and I could still see the memory of the dream in the darkness. It was true. We did somehow believe that ostriches buried their heads in the sand. It wasn't so much a "belief", more like an unchallenged fact. Everyone seemed to know it. Why was this common knowledge? It was strange. It was not a vital bit of information, but it was just something that people knew. The ostriches' silly habits could be seen on post cards, animated cartoons and pictures in magazines, and in books. *Bekalata!* All of these paper products were called *bekalata* in Ntumu. The idea that ostriches did not actually bury their heads in the sand had never occurred to me before. Since the idea popped into my head, it was as if a strange mental process had begun. When I stopped and thought about it for a second, the image of a bird with its head stuck in the ground ceased to be odd and amusing. It became quite ludicrous, even impossible. Was this because now I had planted doubt in my mind? It was as if formerly information on this subject had been filed under "facts" and now they had just been transferred and refiled under "beliefs". Was this because "beliefs" could be challenged whereas "facts" couldn't, and now I needed to challenge the validity of the idea? The questions which I had never asked myself were now being asked. How could an ostrich possibly breathe with its head underground? Somewhere in the past I was told that ostriches did this when they were afraid. If this was a response to danger, then they would be an easy prey for predators and would have been killed to extinction long ago. How could I have held this image in my mind for so long without challenging its validity? Was I now subconsciously challenging my own ideas like these because I was engaged in the conscious process of examining other people's beliefs and assumptions about nature and the world around them?

I was too tired to try to answer my own questions and, mercifully, Fanny would let me sleep late in the morning.

58

ALL CREEPING VINES MAKE KNOTS

Dear Dr Kilngott,

This will be the last letter I will be able to write to you before I send you my dissertation. As promised, I have included here some more equivalent proverbs. If they seem unrelated, it is because they are. I must say that I am diligently trying to finish my submission. In recent months I have all but stopped corresponding with everyone but you.

Recounting stories is a great pastime among the tribesmen and, like people everywhere, they sometimes spin yarns of exaggerated truth. In these cases incredulity is the expected response. The Ntumu do not suffer fools easily. The following pair of proverbs has that "only a diamond can cut a diamond" quality about them and simply convey that "equals can't fool one another".

(123) "Two snakes don't catch one another."

(124) "Phantoms don't play hide and seek among themselves."

These adages are used to show that the listener is not gullible and that he is wise to the truth and is as sly as anyone else. It is a way of saying "Someone who is your equal knows what you know, including your tricks." Another related proverb is:

(125) "A trap made for crocodile catches only crocodile."

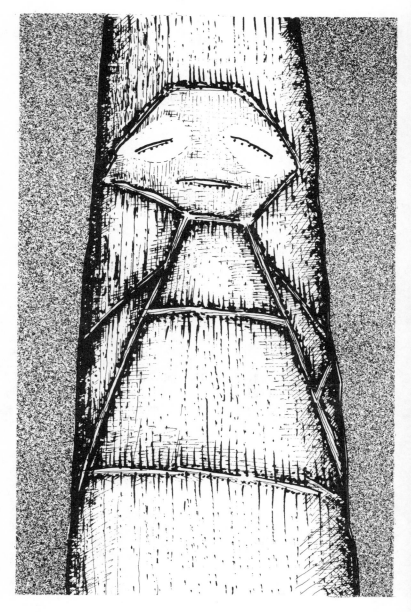

A LEAF OF HONEY

There seem to be several proverbs which approximate the meaning of "Six of one, half a dozen of the other":

(126) "The head and the neck are two different parts but they are connected."

(127) "Eat the iguana as you eat the lizard."

(128) "All creeping vines make knots."

(129) "What is in the chicken enclosure is also in the goat enclosure."

(130) "The herb the mother eats is the herb the child eats."

I found an interesting carving in the jungle this week. When I showed it to my friend Sylvain, he said it was born more of idleness than artistic pursuit. The nearest word to what he called it would have to be "graffiti". The design was cut into the bark of a tree. From the long cuts it must have been done with a machete. The drawing I have enclosed shows that it is rather like a girl in a skirt. Sylvain tells me that this type of carving is occasionally found and everyone in the village has a good idea who makes them. So it seems that this is some tribesman's equivalent of a graffiti spray-painted mural you often see on the walls of subways in New York or on the side of anything without legs in Los Angeles.

Sincerely yours, Joseph

59

THE APPROPRIATE USE OF
KNOWLEDGE

Over the next few days we read our mail. Paul was about to finish High School, or at least was about to a year ago when he mailed the letter. My mother's letter was a ten-page tome in at least three colours of ink. She never wrote a complete letter in one sitting. Days and sometimes weeks separated sections of the letter. Everytime she continued she used a different pen. She had enclosed a load of local newspaper clippings which covered a wide range of subjects and had lots of pictures. After living in the tree-choked world of the rainforest for nearly a year, it was reassuring to see that the California desert was still there. My father wrote that he had been kicked in the chest by a horse and was taking it easy for a while. Dr Kilngott acknowledged the receipt of some of my fieldnotes and commented on my drawings. Fanny was a better letter-writer than I was. She kept track of answering letters to friends and family and maintaining social contact.

The *Secretaire* was still away and we tried not to think about his threat to have us removed from Ma'an. I remembered the dream about the old woman and wondered how I could keep my ear to the ground and know when he was due back. I worried about the *Secretaire* in Nyabessan. I hoped he didn't take his truncheons with him. The Ntumu had some sayings about innocent bystanders and conflict:

"Monkey catches the blame for what the bat has cut down"

and

"Where the goats fight, it is the herbs that die".

304

A LEAF OF HONEY

I hoped he wouldn't take out his anger with me on the villagers there.

I spent most of my time drafting and typing out my final summary of the proverbs I had collected. It was difficult to write in the jungle, it was an environment prone to distraction. I was physically uncomfortable perched in the hammock, balancing my portable typewriter on my lap, but this was better than finding a cockroach up my trouser leg half way through an idea. There were other distractions and interruptions though: chores to be done, water to carry from the stream for bathing and firewood to chop for cooking. Worse than this, would be that often I would run out of ideas. Worst of all, however, was the fact that I had no books I could consult on the subject of the interpretation of oral tradition and world-view. I would have given anything to have access to the University library for just one week or to be able to talk with members of the staff in the Anthropology Department. I hated the idea of re-inventing the wheel and writing down generalizations about tribal world-view that others had undoubtedly already discovered.

I then hit upon an idea. If I treated discovery as the process rather than the product, then the summary could include a narrative which dealt with my process of discovering particular elements of Ntumu world-view. Perhaps the summary could be made more interesting in this respect. It would also allow me to write about the way the tribesmen saw discovery themselves. To them it really didn't matter if a concept was previously known. Concepts were not "unknown" and then "known". Concepts matured with time and were realized. Discoveries were never made in a vacuum. The tribesmen felt that all things were related to and sprang from something else. Discovery was more a process of adding or subtracting ideas, of finding the next link in a chain of concepts or building onto sequential knowledge.

They saw it as a "whiteman thing", the Ntumu equivalent term for "cultural chauvinism", when "European" missionaries proudly laid great claim to the discovery of some spiritual or conceptional "verity" which was already common knowledge to everyone throughout Ntumuland. I decided I wasn't going do the "whiteman thing" and make the same mistake in trying to define their world-view. I would try to describe every inward and outward perception using the images they used. I would describe the physical and social setting and let the proverbs speak for themselves. This would be

305

especially important when describing the relationship between things in nature that they saw. If there was insight to be described then I would try to be as Ntumu as possible in its description.

There wouldn't be much theoretical interpretation. I really wasn't in a position to defend or refute any particular theoretical viewpoint. As an undergraduate I wasn't an entrenched adherent to a particular school of theory. I wasn't a rationalist or empiricist, Marxist or structuralist or anything. I hadn't sold my soul yet. The voice of cynicism still whispered in my ear that some of these approaches were dogmatic and perhaps born of basic conceptional intolerance. In the rainforest, there was ample data around me to address particular elements of Ntumu world-view without resorting to tidy matrixes and formula thinking that was elitist and laced with cultural presuppositions. Fortunately I was still in the field and if I found something confusing, I could simply ask the tribesmen for a statement on the subject. Their answers were always better than my interpretations or extrapolations, anyway.

Ntumu world-view had several major aspects which were clearly interrelated. These included obvious features such as the surrounding physical environment, their sense of time, their social structure and kinship system, and the disruptive external non-Ntumu social and administrative systems which the civil authorities imposed. These were all factors in how the tribesmen perceived the world around them and fixed their position in it. Running through all of these like a connecting thread, however, was something a little less obvious: the Ntumu sense of knowledge. The elders were quite articulate on this subject. To them, knowledge was about finding new ways of regarding old phenomena. Knowledge was not something that was brought into being when it was announced or articulated for the first time among a people who had not heard it before. This was the whiteman way of looking at it. Knowledge was not a finite commodity which people held. Knowledge was not owned. No group of people had a patent or copyright on concepts like unity, peace, love and justice. Knowledge was infinite and existed independently like the sky. The sky above a clearing in the rainforest might be all that could be seen but everyone knew that it was only part of something bigger. Knowledge had an unseen potentiality to it which could only be understood through its appropriate use. This was the key. Knowledge became more manifest in use. Its potentiality shared the same infinity as did reality. It would be simplistic to say that the tribesmen equated knowledge and reality, but knowledge was clearly linked to reality, like shadows and objects.

After each day of writing I would look forward to the night-talks around the fire. In the relaxed companionship of the tribal elders I could ask the questions I had about the nature of reality, knowledge and wisdom. I asked the same questions so often that I was sure they must have thought that I was thick in the head. But they were patient and kind and saw that it was important to me to understand better how the tribesmen saw the world. The elders explained that reality existed regardless of whether or not anyone had an inkling about it. Most of what could be perceived was simply felt and people were usually unable to articulate it, either to themselves or explain it to others. This was the mistake the white missionaries had made. Perception of reality could be simple, reality was not. The tribesmen understood that some people had more capacity to describe reality and knowledge than others. But knowledge was latent or potential in everyone. This was why children sometimes said things which sounded wise. The appropriate use of this potential was what made men different.

Wisdom was designated as the appropriate use of this infinite potential. Anything, any creature, could perceive portions of this knowledge, but the ability to use it wisely was what made people human. This was the underlying conceptional basis of other ideas. How this appropriateness was defined by different groups was what made tribes different from each other. What was appropriate use for some was inappropriate and offensive to others. This was the Ntumu way of explaining cultural differences. This was the Ntumu definition of social diversity. There was a proverb on this subject:

"The world is divided like a cola nut."

The cola nut is naturally separated into individual but tightly-fitting segments. When the cola fruit is peeled, the nut comes apart into a chinese puzzle of inter-locking pieces. When it is eaten it is savoured one segment at a time. It is said that no two segments ever tasted the same. It was a great analogy.

This way of explaining social diversity as separate but inter-locking segments of the same entity also went far in describing the Ntumu sense of unity, social identity and interdependence. When a people shared the same definitions of the appropriate use of knowledge, they were united. They were one tribe.

A LEAF OF HONEY

I learned from the elders that the secret to understanding appropriateness was the awareness of one's ignorance. It unfettered the mind. This is what kept wise men humble and, subsequently enabled them to remain wise. It was important to remember that many people had lived before and many elders had spoken about the appropriate use of knowledge. Wisdom had accumulated. Wisdom required an apprenticeship to the past. This was why young men listened to old proverbs and why old men spoke them.

The awareness of my own ignorance was something I had begun to achieve from living among the tribesmen. I now realized that awareness of ignorance grew exponentially, as the discovery of knowledge grew arthimetically. This realization was a process of learning and apparently was never ending. To the elders, this was the key to individual and collective progress. Personally I was very interested in these concepts but they introduced subjects which were subjective and beyond the scope of the summary I was writing. They would have to wait.

There was a point at which I had to stop writing. I had to let go and hope that I had been coherent enough with what I had already put on paper to describe the Ntumu view of the world. The dissertation was shorter than what was needed to be said. I knew I hadn't addressed important issues like tribal metaphysics, but the Ntumu proverbs didn't say much about cosmology. The universe was mostly what they could see, and the canopy of leaves and the rainforest was its own universe. The deadline was dangerously close and I wanted to give enough time for the summary to reach Dr Kilngott.

I discussed it with Fanny and we decided that I should take my dissertation directly to Yaounde and mail it from there. Ebolowa did not have a good track-record with mail. I would also take the opportunity to look for a job while I was in the capital. Our money was almost finished and we would soon have to cash in the return tickets to America.

On my first trip to Yaounde I had met a man who said that one of the richest men in Cameroon was a Mr Khuri and if I ever wanted a job I should go to see him. I decided that the time had come to try to visit him. Mr Khuri was a Lebanese businessman who owned several wood-related factories in Cameroon. Basically he exported hardwood timber to Europe and the Far East, but he had business interests in many other things.

A LEAF OF HONEY

I arrived in Yaounde on a Friday morning and after mailing my dissertation I went to look for the offices of Sintrabois where I was told I might find Mr Khuri. It was a modern office set back from the road. I didn't have an appointment to see him, so I was asked to sit in an outer office until he had a moment to see me. I sat there for an entire day reading the same French forestry magazine over and over again. About twenty people with appointments arrived and went in ahead of me during that time. Just before closing time at five, a receptionist called me and escorted me to Mr Khuri's inner office. The room was palatial, both in size and furnishings. The receptionist seated me. An immaculately groomed middle-aged man entered from a side room and sat down behind a perfectly polished desk the size of a ping-pong table. He wore a silk shirt open at the throat and a gold medallion.

"You have five minutes," said Mr Khuri.

"I would like a job," I said simply.

"What can you do?" he asked. I began to tell him about my academic qualifications, but he cut me off in mid-sentence.

"Just tell me what you can do," he interrupted. I quickly ran down a verbal list of design and engineering skills I had picked up which included some of the machinery I could run. I also listed the teaching, foundry, welding and drafting jobs I had had. I specified the languages I could speak. The last one I mentioned was Ntumu.

Mr Khuri reached over and hit an intercom button.

"Anton!" he shouted. In ten seconds a young man presented himself in front of the boss's desk.

"Anton, speak to this man in Ntumu!" he shouted. The young man quickly turned to me and greeted me in Ntumu. We rapidly threw questions and answers at each other for a moment until Mr Khuri shouted "Enough! Go back to work!" The young man flew out of the room without a word. I could see that colonialism was still alive and well in Sintrabois.

"So you speak Ntumu. Can you operate an automated power lathe?" he asked, showing me a diagram he fished out of a pile of papers on his desk.

"Yes," I lied. I needed a chance at the job. I hadn't operated a lathe since my woodshop class in high school when I tried and failed to make a walnut salad bowl for my mother. I had never even seen the type of huge, complicated lathe he showed me a picture of. I hoped the man standing next to it in the diagram was unusually short and in real life the machine wasn't really that big.

309

"Fine. Meet me Monday morning at the furniture factory. my secretary will give you the address. Goodbye." He reached over for the intercom switch again and shouted someone's name. I left silently and closed the door behind me. It had been exactly five minutes.

I stayed with some friends over the weekend and on Monday morning I arrived at the factory gates an hour before they opened. I didn't want to be late. At seven a huge truck arrived driven by someone whose cocky self-assurance reminded me of the man I shared a gorilla fist with. This was followed by a mobile crane. On the flat-bed of the truck was a massive piece of equipment under a tarpaulin. It had a familiar shape. If this was the lathe, the man in the diagram wasn't short, he was a giant. Inside the gates and high surrounding walls the factory was open with no interior walls. From where I stood at the gates, I could see about fifty different pieces of wood-shaping machinery. Workers soon began to accumulate and at seven-thirty the gates were opened and more than three hundred Cameroonians clocked in. I pushed my Yamaha inside and parked it next to the factory office. I waited beside the motorcycle until Mr Khuri arrived in a metallic gold Mercedes 450 Coupe. As he drove past, he motioned for me to follow him. He parked his car under the roof of the factory and got out. By this time the Cameroonians were already at their work stations and they turned and nodded or lifted their hats to their boss. Mr Khuri said good morning to me and I nodded back. He called the truck driver over and told him to bring the lathe and crane in the gates.

"I brought this machine here today especially to see you operate it," he said to me. "It has taken a crew of men two days to disconnect, load and transport it here from my factory in Mbalmayo." The driver undid the ropes and the tarpaulin fell away. I felt sick. The lathe was a monster. It was bigger than his Mercedes and had twenty different levers and cutting points.

Mr Khuri pointed to a spot on the factory floor near to where he parked his car.

"Install it there," he commanded. "I will be back at three. Have it set up and ready to go by then." I shuddered as I watched him get in his car and drive away.

What had I got myself into? We used the crane to lift the machine as near the spot as possible and lowered it onto some steel pipes which acted as rollers. With twenty men we pushed and levered it into position, inch by inch. It was like moving a stone block in the age of the pyramids. I took the electrical panel off the back. The lathe had a polyphase motor system and required a staggering 440 volts to operate. I directed one group of men to set mounting bolts into the concrete floor and another to patch in a power cable from the mains transformer room of the factory. The complex control panel was intimidating. If operated correctly, this lathe could probably make anything. The switch required a key to turn it on and looked like the arming device of a nuclear weapon.

Miraculously, by three o'clock it was set up. Mr Khuri arrived on time and parked in the same place. He had brought with him a handle.

"Cameroon imports all its hoe handles. I want to take over this market. I want to produce hoe handles here at this factory." He gave me the handle. It was round, tapered and smooth. "I bought that one this morning. As you can see, it is made in France. Set up the lathe to produce this hoe handle."

I unbolted the guide-bar off the lathe and ran to the machine workshop of the factory. Mr Khuri went to the factory office. It took an hour for me to design, acetylene cut, grind and polish a reverse image template to match the hoe handle he gave me. When I got back, I found that he had ordered one of the workers to cut fifty wooden blanks for the lathe. They were neatly stacked beside the machine. I had expected that Mr Khuri would go away and come back later, perhaps the next day to see the finished product. Instead, he leaned against his car, a safe distance from the machine, crossed his arms, looked at his gold wristwatch and said "Now make me one." The moment of truth had come. He was going to stand there and watch me, watch me make a fool of myself.

With trepidation I turned the key and pressed the power switch. The motor made a sound of awesome power. The monster was now armed. I put the first wooden blank in the lathe, adjusted some of the cutting points and hit the start button. The wood disintegrated into a shower of splinters. I swallowed hard and reached for another blank. The second one flew out of the machine and hit the roof overhead. I made some more adjustments and this time the machine only sliced, diced and shredded the wood. The vibration at the cutting face was terrible. I continued to adjust the speed of the machine and the position, angle and sequence of the cutting points until I had reduced all fifty blanks of expensive wood into a pile of mangled sticks, wood shavings and sawdust. Mr Khuri never took his eyes off me. No matter what I did, I couldn't get rid of the vibration. At last I handed him the product of my fiftieth attempt to fine-tune the lathe. It was the most appalling hoe handle ever made. Even my high school woodshop teacher would have failed me. It was ragged and distorted and totally unmarketable. Mr Khuri held it in one hand and compared my product with France's in the other.

"Not very good, is it?" he asked sarcastically. That was it. Even without his tone I knew that I had blown my chance of getting a job. I could see the disappointment in Fanny's face when I went back in failure. Mr Khuri was a powerful man and I had cost him a lot of money to arrange this demonstration. He could probably make sure I never got a job with anyone in Cameroon. However Mr Khuri seemed to be waiting for me to say something, to give him some kind of explanation.

"Mr Khuri," I began, "the diameter of the shaft is too small in proportion to the length you specified. The handle develops a resonant vibration against the cutting face that cannot be controlled." Mr Khuri smiled sardonically. Even I found this hard to believe. A machine this complicated should have a mechanism to overcome something as simple as this. The problem was, I hadn't found it. It was a waste of time trying to describe the technical difficulties I was having. He wasn't interested. I decided to just say what I felt.

"*This* machine cannot make *that* handle," I announced simply. It sounded terrible, like I was blaming the machine to cover my own ineptitude.

"I know that," he said looking at his watch. "And it only took you forty-five minutes to discover it. It took my former technical director of engineering, whose job, by the way, you now have, three months to discover that same fact. That was after he assured me that the lathe would do the job before I ordered it from France."

I was stunned. He turned on his heel and got back in his car. Through the opened window he reached out and offered to shake my hand for the first time."

"By the way, what's your first name?" he asked. I told him. "Well, Mr Joseph Sheppherd, come and see me in the morning and we'll see how much you're going to cost me."

Operating the lathe and making the hoe handle wasn't the test after all. Discovering the problem with this machine was the real test. I could see how Mr Khuri had become so rich. He was devious, cunning and shrewd.

On the way home I examined what had happed. Somehow, I had won a job for which I had little or no experience, simply because I had some ability to consider possibilities beyond those posed in the questions asked of me and to reach plausible conclusions based on limited information. This was not a particularly unique skill in America. Obviously in Sintrabois it was. But in the land of the blind, the one-eyed man is king.

When I reached Ma'an, I sat Fanny down and told her that I had a job with an expatriate contract which included a good salary, a house, a car and a two month paid vacation every year. She didn't believe me.

"I hope this makes up for making you live in this hut. Say goodbye to the cockroaches and start packing" I said. I don't think she believed me until it was actually time to get in the bush-taxi and leave Ma'an. We gave almost everything away. All of the household items, including the food that still remained in the square green bottles, we distributed among the widows of Ma'an. We took the *push-push* loaded with gifts to Meyo-Ntem and said our last goodbyes to our Ntumu clansmen. As we left, it was one of the most moving experiences I have ever had. We cried as we listened to them sing our names as we rode away.

The next day I put Fanny and Anisa in the bush-taxi with our clothes and fieldnotes. I waited a long time after they left before I could got on the motorcycle and followed them. I wanted one last look. Somehow I knew that this would be the last time I would see the "crossing of paths". Life in Ntumuland had been an adventure. As I rode the Yamaha east through the rainforest for the last time I didn't know that life in Yaounde for the next three years would be as big an adventure.

60

THE PROVERBS OF THE RAINFOREST

Dear Dr Kilngott,

Thank you for the good news. Quite honestly, at the beginning of my research I wondered if I would even finish at all. I had a lot of difficulties getting started which I never shared with you but, more importantly, I also seriously underestimated the amount of work there was to do. The tribesmen have a better way of saying it:

> (131) "One can't realize the size of a bundle while it is on the ground in front of you."

Now that I have picked it up and carried the "bundle" for a year, I am beginning to understand something about the size of the task I undertook. I have discovered that any analysis of ethos will expand with time and that bundles get heavier the longer you carry them. After the five hundred or so proverbs I have recorded and investigated, I am certain that I have only collected a few scattered leaves without discovering the tree they came from. There are still many more out there to be discovered.

When I read your letter and looked at the diploma you enclosed, it was hard to believe that it was mine. I was amazed to learn that I had graduated with honours. I would have liked to have been there when they passed them out. I can't even remember what I was doing on graduation day while the rest of the seniors at the University were in gowns and mitres receiving their diplomas. Looking at this diploma, I can see that it was worth all the work. I would say it was more than a fair exchange: a ream of badly typed paper for a scroll of parchment. Having had a chance to reread the carbon copies of what I have written, I am appreciative of your compassion in receiving a dissertation so over-burdened with spelling misstakes. I don't know what excuse to give other than I am a product of the California elementary school system. The fact that I typed it sitting cross-legged in a hammock by lamplight and that the vermin ate most of the section from L to P in my dictionary had nothing to do with it.

Dr Kilngott, thank you for being my supervisor. I know that I should have thanked you long before this. I would also like to thank the staff of the anthropology department for allowing me to come to Africa as an undergraduate. We may not have agreed on everything, particularly on my religious beliefs, but I learned a great deal while at Riverside. Please thank them for me. As my supervisor and friend you prepared me well. Out here among the tribesmen I survived socially because you provided me with an adaptive understanding of how tribal societies function. It was also good that I had you to write to rather than trying to explain what I was learning to an unknown audience. Just knowing that there was someone I knew reading the material I sent was comforting. Your occasional letters brought me more encouragement than you can imagine.

As you know, I have decided to stay on in Cameroon for a while longer. Rest assured that I have not gone native. Quite the opposite. I have landed a job in engineering with a forestry company called Sintrabois. Actually having learned Ntumu helped me get the job. I am discovering that there is not much anthropology in engineering or money in anthropology but there does seem to be quite a lot of money in engineering. Forgive me, but after a year of leaking roofs and strange food I am suddenly shamelessly attracted to materialism. I am sure it will pass. I have not lost sight of my hopes of ultimately getting a job in socio-economic development with one of the foreign aid agencies and in my spare time help out in any way I can in the growth and maturation of the Baha'i Community here. As a religion, we are still young here in Cameroon, less than thirty years old. Eventually the Baha'is will be able to sponsor grassroots development projects of their own. When that happens I will be well trained for the job. In the meantime, I am still here.

In retrospect, the time I have spent in Meyo-Ntem and Ma'an has been in many ways the most meaningful year of my life, a time of preparation. These villages have become home and my tribal neighbours my best friends. When I had to move on, part of me

315

stayed in the rainforest and I am sure that the memory of it will travel with me like a shadow and companionate wayfarer. I have begun to comprehend the nostalgic saying:

> (132) "The morning leaf is always wet, a man must stay long in a place."

As the chief of Ma'an said to me once:

> (133) "One never throws away the walking-stick before meeting the earliest wayfarer on the path in the morning."

I hope that what I have learnt about the Ntumu people will someday be published. The Ntumu acumen, like all wisdom, needs to be shared. Sadly the tribesmen are beginning to move from their villages in the rainforests to the big cities and are being assimilated into the amorphous culture of urban survival and hopeless poverty. Recently, I have run into some young Ntumu tribesmen here in Yaounde. They were different. They looked bewildered and lost in a world with a visual horizon and no trees. When I asked when they would return to Ntumuland, they were quick to say that they had come only for a visit. But the capital is a trap. After a while it becomes socially and economically impossible to leave. I doubt they will ever return to the jungle. And they are not alone, with the arrival of each Ntumu youth the distinctive soul of the rainforest tribe is diminished, both in number and quality. These tribesmen soon lose their calmness, quiet dignity and humble sagacity. All the things which their elders taught and valued as good. They no longer hear their proverbs.

It is sad when goodness and wisdom are diminished in the world. Now, more than ever I must keep my promise to the tribal elders and safeguard the proverbs of the rainforest. If they are not published I fear that this part of their culture will be lost. The social environment which perpetuated their oral traditions is eroding. It is now time to write them down. The only comfort I have is that part of the Ntumu culture will be preserved and that to some degree their experience will permeate other societies which read it. It is possible for the wisdom at the root of the proverb: "Man is a leaf of honey" to be understood by anyone. It is universal. We are all leaves of one tree.

Sincerely yours, Joseph

JOSEPH ROY SHEPPHERD was born in the United States in 1949 into a family of Californian cattlemen and fruit farmers. All his life he has been interested in the diversity of culture and language. He has travelled extensively through more than 50 countries and served as a Baha'i pioneer in Guatemala, Colombia, Cameroon and Equatorial Guinea, where he worked for two years as Anthropological Advisor to the government and Curator of the National Ethnological and Archaeological Museum in Malabo. He received his Bachelor's Degree with honours in Anthropology from the University of California and his Master's Degree in Archaeology from the University of Cambridge. He is presently involved in projects of social and economic development and writing his Doctorate. He lives with this wife and children in Buckinghamshire, England.